Pakistan's Development:
Economy, Resources & Technology

Akhtar Ali

Research on Economy and Politics of Pakistan - REAP

About the author:

Akhtar Ali is a management consultant, having broad and diversified professional training and experience as consultant, top management executive and research scholar. He has authored many books, publications, studies and journal papers on the subjects relevant to the book at hand. He is a former research fellow Harvard University *and has lectured at prestigious civil and military institutions in Pakistan and abroad.* **Akhtarali1949@gmail.com**

Books by the same author:

1. **Pakistan's Nuclear Dilemma: Energy & Security Dimensions.**

2. **South Asia: Nuclear Stalemate or Conflagration.**

3. **The Political Economy of Pakistan: an Agenda for Reforms.**

4. **Nuclear Politics and Challenges of Governance.**

5. **Pakistan's Energy Development: the Road Ahead.**

6. **Pakistan's Development Challenges: Federalisms, Security and Governance**

About Reap

This study has been done under the auspices of REAP. REAP, originally known as Research on Armament and poverty, has been rechristened as Research on Economy and Politics (of Pakistan). REAP was founded in early 1980s, and has organized and published many books and publications, including this author's previous books. reap@gmail.com.pk

Contents

Akhtar Ali

Preface

Whenever one writes a book, some issues are left out for one reason or the other, which impels one to do something about it, and it usually results in another publication. This book has been produced in similar circumstances. I wrote two books recently; (1) Pakistan's Energy Development: the road ahead; (2) Pakistan' Development Challenges; federalism, security and governance.

The issues covered are multi sectoral and multi-disciplinary. However, the issues covered are vital and should be of interest to a wide range of audience who may have interest with Pakistan and its economy and well-being. Such issues as management of floods and of Science and Technology may look to be different but are stitched together in the development issue theme. Same goes for other topics such as mineral and energy resource development

These are selected issues only and not all the issues. Selected, because I have no pretension of knowing all and everything despite a wide and varied agenda included in this book; the problems of the countries are varied and numerous. And some of the issues have been covered in the recent publications as mentioned earlier. Except for the "Ten Commandments" part, the enlistment does not mean a priority list, although some of the issues such as energy must be in the priority of our government and leaders. The discussion has been structured in three sections; a) Economic Policy; b) Resource Development; c) Science and Technology. A post script has been added which contains several chapters dealing with a variety of issues including a proposal for manifestoes of political parties.

I am grateful to Mr. Wamiq Zuberi editor and publisher of Business Recorder who provided generous space in his newspaper where a significant portion of this book has been published as individual articles. I am also grateful to Dr. Jawaid Anwar, President Ma'arif Foundation to reproduce a chapter in this book which was originally written for their annual publication Muslim World Source Book

My wife Dr. Meher painstakingly edited the book, and offered fresh ideas and critique for which I would remain grateful as ever. Schanze's usual outdoor trips in the evening to relatives and friends were interrupted, which she bore with amazing patience. She deserves my special thanks. And thanks to my house girl Fazeela also who was never hesitant in offering fresh and copious cups of tea and Juices. Last but not least Mr. Rashid Abbasi word processed and organized the write-up. It is my fourth book which he has handled in such a sincere manner.

Akhtar Ali
akhtarali1949@gmail.com

14 August, 2011

1   Introduction

The issues covered in this book are multi sectoral and multi-disciplinary. However, the issues covered are vital and should be of interest to a wide range of audience who may have interest Pakistan and its economy in and well-being. Such issues as management of floods and of Science and Technology may look to be different but are stitched together in the development issue theme. Same goes for other topics such as mineral and energy resource development.

Some of the chapters such Land Reforms & Government Land Distribution as Land Reforms was written earlier and has been updated with new data and tables in the new context. The rationale has been revitalized by the continuing and unabated terrorism. The perpetrators are not only religious fundamentalists but are also the poor and the landless and their younger family members. The struggle for land and resources and against poverty has already entered in its violent phase. It only has a different vocabulary and symptoms. The root cause is the same. Ultimately settlements may have to be made in terms of ideology and as well as land redistribution. This may at least reduce the copious supply of suicidal attackers, who while motivated by a deviationist ideology may be equally motivated by the lack of hope in the material circumstances they have to face. Land can give and spread the hope, optimism and good will that are so badly needed by this country. In some ways the Land Reform discussion appears to be of no use in the circumstances, when the main actors the landlords are not even prepared to pay their dues in terms of the income tax. It is not a tax on agriculture; it is a tax on income. Any one who earns an ordinarily taxable income pays it , irrespective of the sector or class or region. Land is still being utilized inefficiently. Inheritential distribution may have divided smaller landholdings, but the large estates are still there in Sindh and Southern Punjab and the strangleholds of the Sardari system in Balochistan.

Agriculture has a share of 26% in Pakistan's GDP and employs 38% of the work-force. The sector has a potential of growing at rate of 5% p.a. as it did in 1960s earlier. Low growth rates in the economy in general and in agriculture has significantly contributed to poverty and unemployment. Poverty in Pakistan, as measured in 2007-08, was at 26%, which should have increased in the wake of floods and the economic crisis, and has reportedly returned to the previous high levels of 33-38 % of 2001-2002. Rural poverty has always been high in Pakistan at 40% plus. A major reason for it has been the landlessness and low employment. A good 10.36 % of the rural house-holds are landless peasants and another 57% (35.1 % of total population) are under-employed and under-paid non-farm laborers. Both of these groups could benefit from higher agricultural growth rates and Land reforms and land redistribution.

Higher growth rates would create employment in farm and non-farm sector and would increase wages and incomes. Both growth and equity policies can be mutually reinforcing. Our argument is that the Livestock sector in Pakistan has a contribution of 47 % in the agricultural output, which has been mostly contributed by small holders or the landless, having 2-5 Buffaloes. If 1-1.5 Acre plots are distributed to this group of the landless and the non-farm workers, under a land reforms scheme, it would contribute to both, output and equity. Similarly, the proposed beneficiary group could also participate in high value horticultural sector, which has been shown to have a growth potential of 5.0% p.a. A reasonable land reform component along with the distribution of state land to the rural and possibly urban poor could go a long way in reducing the endemic poverty in this country. Many recent writings have indicated the destabilizing potential of the rural and urban poverty and disparities. Even the Taliban issue is interpreted as having linkage to poverty and deprivation. This creates a new logic and rationale for land reforms which may not only be restricted to land distribution but should go well beyond towards improving upon the tenure issues. The author strongly argues against the so-called market efficiency and growth-sans-equity policies e.g. Egypt which have worsened the poverty and inequity conditions.

Public works programme like improvements of irrigation, water harvesting and small dams and irrigation in Barani areas, and road-building and other construction projects could improve unemployment and under-employment conditions among the landless and non-farm workers, which would not only increase wages and incomes of these groups, but would generate the necessary market forces and pressure for equitable improvements in the share-cropping terms and land rentals.

Pending a wholesale land reform, whatever land can be distributed under the relevant socio-political constraints, is a praise-worthy and laudable activity, as it brings happiness and prosperity to the poor, as would be evident from an Oxfam report on the subject which has been reproduced at the end of this discussion.

There is a lot of surplus government land which is usually kept safe for projects or vested interest. We have seen how such land has been in the past and would continue to be allotted to the powerful and the civil and military elite. Hiding behind the argument that there are too many landless, and hence no amount of land would be enough to meet their needs and thus withholding land from them is a convoluted logic. This is like as the Holy Quran says: There were two brothers; one had ninety-nine sheep and the other had only one sheep; the one having 99 sheep asked his poor brother to give his lone one sheep to him to make his total add to 100. Quran curses such people promising destruction in this world and hereafter.

Thus there is a lot of merit in the existing government program which should be continued and extended as much as it is possible with transparency and without nepotism. Problematic and useless land should not be given, for the required capital to improve it may not be available with the *hari* and *Kisan*. I am not sure if *Kisan* in Punjab and other provinces are also benefitting under similar land distribution programs. Punjab, esp. Central Punjab is short of uncultivated land. However, southern Punjab should have significant newly developed government land. Although the chance is that quite some of it has been already allotted to the elite and the vested interest. Their needs are never satiated. Older ones die with the lands and the newer progeny springs up every thirty years with new demands of land. There is no dearth of Land in Balochistan where a mere 6 million people are populated in almost half of total Pakistan's area, although developed land may be short there. NWFP is generally short of land but there is unutilized belt in tribal areas and the adjoining settled areas.

The Energy and Resource Issues

Pakistan is importing 10-11 Billion USD worth of oil and its products every year, while it sits on unexploited Thar coal resource worth more than the combined Oil and Gas wealth of Iran and Saudi Arabia. And it has to ask for IMF's dole for a payment deficit of a billion dollars each. There are many recommendations that have been provided which the policy makers and other stake-holders may greatly benefit from.

Similarly, although to a lesser scale, a good offer of Direct Foreign Investment in Rekodeq for Copper and Gold mining project has been opposed by a combination of vested interest, ill-advised well-wishers and what not. Again a well-earned foreign exchange prospect may remain buried for ever, but for the patience of the investors who have been made to run into legal battles of all sorts .People must know the facts, and that is what has been done by including several chapters to bring forth the correct perspective.

A foreign company Tethyan   has completed exploration of the resource located in Chaghi, the famous place where Pakistan's first nuclear explosion was carried out, and has prepared and submitted a feasibility study for consideration and approval of the government of Balochistan. The company claims, and perhaps rightly so that it has spent some 200 million US dollar on the project studies and exploration over the past several years. The company expects that it is given mining rights pursuant to its exploratory efforts and investments. The company proposes to bring a foreign investment of 3.2 billion USD and has provided for spending 50% of the investment on local procurement of goods and services. For seemingly archaic confidentiality reasons, the company has refrained from revealing its feasibility study, which has created doubts and controversy among the mind of general public. The project is being opposed by many quarters. This article takes account of the debate and the arguments, attempts to build a picture of the project in terms of real numbers, develops proposals on royalty issue based on international practices and in conclusion broadly supports the project, while advising Government of Balochistan to avail the services of third party experts in contract negotiations with the company.

Present mineral sector output in Pakistan is a paltry 0.4% of GDP, way below its potential variously estimated at 2-3% of GDP, which would mean an annual output and exports of 5000 Million US dollars. By comparison, IMF contribution to foreign exchange deficit is slightly more than 1000 million USD. However, mineral sector has been stagnating due to low technology and small scale mining and that mostly in non-metal sector. Except for Saindak with an output of 16000 tons of blister Copper, there is no sign of large scale mining, benefiting from foreign capital and technology.

TCC-Rekodeq is a good window of opportunity; Pakistan has been waiting for years. With a foreign investment of 3.2 Billion USD and an annual output of 220,000 tons of Copper and 16 tons Gold ,resulting in annual exports of more than one Billion USD, it is a project of international scale in every respect.

The project has been opposed on many counts, the most significant ones are as follows; a) the monetary terms offered by the foreign JV TCC are not adequate; b)we can do it on our own and make more money; c)there should be local processing done within the country instead of the export of raw concentrate. The alternative cited is an ECNEC approved project.

We have studied the international Copper industry and its workings including several large scale projects in the pipelines. We have examined the PC-1 of the ECNEC Copper Rekodeq project and other claims that have been made in this respect. We have also studied the data of Saindak Metals in so far it is publicly available. We have also examined the TCC project data, mostly based on the data and info available on the company website, and some press reports containing some useful data. We also had had an opportunity of examining the data from Aynak project in Afghanistan, which contract has been recently awarded to MCC of China.

The ECNEC project is very small with a daily ore output of just 5000 tons, as opposed to 110,000 tons per day of ore output of TCC proposal. It is even smaller than the existing Saindak. ECNEC proposal relies on small scale mining of the local mining companies. It is doubtful, if even 5000 tons of ore can be mined by the local sub-contractors. Understandably, its cash cost per ton are very high, i.e.3158 USD per ton, several times higher than international cost including those of TCC. It is widely known that small scale mining operations are uneconomic and the ECNEC project only supports that. There is a high probability that this project runs into snags, cost over-runs and lack of output. There may be a good chance of success, however, if the ECNEC project restricts itself to mineral processing, a point that we are going to take up later in the chapters. A chapter has been added on Mineral Policy, to understand the larger sectoral and policy issues and offer some recommendations in that respect.

The Ten Commandments

I wrote "Ten commandments for the government "during the early part of their present reign, outlining some urgent do'es and don'ts, which is reproduced in this chapter. Government perhaps was already thinking on the line and seems to have taken steps in that direction. Later, some little variant of it was echoed in the Ten Points Agenda of the PML (N), which fortunately did not result in political instability and destructive politics. It appears that the deliberations resulted in some deeper understanding of the issues and argued for patience. I also wrote in this respect which was very kindly published by Business Recorder as a series of articles. The same has been included in various chapters with some adjustments.

These are selected issues only and not all the issues .Selected, because I have no pretension of knowing all and everything despite a wide and varied agenda included in this book; the problems of the countries are varied and numerous. And some of the issues have been covered in the recent publications as mentioned earlier. Except for the "Ten Commandments" part, the enlistment does not mean a priority list, although some of the issues such as energy must be in the priority of our government and leaders.

Science and Technology may be esoteric, but the need and importance of it is easily understood. Without Science, Technology and its precursor the Education, no development is possible. It can be borrowed in the interim, but a part of it has to be developed locally. There is a merit to the local development of Science far transcending the ego or pride issues. If nothing else, local Science would result in affordable costs of input and wider availability. National priorities and urgencies are different for nations depending on the stage of development, resource endowments and meant other things.

Pakistan's achievements in this respect are not many or remarkable, except perhaps the development of nuclear weapons, which although cannot be called totally indigenous, is a proof what a national consensus and persistence can deliver. The need is to be felt and recognized. This is the lesson. Genuine needs of the people have to be assessed and prioritized based on what can be done. Excellence of a few cannot be enough; neither should there be socialism shy of rewarding merit, efficiency and hard work. For an unfortunate period elitism has been pushed on Science, no more. Primary Education and then Secondary Education and then the Tertiary Education; these should be the priorities in order, forming a balanced and stable pyramid having a long and short potential. Military dictatorship is bad for science, bad for education. Education is both a precursor and fall-out of democratic dispensation. We would have to have more primary school teachers than security personnel; we cannot afford both in large quantities. A balance has to be established .Strategy connects ends with the means. If there is a disconnect, it is no strategy. Some deep thinking is required in this area.

The issue has been covered with some length under the caption of reducing government expenditure and balancing the budget.

My advice to go slow in Taxation, in the perspective of large budgetary deficits the country is facing, may sound strange to many. I have compensated this by calling for income tax on agriculturists. The pursuit of balancing the budget and documenting the economy should not kill the goose that lays eggs. A significant part of our economy is based on small enterprise and small trade and retail. The literacy rate is low and the ability to maintain accounts further low. Moreover, the local retail sector runs on one of the lowest margins in the world due to fewer overheads. Secondly, it is the classical African question and the rise of capitalism. The acme of capitalism requires low taxation and low tariff. Leaving some sectors and segments from near-perfect tax extraction is our way of following the capitalistic decree, leaving the surplus with those who would reinvest and contribute to growth. In our present socio-political conditions, a large part goes to the non-productive expenditure and corruption in projects and businesses. An enhancement of the tax pie is to contribute in the growth of these factors. The logic and rationale of these is discussed in more details later in this chapter itself and elsewhere.

Perhaps the single-most stumbling block to our growth, development and betterment is the "persecution complex" and, "conspiracy theories", which shifts the blame of our woes and problems to outside forces and diverts attention from the vested interest that manages to keep its stranglehold on us. And a firm belief in a zero-sum game is another pet assumption, that they grow out of extraction from us, and that if we grow they would be poor. There is an implied assumption that we are one of the most resourceful countries of the world, which is very far from the truth. Admittedly, there are resources that ought to be optimally utilized such as of Energy Resources, but on a world scale we are one of the poorly endowed countries. We do not have enough land and water, which are the two fundamental indications of resource endowment. We have included a chapter on the development and growth of the Muslim countries. We find that some Muslim countries have really progressed and are showing remarkable achievements. Take the example of Turkey and Malaysia, the former is already a 1 trillion US dollars economy, on the way to join the big league. Malaysia, a tiny country, relatively speaking, has done wonders. We have provided data on ten sample Muslim countries, which amply demonstrates our stagnation and lack of progress on a relative scale, despite the claims of successive and intermittent but constant military rules.

It is never too-late. The journey to progress and development can be initiated. There are at best some mixed signs. Political parties, at least some of these, have learnt lessons .More cooperative or less-destructive politics has been shown. More improvement is required in this respect. The specter of another round or perpetually intermittent rounds of the military rule is not over yet. We are still confused on the role of military in the running of the country. Those very forces, which have forcefully opposed the idea of a National Security Council, providing a limited but structured role of the military in national emergencies, have spoken of the need of involving the latter in a dialogue. Political parties are still week institutionally and in the strangle-hold of individuals and families. There is no real drive to build roots in the masses and increase their role in the political process, beyond voting .We do not need one big Messiah to disrupt the political process, but we may need a lot of those who cause change in their respective domains. We need a wider conscientiousness among the political forces and the powerful elements that growth is mutually beneficial and that sharing is beneficial; some kind of national renewal ala Japan, which once was in the clutches of the war mongering feudals and super-patriots. They got converted and are today part of the industrial miracle. The same group in this country can indicate its willingness to do the same by agreeing to the income tax on agriculture and some meaningful land reform that gives a small piece of land to the landless. The beginning has perhaps been made by the announced support for income tax on agricultural incomes by the scion of a big landlord family –the Shah Mahmood Qureshi, a PPP stalwart and former Foreign Minister.

There are widespread demands of improving governance performance. It appears that some major policy steps and reforms package may have to be launched courageously to assuage concerns in this respect. All policy reforms of any significance carry risks of annoying and even antagonizing some sector or group. Those risks have to be taken. The risks in not taking the measures and appear to be doing something meaningful are probably more.

These are my humble submissions to the Government of Pakistan, especially in the aftermath of the floods, which would have been required to be implemented even before the floods. The list could have been longer, but has been kept brief. More will follow in this series:

The Ten Commandments

1. *Reduce budgetary deficit; the choices are not many; reduce military expenditure or bring agriculture into the tax net.*
2. *Overhaul the education system and increase public spending on education to 4% of GDP in the next five years.*
3. *Bring meaningful reforms in the Banking sector, bringing lending interest rates and banks margins down, and balance the lopsided free for all. Improve cheap credit access to the poor and small businesses.*
4. *Pay attention to Energy Sector: develop local energy resources; fast track Thar Coal with Chinese assistance with a package deal of 5000 MW; solve hydro royalty issue of KP ala Indian model of 12% free electricity.*
5. *Launch some significant initiative on Land Reforms and Land Distribution. Introduce land co-operative schemes. Start with allotting government wasteland to the poor and the landless. This would solve the Balochistan issue as well where large plots (10 acres) could be distributed among all Baloch households. Elsewhere consider 1-2 acre plots for agriculture and 500 sq. yards for House & Garden schemes in rural areas.*
6. *Consider housing reforms in urban areas on similar lines; allot 80-100 sq yards subsidized plots on government lands. Introduce and pursue jobs creating economic policies supporting SMEs and micro enterprises. Provide affordable work space; introduce high-rise industrial estates for small enterprises; provide lockers spaces for vendors.*
7. *Broaden and strengthen EOBI programme to include the construction workers, informal sector and house workers by levying a cess on imports and on relevant production such as that of cement.*
8. *Revive Ration Card scheme of the 1960s (for cheap ration) for flood victims and for the others for cheap rates from the utility stores.*
9. *Encourage and facilitate labor intensive sectors and industries; Aqua fishery for flood areas and cage-in-sea fisheries in coastal areas of Sindh and Balochistan. Launch widely dispersed cost-effective construction projects (road –building, drip irrigation, relining water-courses, community centers, agricultural storages for local and rural needs to be handled locally.*
10. *Expand trade with India while protecting the local industry; it is to Pakistan's consumer and industry advantage, who will pay less and save on transportation.*

In the aftermath of floods

Chapter 12 deals with the scientific, management and economic aspects of the recent floods. Floods have devastated Pakistan directly and indirectly. Nearly one-fifth of people and area have been affected. Human, cattle, crops, homes, schools and infrastructure and what not have been destroyed. Damage and loss assessment is yet to be completed, however, there are varying estimates ranging from 11 to 45 billion US dollars. As it is Pakistan was reeling from the affects of two or more successively bad years due to international recession, oil price hike and political transition. Floods have worsened the situation further. The initial psychological and physical shock was so much that some people even doubted that Pakistan would be able to survive at all. These doubts are not new and the flood shocks have even exacerbated those.

Floods visit every community where there is a river. For centuries of human experience and history, floods have been considered a blessing which brought a new round of fertility. There used to be no fertilizers, floods brought fertile soil along and spread it on the shore. The problem is due to the burgeoning population. In the last sixty years alone, Pakistan's population has increased manifold, mounting pressure on both rural and urban land and areas.

The intensity of floods was colossal. According to initial estimates, 45 MAF (million acre feet) of water gushed out in a few days, as opposed to normal average flow of 100 MAF in one full year. This was certainly the most severe flood in the history of the land of this country.

Admittedly, floods devastation could have been much lesser, had we been a little more organized and a little less corrupt and inefficient. What a forlorn hope. Most technology to forecast floods and deal with it exists in the country but utilized with wanting efficiency. Investments in Dykes and Levees have been made over the years, but got weakened and dilapidated due to poor maintenance as a result of corruption of the irrigation department. On e of the most corrupt in a country which has the "honor" of being listed as one of the most corrupt countries of the world. Sindh has suffered much more due to this corrupt officialdom. In Sindh, doctors and teachers do not go to their workplaces and draw salaries. It is ghost schools and health facilities all over. Nationalists in Sindh would have pushed the entire fault to Pakistan and its federal (Punjab) government, had Sindh not been ruling in the center and elsewhere. A separatist movement would have been launched. Thanks to the present democratic set-up. This is another reason that many patriotic and sincere Pakistanis argue and wish that the current political dispensation should be allowed to continue and complete its full term, which it has legitimately earned, despite the purported faults and issues. Sky is not falling; it would have fallen in their absence of those who pronounced "Pakistan Khappe" in a situation when they had all the power and potential to play foul.

It is not easy to run this country in these circumstances. Perhaps those who are destabilizing the system in the hope of coming to power through back doors do not quite appreciate it. So is the power of power. It is a mix motley crowd consisting of naive and innocent middle class professionals clamoring for reform and revolution and a less mature media led by inadequately informed anchors, some of whom clearly running their personal vendetta. In the background there always are undemocratic forces, both within and outside the establishment. The establishment established long ago by the so called," gang of four', led and left by the Governor Ghulam Mohammad. Younger people wouldn't know and appreciate what I mean.

Government of the day has great responsibility to discharge despite onerous and mounting problems. For its part, it should maintain its politics of consensus despite problems and difficulties. Opposition has a difficult role and task to perform to which it has not been quite used to and for which there has not been a tradition. To maintain and support the present set up without letting them winning the next election. It is indeed a tight rope, and the chances and incentives and detractor too many to cause imbalance and a fall. Mr. Nawaz Sharif has an opportunity to live for history and not for power. He has done well up till now and should continue doing so. He would earn more honor and respect without power than with it. He has already done so.

Improving governance performance

Often it is argued that in Parliamentary democracy, ministers come from their districts through popular votes. They are often not well versed with the ministerial tasks they are entrusted with. Consequently a case is made either for the Presidential system in which ministers are not elected but are selected by the president usually on the basis of expertise cum political association.

Or military dictators emerge offering expert ministers as a better alternative. Can ministers deliver in the parliamentary system while lacking in expertise? The case of Lalloo Prasad, the former flamboyant

Chief Minister of Bihar province in India, proves that ministers can deliver. Lalloo turned around Indian Railways recently, turning a loss giving entity into a profitable organization and that without increasing the fares. In India ministers have been delivering well over the years despite the so-called cacophony and rambling of democracy. It has been marching ahead on fast track over the last decade with a growth rate of 10% plus as opposed to our boom-bust economy artificially primed by military dictators which often runs into snags thereafter.

There is a strong case for our ministers to improve performance. After all they are a motley crowd of a century plus permitting build up of expertise and specialization having large cabinets is often a need of fledgling democracies garnering and building a strong base of support for the government. Only a minister is added. Often the administrative departments are already there irrespective of a separate minister. If ministers behave frugally, and the whole system is reorganized on frugality and cost consciousness, it can be affordable. So the problem is not with having a large cabinet, it is with the general culture of profligacy. The most frugal government expenditure system is of the United States. High ranking US officials are found travelling in "tubes" in Geneva. Their Pakistani counterparts often are provided with rented Mercedes.

Similarly much criticized foreign trips and travel could be made more cost effective, if no extra payments are made other than a frugal daily allowance, and embassies are forbidden to afford extra cost. All legitimate costs can be affordable and justified; if there is efficiency and output. Without output and performance, even a zero cost would be a liability. So buck up Pakistani parliamentary ministers. Introduce frugality, innovation and efficiency.

Fighting the menace of Terrorism

Terrorism was originally conceived as a political technique by Hassan Ibne Sabbah in Iran many centuries ago, and then developed and perfected by Palestinian struggle against Israeli Zionism earning it legitimacy. Ironically Americans encouraged and even forced terrorism to be adopted by Pakistan and other Muslim country collaborators to fight its proxy war in Afghanistan against the Soviet invasion of Afghanistan. The genie is out of the bottle and Americans and the world are suffering from and under it. Ironically the liberal forces in Pakistan who tend to side today with the Americans, opposed this proxy war and terrorism then and do that now.

Pakistan's national interest did not suffer, as per this view, due to Soviet presence in Afghanistan. Soviet encroachment was a threat to the western or American interests. For Pakistan, Soviet Union was too big to be a threat. Pakistan had to learn to live with its great neighbor, no matter how far or how close it became to Pakistan's boundaries. And at the risk of surfeit of irony, those very forces which supported the US and earned a lot of political and financial gains, are either supporting, abetting and undertaking terrorism in a spectrum of varying mix. General Ziaulhaque, who had earlier finished up PPP government and its leader Zulfikar Ali Bhutto, benefitted most and pushed PPP in a camp opposing the US campaign. Enemy of a friend is an enemy, and thus PPP was persecuted. There is no historical or philosophical reason for the PPP government to side with the US action and campaign against terrorism, except for the momentum of the past and national self interest.

On the other hand American interventions in the last decades have hardly benefitted any body. First of all, war on Iraq was begun on the false pretext of weapons of mass destruction. Consequently terrorism entered Iraq, and now Americans are leaving with a week civilian government, and a highly polarized Iraq under severe Iranian influence of Ahmadi Najad. In Afghanistan also, there is hardly any success. US intervention there has only managed to spread and spill over the problem to Pakistan. We are in it with the US and we cannot unilaterally withdraw from it and neither would it be desirable from the point of view of our own national interest. President Obama is committed to withdrawal from Afghanistan. US has finally allowed President Karzai to talk to the' good' Afghans, something which Pakistan has been long arguing for.

Pakistan Government should encourage and further this process, paving for the exit of the US from Afghanistan. It may be worthwhile counseling them, if they are amenable to, to spend some savings from the presence and war in Afghanistan, on the economic uplift of the region. They escaped swiftly earlier, without treating or disposing their refuse. They may not do it now. But they should do more, spending more on the causes than on treating or facing consequences. Europe may not have been the same peaceful ally as it is today, had the foresight of Marshall Plan was not there. Our government should actively work towards this and handle the negotiation and conduct of policies in a manner that does not penalize Pakistan, in the event of the flow of American largesse. We need it badly.

Cultural adjustments with Terrorism- some unconventional ideas?

Terrorist have not spared their Muslim brothers during or after these floods. Are they really Muslims? They are but they are misguided *mufsideen.* Who were Kharjis and what they did. This is not difficult to identify this old strain in Muslim society. They attacked *Data Darbar* earlier and now yesterday they again struck at Abdullah Shah Ghazi's shrine and have accepted responsibility. Some or most fundamentalist parties and persons blame foreigners including the US for these atrocities, even after their admission. There cannot be more thankless and unimaginative people than are among us to blame America for this.

There may not be any compromise with the terrorists but there can be a compromise with their front men and protagonists who are not directly involved but have considerable sympathy with the terrorists and their Jihad. Most fundamentalists avoid openly condemning terrorists may be due to the fear and more probably because of a common theme that the Pakistani state is almost a *Darulkufr* and it should be destroyed in its present form to be replaced by an Islamic system of their type where women are flogged and daughters kept away from schools. We may have to think about their ideology and thought process. Most poor people and by definition the majority of Pakistan seems to be in their favor-the fundamentalist clergy. Terrorism is expanding, it is not abated. Even if they are in not such a majority, as it may appear apparently, they are in significant number. Some accommodation has to be sought with them. Democratic conduct also requires that the liberals show some sensitivity to their version of ideology. This is not enough to say that we are all Muslims. The differences in approaches and understandings are great.

Surely some mid-ground can be found. The background talks that are going on with some of the good terrorists or our own terrorists should be accompanied by some negotiations on philosophical and ideological issues with their front men. Some cultural adjustments would have to be made. Flagrant demonstration of flesh business by a section of the media must end. Democracy does not, at least the stage we are in, does not need that kind of freedom. Many other flagrant demonstrations of western culture may have to be suitably curtailed. It is often speculated that documentary and media evidence of objectionable materials and other unnecessary carnal exhibitionism is used by the terrorist organizations in their training and indoctrination.

One may argue and perhaps quite justifiably that it may be downward slippery ride to the abyss. For the likes of fundamentalists and terrorists we are facing, even Saudi cultural restrictions are not enough. On the other hand Muslim liberalism may have to also define as to where culture stops and flesh business begins. At this moment, it is also a slippery ride into the western permissiveness of 1960s.

Certainly, this government has to tackle many problems, many being simply inherited. All people and parties should be cooperative and show some compassion and sympathy than simple and cruel opposition, criticism and condemnations.

SECTION-I

Economy

2   Promoting Social & Economic Welfare

Economic Management & Policy: some unconventional wisdom

In Pakistan, it is said, the savings, investment and tax collection are one of the lowest in the world. Of course, this is the formal economy that is talked about. Informal economy is different, and almost equal in size if not more than the formal economy. There is massive tax evasion, often abetted and even forced by the tax collection machinery. The surplus is devoured by the tax collectors. More taxes would be collected if , theoretically speaking , there is less corruption by the tax collector, as the money that otherwise goes to the pockets of the tax collector would otherwise go to the government. On the other hand, there has to be tax collection machinery, without which there may not be tax collection at all—for lack of fear and lack of the system.

However, we would examine here whether lesser tax collection minus corruption of tax collector is that bad as it is often claimed. Lesser tax collection means lower effective tax rates. Lower taxes have been considered a boon for the economy, according to a powerful conservative economist ideology. Their classical argument is that lesser tax means more money with people which results in private spending and demand for output and services which boosts the economy. The counter argument of the non-conservatives (Democrats in the US) is that lesser taxes mean lesser money with government and thus lesser socially beneficial programs for the poor and the disadvantaged.

In Pakistan ,many argue, that more taxes and government invariably ends up fuelling arms race and military expenditure, which many governments have only dreamt for reducing but could not due to the powerful military establishment and their perceived genuine needs. And what is left ultimately ends up in unnecessary government consumption and bloated bureaucracy. Very little goes to the social sector. The numbers are there to certify this claim. More taxes and more collection   may simply go towards the building of an elitist state.

As for the economy and the livelihood of the poor people of Pakistan, it has been built on the back of the informal economy consisting of the small and medium enterprises. Who normally do not like the taxation system, not because they are any greedier than others, but because it is cumbersome, inefficient and corrupt? They do not have the time and patience for it. What is the result? Their unpaid taxes do not end up abroad. They usually invest it in their businesses create output and employment. After all where would the capital and wealth come from and accumulate to create a pool of businessmen and investors, if half of their income is siphoned off tax free. The corrupt official keeps his bribes tax free. No wonder, there is no dearth of former tax and other civil and military officials and their scions running big businesses.

Small businessman would be paying their dues as well, if there is a reformed system. Till such time he should not be bothered, under the garb of documentation of the economy. It is not easy to keep books of account for those whose life is so tied down to their business affairs which is already made so difficult by the system which requires them to keep inspectors and officials from some sixteen departments happy and in good humor.

Pakistan is passing through a difficult time. Even before the floods, 25-30% of its populace was living below poverty line. What would happen after the floods is any body's guess. It would be advisable that the government takes up the matter with the IMF and the US and European governments, and try to prevail upon them to spare us or soften their conditionalities in view of the highly stressed social and economic system that prevails in the economy. After all they want to help us recover and get their money back and contribute to the stability of the world system. IMF intellectuals would be requested to get a deeper insight into our societies in order to be of some help. And help they certainly can.

Taxing Agriculture and the Land Reforms

Taxing agriculture has been long demanded by the people and professional economists including veritable international bodies. Agriculture accounts for one-fourth of Pakistan's GDP. There are 30,000 agricultural households having large estates of 500 acres or more. A large number of them come from upper Sindh and southern Punjab. Most of the times the argument for not taxing agricultural incomes was the skewed terms of trade due to low domestic prices for the crops. Now the prices have been brought in line more or less with international prices. Even otherwise, whatever, be the economic or pricing policy regime, if some body is earning income that is otherwise and normally taxable for others ,should pay his dues.

Paying taxes has a psychological under tone, and that is submission to the state and government. Perhaps it is too much for the feudal that has been lording over the districts and has even managed to cannibalize democracy for his ends. This would also bring some balance into the political system. We have suggested earlier that a collection of measures could be taken that may discourage large landholdings and pave the way towards land reforms and transfer, without coercive means. The time for agricultural tax and land reforms has come. Something will have to be done willy-nilly by the politicians. Otherwise a future military usurper may find it as a wonderfully legitimizing tool. Future military interventions may not be traditionally oriented seeking support of the vested interests, but may contain a revolutionary flavor ,if not fervor and if not out of conviction but for shear political purpose. I am not at all making a case for military takeover; far from it. I am advising the politicians to close this gap which may otherwise be used by the usurper.

Political requirements and essentials

Floods have devastated Pakistan directly and indirectly. Nearly one-fifth of people and area have been affected. Human, cattle, crops, homes, schools and infrastructure and what not have been destroyed. Damage and loss assessment is yet to be completed, however, there are varying estimates ranging from 11 to 45 billion US dollars. As it is Pakistan was reeling from the affects of two or more successively bad years due to international recession, oil price hike and political transition. Floods have worsened the situation further .The initial psychological and physical shock was so much that some people even doubted that Pakistan would be able to survive at all. These doubts are not new and the flood shocks have even exacerbated those.

Floods visit every community where there is a river. For centuries of human experience and history, floods have been considered a blessing which brought fertility and prosperity. However this was a flood of colossal magnitude .Some 45 MAF (Million Acre Feet) of water flown in a few days as compared to 100 MAF throughout the year, which is a normal average. The flood devastation would have been much lesser had we been a little more organized and a little less corrupt and inefficient. a forlorn hope. Most technology to forecast floods and deal with it exists in the country but utilized with wanting efficiency. Investments in Dykes and Levees have been made over the years, but got weakened and dilapidated due to poor maintenance as a result of corruption of the irrigation department; One of the most corrupt in a country which has the "honor" of being listed as one of the most corrupt countries of the world. Sindh has suffered much more due to this corrupt officialdom.

In Sindh, doctors and teachers do not go to their workplaces and draw salaries. It has ghost schools and health facilities all over. Nationalists in Sindh would have pushed the entire fault to Pakistan and its federal (Punjab) government, had Sindh not been ruling in the center and elsewhere. A separatist movement would have been launched. Thanks to the present democratic set-up. This is another reason that many patriotic and sincere Pakistanis argue and wish that the current political dispensation should be allowed to continue and complete its full term, which it has legitimately earned, despite the purported faults and issues. Sky is not falling; it would have fallen in their absence of those who pronounced "Pakistan Khappe" in a situation when they had all the power and potential to play foul.

It is not easy to run this country in these circumstances. Perhaps those who are destabilizing the system in the hope of coming to power through back doors do not quite appreciate it. So is the power of power. It is a mix motley crowd consisting of naive and innocent middle class professionals clamoring for reform and revolution and a less mature media led by inadequately informed anchors, some of whom clearly running their personal vendetta. In the background there always are undemocratic forces, both within and outside the establishment. The establishment established long a go by the so called, "gang of four", led and left by the Governor Ghulam Mohammad. Younger people would not know and appreciate what I mean.

For its part, government of the day should keep pursuing its policy of persuasion and consensus, despite miscreants inside who lack broad vision and are grounded in their districts and at best in provinces. Opposition has been playing a positive role to the extent it has been humanly possible for them. They have a tough and tight job and a rope to walk on. They have to work for and with the democratic system and yet win the next elections. It is not easy and would not be easy to maintain the fine and tight balance. After all democratic traditions and practices have not been allowed to take roots.

The case of the poor

For long in Pakistan, poor has been neglected. Only lip service has been made towards the poor. Only bare minimum has been done ,as is indicated by the persistent short fall in the spending in social sector , and even then a skewed distribution against the poor has been maintained ,if not by choice then by default. This may not be tenable anymore in the aftermath of floods without compromising the supreme national security interest of Pakistani state. It has occurred earlier in the case of East Pakistan-Bangladesh. It can occur again, possibly under different consequences and configurations and circumstances. Economic policy should now be conducted in the favor of the people and the poor. We have Taiwan model where small enterprise was promoted and we have South Korean model which relied on large industrial conglomerates. Both countries developed and prospered. Our conditions are more akin to Taiwanese model due to large scale dislocation and poverty. Direct income, employment and welfare of the people should be a priority than the trickled down effect of an elitist system. Trickling is often too little and too late.

It is not a vague political economy. The choices are often stark and clear; do you invest in Lahore-Islamabad freeway reducing the travel time of the elite on a comfortable journey as opposed to investing and improving the GT roads where the people and goods move; do you invest in beautification of Lahore at the expense and funds of lesser areas of southern Punjab ;do you spend foreign exchange in new cars and luxury goods while ignoring and discouraging capital goods that may be used by the SMEs ;do you let banks and brokers earn excessive profits at the expense of SME borrower who has to pay interests of over 20% to the same banks, as has happened in the days of Musharraf; Do you accept some load shedding vis-à-vis installing expensive peak power; do you extend credit priorities to the large and rich sector or prefer cheaper credit for the small farmers and the SMEs; do you allow small enterprise to wind up successively in face of monopoly capital's expansion or do you reserve some space for the SMEs, as has often been done in our neighborhood.

Often it is said that Lassaize-fare economies often work out and often market based solutions are efficient. Perhaps no more; direct attack on poverty with sympathetic treatment to the poor's economy would have to be made in the prevailing situation. We do not have time to further linger the misery. However, when I argue and emphasize in this respect, I also do not lose sight of sustainability and affordability of reform steps. Rash and un-thought through steps only based on confusing ideologies can be a recipe for disaster, as has happened before in the case of whole sale nationalization.

Impose both: Flood Tax & Income Tax on agriculture

Flood Tax is being contemplated by the government. Normally nation would have gladly accepted the additional load. However, there are several reasons that voices have been raised from popular circles against it.

Firstly, if it is levied on imports, it may be akin to be a tax on poor and the rich alike and may contribute to inflation. Secondly, if it is on income tax, it would mean milking only those, especially, the salaried class which is paying its taxes without default. Thirdly, it has been argued and demanded that tax net should be expanded and exempted sectors brought into the tax net. Income tax on agricultural incomes and capital gains on stock shares are the two major exemptions. Debate has even extended among donors and public abroad, who think that Pakistan should start bearing its own load and shun the policy of foreign dependence on all kind of aid, flood and otherwise. The taxpayers in the west complain that if Pakistan's rich are not paying their dues, why their tax money should be helping Pakistan.

Prime-minister Gilani has announced that some difficult decisions may have to be taken and that he was ready for that. Let the agricultural income tax be one of those decisions. Any body, who earns taxable income, should pay income tax as others do. There used to be an argument against this, citing low and depressed crop prices paid to the farmer. No more is that case valid today. International prices are being paid despite poorly paid agricultural workers and sharecroppers.

And it sends a wrong signal and a depressing one, spreading despondency and estrangement. Bulk of Pakistan's ruling elite comes from the agricultural land lords. It is extremely disappointing that they exempt themselves and shirk in sharing the load. Initially, lower landholdings could be left exempted and taxation may start from 50 acres and onwards. Agriculture accounts for 25% of Pakistan's economy, and should be able to add significantly to the government revenues.

Although I am personally not a taxation enthusiast and I have made my views for lower taxation in Pakistan elsewhere, arguing that economic growth could also be laid by private consumption. It is also a sad fact that in Pakistan tax collection is at a dangerously low level of under 10%.Exemptions, especially in agricultural sectors not only reduce revenue but are a major source of tax dodging and concealment of income. All kind of incomes are grouped and hidden under exempt agricultural income. If you are a landlord, no question asked. This must go.

Flood tax may only be tolerable by the public in general and taxpayers in particular, if income tax on agriculture is imposed simultaneously. Finally rulers should declass themselves. Their job is to act in the common national interest .It is another story that democratic governments are so much pressurized by the vested interest from the beginning demoralizing them so much, that any intention or incentive to bring in critical reforms is severely discouraged. Despite such difficulties, government of the day must act in national interest and show courage and determination.

Introducing reforms in the banking sector

Banking sector unduly prospered in the reign of Musharraf-Aziz Qureshi. In order to get acclaim and recommendations from powerful financial lobby, national and international (it is well integrated), it is found essential by illegitimate regimes pursuing temporary bonanza and ratings, to patronize and unduly benefit this sector; result being buoyancy in banking and purely speculative stock exchange. International press and media start publishing photos and shower praise. Often ratings improve mostly because of the psychological factors. Boom is brought to be followed by a subsequent bust as has happened in the past and also most recently. Although the recent bust has been related with international factors, while it is also true that slowdown had already set in by 2005.You can only go so far by superficial laissez-fair and by utilizing earlier installed capacities and investments. Why is the boom not sustainable? Perhaps the bust is implicit in the boom?

Hot capital attracted by a purely speculative market goes away at the slightest indication, robbing the small investors of their investments by causing planned and unplanned crashes. Stock markets based on long term investments and yields may be of some benefit to the economy, contributing to the welfare of investing public and creating jobs and economic activity.

If there is to be an improvement in the performance of the financial sector, the interest rates should have come down along with the cost of intermediation. Lending rates hover around 18-20%, while the deposit rates seldom exceed 10 %.This is among one of the highest bank margin, indicative of underdeveloped and inefficient financial and banking sector. It discourages both borrowing and deposits and only encourages bankers. No wonder banks in this country have earned huge profits. The artificial boom, call it free-for- all, caused distortions in banks factor market. Ordinary run of the mill managers started demanding and managed to get impossible salaries. After all, the loot had to be shared. It was shared by their patrons, banks and the employees.Net losers being the depositors and the economy.

This is the time to correct the excesses of Musharraf regime and bring in some real competition and controls in the sector so that the lending rates come down, removing one of the major stumbling blocks in the competitiveness of Pakistani exports, causing trade gap, foreign borrowing and more inflation. However Pakistan interest rates are not high due to inflation, as the deposit rates are comparatively low. It is the bank margin that makes interest rates high, I must say, at the risk of being nauseatingly repetitive. There is no need to be disruptive and rash. Some adjustments and reforms can definitely cause improvements without rocking the boat. A high level committee of the stake-holders incorporating some genuine reform and socially oriented intellectuals and professionals should be formed to address the required changes.

The Food Prices Issue

In case of Food prices, there is a strong case of targeted subsidies for the very poor. Tandoors of Punjab governments have not worked well, although it is politically very attractive to sell hot Roti at cheaper prices. Nor can the Utility Corporation be effective without a formal rationing system. There was rationing on flour (Ata), sugar and rice up till late sixties, although mostly for demand management purposes. It worked petty well without the help of today's computers. There used to be a Ration Card and plenty of ration shops run by the private sector. The same can be done much easily in these days of computerization and other possible controls. Cheaper food items could be sold in poor neighborhoods at subsidized prices.

Food prices would be lower, in a sustainable sense, only if agricultural productivity and efficiency goes up. Agricultural productivity in Pakistan is less than 50% of that in the comparable countries and the average Agricultural productivity being similarly lower than the best within the country. This indicates great potential and scope for improvement. Similarly, a lot of water is wasted by the agricultural sector, resulting in lesser availability and lower water productivity.

Creative solutions are always possible. Look at the Sunday bazaars which have played a good role. Middleman profiteering is notorious in Food sector. Even in advanced countries, there are cooperatives working at large scales to eliminate the middleman. We hear of only scandals in the cooperative sector that we have seen in this country. Agricultural input prices can be controlled through buying cooperatives as well. Cooperatives avoiding wasteful competition and selling costs can and do result in lower costs and economic efficiency. Reduction of marketing risks enables attracting capital at cheaper rates than the corresponding rates for a commercial operation. One may note the following examples;

- In Brazil, cooperatives produce 72% of the wheat, 44% of barley, 43% of soya, 39% of milk and 35% of cotton and 21% of coffee resulting in exports of 1.3 billion US$.
- In Japan, agricultural cooperatives report output of US$ 90 billion, with 91% Japanese farmers as members.
- In Finland 74% of meat, 90% of dairy products, 50% of eggs, poultry and 34% of forests are controlled by cooperatives.
- In Korea, agricultural cooperatives have a membership of over 2 million farms (90% all farmers), and an output of US$ 11.00 billion and 70% of fishery products.
- In Norway, 99% of Milk production and 76% of timbre is coming out of cooperatives.
- In India cooperative movement has had considerable role and success in improving the Indian economy and social conditions. Two cooperatives have had country wide out reach and are known world wide. One covers milk and dairy and the other fertilizer. Gujarat Cooperative Milk Marketing Federation (GCMMF) markets its milk products with the trade name Amul, with turn-over of around 1.3 billion US dollars. It has 2.7 million milk producer members in 13141 village societies. In addition to marketing milk, it owns processing plants, markets a variety of milk products like cheese, butter, chocolate and ice cream. Even multinational firms are scared of its distribution network and competiveness and quality.
- Top 300 cooperatives called "Global 300", and an annual turn-over of US$ 963 billion, almost equivalent to Canada's economy which is 9th in the world. The list includes Switzerland largest employer

"Enpore" largest dairy business, France's largest bank, the largest rice company, Japan's largest agri-cooperative Zen Noh with a turn-over of US$ 54 billion.

Federal (GOP) and provincial governments can stabilize and reduce prices, increase employment, improve worker welfare, enhance economic output and exports by launching a major initiative in the Cooperatives In all such areas which are labor intensive, cooperatives can be a useful agent; also to provide economies of scale bringing consumers together to create a large market; bringing producers together to support them with market, technology and information. Establishing cooperatives and putting them together is a lot easier than SMEs where greed, secrecy and taxation issues do not let them go very far. However this should not be taken as a discouragement of SMEs which has a role for itself for those with money, ambition and enterprise.

There is also a great need to reduce the cost of transportation and logistics. Improvements and energy efficiency in transportation fleets, improved farm to market roads and a better functioning railway system can all play a role.

Concluding, there are no easy or command options in reducing costs and prices. But it is certainly possible. Governments of the day, today or tomorrow, would need peace of mind to be able to think and launch and implement creative solutions. If they are embroiled in daily challenges and uncertainties not much would come out. Pressure for the betterment, in fact, would have counter-productive effect. While democracies work and thrive on controversy, contention and opposition, there is also a role and value for constructive engagement. To a certain extent, Pakistan political process has acted positively in this respect. Politicians may be encouraged to continue the same path without abandon or feeling shy due to the distracters. Reduction in government expenditure is dealt in the second part of this two part article.

Sugar problem: People vs Elite?

Sugar problem is poised to emerge again and again. Sugar in some periods has been sold at Rs.100+. And it was not available at all under Supreme Court edict and government's somewhat lame crack-down on sugar mills, traders and other hoarders. Sugar is an essential food item and more for the poor, whose staple diet is bread (Roti), onions and tea. Sugar is a great source of energy and enthusiasm for the poor workers.

Why does the government and Supreme court could not do much to address the problem?

I have not personally investigated the problem but keep reading about various aspects of the problem. The major argument is that one cannot fight market and the greed. When prices are high in international market, and domestic controlled prices too low, either price control would be defied, or hoarding and smuggling would take place. Government can do very little about it, it is argued. But do consumers get the benefit, when international prices are low. Consumers can get benefit if it imports the foreign sugar at the right time and in right quantities which it somehow fails to do. Sugar mafia somehow manages to put a hammer in the process and contentious debates ensue as to who was responsible.

There is a simple answer, may be a little too facile, but still reasonable and defend-able; sugar mills are owned by the political and even military elite. In the days of General Ziaulhaque, there was a Parchi system under which most politically desirable and powerful politicians were given loans by the DFIs and banks; one parchi for banks and another for HMC and KSEW who mostly supplied the machinery and installed the plants. The beneficiaries were mostly the right wingers and today's principled politicians of PML (N) and not very principled PML (Q) leaders, who were together in those days. A whole new political class was developed and strengthened in the country to support the military general. Then came the PPP government of 1988 which repeated the sugar mill parchi syndrome with a vengeance. Mr. Zardari and his associates benefited this time to complete the circle. As a result a sector developed which predominantly is owned by the political elite, who rule the country .Whether democracy reigns or dictatorship, one powerful group defending the private interests of the sector is always there. Opposition also has its representation in sugar mafia. So it is people vs elite. And they say jo maza haram kamane main hay wo halal main kahan and who says it is haram?

Those who are older like me would remember the famous Ration Shops in General Ayub's period. Every Mohalla used to have a ration shop and every family used to have a ration card which also used to double as an identity card in those days when NADRA and NIC were not there. In those days of no computers, families and there ration shops were registered with nearby ration shops which supplied *ata*(flour) and sugar for fifteen days of a family quota defined by the government. I remember going to these shops regularly fortnightly and get the ration, on payment and not free, as same may be akin to dream? This was a stable system and worked well without computers to keep a tab on misuse. No big scandal was reported, although in such regulatory and control system some misuse is expected. The ration shops were in private sector and worked under government license. Today a near equivalent of Ratio's shops is the Utility Store owned by the government but no ration cards and fixed quotas. As a result Utility store sells to the hoarders and every body else till the supplies lasts and most deserving consumers do not benefit from the concessionary rates.

It is time to revive ration shops and ration cards and include utility stores in the system as well. Poverty and food items pricing and scarcity issues are not expected to go away. I have discussed this issue in my book: Pakistan's Development Challenges as well.

Floods Recovery: land reform, water rights, in-land fishery and white revolution

We should be coming out of floods soon, as at least in Punjab people have started returning home to start planting for the next crop. In Sindh also, people are expected to start returning. Flood victims will have to be rehabilitated, as they have lost almost every thing; houses, cattle, food stock, plantation, crop etc. It is an extremely difficult task. Most of the affectees are small farmers and the landless poor, operating in the Kachcha areas. Next crop is to come in six months, and the affectees have to eat and survive in this period besides providing inputs to produce their livelihood.

In this article, I would like to discuss some of the options and approaches that could produce some results in near term, although may take some time, and may not be implementable immediately. However, as I have pointed out elsewhere, government(s) can utilize this calamity as an opportunity to launch some fundamental reforms in the economy and agricultural sector in Pakistan.

Let me first of all and at the first opportunity explain what is meant by "white revolution", as some readers may be concerned and nervous over the word revolution. White revolution is a term referring to the prospect and potential of very high increase in milk production in our country. For almost a decade, we are talking about the white revolution by launching innovative development and assisting programs in the live stock sector. With more than 200,000 cattle having been lost in the floods, the dream of such a revolution seems to have receded further into the oblivion. However, a more distributive and broad based programme could be launched by providing a pair of cattle under some loan scheme, along with a small piece of land. By some magic ,if government manages to get the money and credit from abroad and lends it to small farmer, where does the land come from.

I have discussed elsewhere the possibilities of launching land reforms, in a limited fashion, which may be politically feasible. I would not elaborate it over here, except that the Government(s) can speed up and rather broaden the land distribution programme that had been in the pipeline in Sindh, before the floods. Same can be done at much broader and wider scale in Balochistan, where only 5-6% of the countries population lives on almost 50% land mass of the country i.e., one million households vs 25 million households elsewhere. I have similarly argued for water rights for the landless from all the future irrigation network expansion of the future, and further increase in irrigation water availability.

Let us here focus on the flood water. Many water bodies in the country and especially in Sindh and Balochistan ,which had become almost extinct due to lack of water, should have been revived and rehabilitated by the excess flood water. In lower Punjab, farmers are reportedly offering higher bids for leases of these water bodies with their enhanced fishery potential. New areas with deeper land where inundation has been very high could possibly convert to new water bodies. In many countries like Bangladesh, Peru and Brazil etc aquatic fishery projects have been launched successfully in the flood plains under community based systems.

Traditionally in-land water bodies are auctioned and given out on annual contracts to often rich and well-connected contractors who try to maximize their fish catch, small artisanal fishermen from their subsistence activities. As it happens conventionally in Pakistan, a lot of money and income goes into the pockets of those awarding the contracts and their patrons. Very little income is received by the government. Provincial governments should consider awarding communal or cooperative ownership or fishing rights to nearby and traditional communities along with assistance and extension providing hatcheries and feed supplies under some credit schemes. New water bodies may be created by trapping the flood water and connecting it with river through channels. In Haiti a similar project has been launched under Clinton Global Initiative, about which a film has been shown recently on CNN.A similar project could be launched in Sindh and elsewhere in the country. Through such innovative schemes and projects, one could mitigate and alleviate the disastrous consequences of floods to our people and the economy. However we must move fast, and move optimistically in a positive way, looking for wisdom and approaches from whatever directions these may be available. Fortunately, world today is a global village and technology and wisdom is available to meet the challenges. World community appears to be quite eager to help, if we are eager to help ourselves.

Fishery cage aquaculture for sustainable livelihood for the poor, landless and flood victims

Fishery aquaculture has existed in Pakistan for quite sometime now. In this one literally grows fish from small fish media called fingerling, the latter being produced in hatcheries. Fishery aquaculture is, however, quite expensive business requiring land, pond excavation, water pumps and drainage system and in some cases even expensive oxygenation. Fish feed is also to be provided. In Punjab, fish aquaculture has grown quite significantly to meet demand mostly from middle and upper classes.

In coastal areas of Sindh and Balochistan, natural fish is caught under traditional net and line method using fishing boats and trawlers. It is an open access system where Pakistani vessels have equal access under a nominal registration fee system. Fish catches and yields from the sea has bee dwindling through out the world including Pakistani coasts , creating a space and demand for other fishing techniques, one of which is fish aquaculture as discussed before.

Lately Fisheries Development Board has announced a project named Cage Fishery Development. In this technique fish aquaculture is done in inland water bodies, open riverine or sea water in metal or plastic net cages. Because in open water, fish grown by fish farmer is free to go away otherwise, it has to be caged. With cages many individual and groups can pursue aquaculture in a common water resource, otherwise one has to excavate his pond or may have to contract or lease the whole water body.

Cage fish aquaculture is relatively a new technology developed only since 1980-90s. Highest development and production of cage fish culture has taken place in China, where demand for nutritional protein is high due to an expanding population base. In Nepal, cage fish culture has been introduced to provide livelihood to displaced communities of a dam project. In Indonesia and Thailand, Tsunami victims have been supported through in-cage fishery aquaculture initiatives. Most recently, Clinton's foundation Global Initiatives has launched a similar project for Haiti Earthquake victims and has reportedly been received well by the stake holders.

Currently the initiative launched by Fisheries development Board (FSB) is geared towards larger projects and investments. FSB has created a network of facilities to promote fish production through this method. The in-cage fishery aquaculture is feasible both for large scale as well as at micro and individual level. FSB and provincial governments would be strongly advised to launch a small scale initiative for the poor farmers, rural poor and the landless peasants and now the flood victims. A package consisting of 4-5 fish cages of one cubic meter volume(one meter all sides),and monthly feed supplies and a starting stock of fingerling could be provided to the target group in all parts of the country in flood areas and in coastal Balochistan. Water bodies may be allocated to farmers groups and associations or on individual basis along with the aforementioned inputs. A training and demonstration programme should also be launched .Chinese government may be requested to provide assistance in this respects. They have a lot of experience in this and offer inputs and services at less than % prices.

This is no alternative to land reforms, in absence of which at least water bodies like rivers, canals and lakes could be leased to the poor for in-cage fish aquaculture production, which would earn them cash and as well meet the nutritional requirements. NGOs should also pay attention especially for the flood victim poor. Women who currently are at a disadvantage in the fisheries sector, because in our social and religious traditions, women do not go out on boat for fishing, in-cage fishery would provide an alternative inroad into this sector.

Community based fisheries management

Fish consumption in Pakistan is one of the lowest in the world i.e.1-2 kg per capita per year bringing down nutrition levels among people to one of the lowest also. This is not a habit issue, which at best is a chicken-egg problem. This is despite, a 1000 km+ coastline and four rivers and thousands of miles of canal network. There is a tremendous potential in the sector to contribute to the livelihood of the poor, if not for boosting exports which any case robs the poor of its potential food that may be available otherwise.

Most of the coastal fishery is under open access system which is normally exploitative maximizing output and profits without any regards for resource conservation, sustainability and stewardship, although there are some regulations that provide for the former with a varying level of effectiveness. If a resource is owned by a community, it may forego consumption or injurious exploitation, for the sake of tomorrow's consumption and needs. In open access system, it is generally free for all and no such incentives for resource conservation and stewardship or management exist, except for some labeling systems that are in a stage of infancy.

Similar is the situation for inland fisheries resources and water bodies which are contracted out by WAPDA and provincial governments as per their domain and ownership. Except for some limited revenue, the characteristics of contractor-ship are the same as in the open access system. Even the purported and potential revenues are siphoned off by the corrupt bureaucracy and their politically influential patrons.

Community base fisheries management has emerged as a viable alternative management system, although promoted more for environmental reasons than any thing else. Our focus here is to utilize this approach towards the following social and economic objectives:

1) to broaden the claim and stewardship of the poor and the landless on the resources.
2) to dilute feudal structures and reduce dependence of the people on it.
3) to increase nutrition and income of the rural poor.
4) to increase output, efficiency, economics and resource conservation.
5) and for the time being ,contribute to the revival of rural economies after the flood disaster, with which we have dealt with elsewhere.

However, there is a great risk in all community based systems to be hijacked by feudal vested interest through proxy and background manipulations and machinations. The very purpose of broader social and economic upliftment is gone. Commercial and administrative systems have been and are an improvement of the classical and traditional master-client system of landed interests which try to reemerge under new names of community organizations. Policy designers have to be watchful.

The opportunities of improvement are many. Small steps with continuous improvement and innovations at a broad scale in most parts of the economy can add up to bring about a major impact on the economy and well-being of the people. The tragedy is that people seem to be losing hope and confidence that things would work out. They wait and dream and hope for a great tumultuous type of change delivered by a Messiah whose time is either gone or has yet to come.

Some phony messiahs are touting themselves as the real ones. Others are waiting for an Islamic system and their other brother's want to fast track the same through their suicide attacks. Some nihilists are looking forward to total destruction, so that a new order emerges from its debris. There used to be communists of the yesteryears, whose dreams were overrun by the collapse of the Soviet system. Still possibly, the only real communists are found in Pakistan and India. Fast growth phenomenon of fascism was defeated at the altar of misconduct of Adolf Hitler, and the new proponents of it in the form of military dictators of ours have not been able to offer a panacea, except to offer themselves again and again. So there is no panacea, magic or secret recipe for social and economic development. It comes about piecemeal, in small steps but through a continuous and sustained effort.

In Pakistan, we have been talking about various initiatives for a long time. No sizable initiative after Poultry Scheme has been implemented. All that is done is that some demonstration projects are launched under foreign aid and through foreign consultants, without conviction or commitment. There is no follow-up and no policy and action for launching such schemes and initiatives. There is abundance of doubting Thomases and skeptics for whom nothing is possible or feasible, except the continuation of their perks and benefits. On the other hand so many challenges and demands on newly elected political leaders are created that they are paralyzed in fire-fighting and so much impatience is shown as to create despondency, while military rule is tolerated for long times. People of Pakistan must understand these machinations and put their weight behind democratic political order. On the other hand, political parties should induct technicians and experts, who should remain busy in their development work without bothering about the daily political ups and downs. It is only then that a legitimate and sustainable development and improvement cycle would come into full gear.

Insuring the poor

In 1996, I wrote a book," The Political Economy of Pakistan, An Agenda for Reforms and Restructuring", in which I made some submissions and proposals in this respect. Personal Insurance is not a very popular concept in Pakistan. Mostly industrial assets and vehicles are insured against theft and fire etc., and that for banking reasons mostly. Employees Old Age Benefit Insurance (EOBI) was launched for the benefit of employees in manufacturing and services sector. To date 400,000 workers are benefiting under the scheme with health coverage and old age pension. Mostly large companies have come under the ambit of EOBI. There is massive corruption in EOBI, wherein the EOBI inspectors and officials collude with company owners to under-register and under-pay the annual dues. Still EOBI is providing some benefit and coverage to the poor workers.

Industrial workers in the organized sector form a very small part of the workforce. Bulk of the workforce is engaged in the following sector; a) agriculture, b) construction, c) service and trade, d) domestic workers, e) self employed and informal. Most of the workers in these sectors are not formally employed as company employees. They are mostly paid on contract or daily basis. Something should be done to cover them in some sort of Insurance scheme. In the current economic thinking, in addition to the long drawn trickle down effect, direct support to the poor and building social safety nets have become an accepted approach. Benazir Income Support Program (BISP) has been launched and is being widely acclaimed domestically and by international donor community.

Lack of formal employer is a major constraint to expanding insurance net to the aforementioned sectors of agriculture, trade, construction etc., wherein the employers are too many to deal with. Levying a modest insurance cess (tax) on agricultural commodities and construction material could be a feasible way of mobilizing resources for this purpose i.e., paying the premium for insurance. Ready candidates for such cess /taxation would be cement, steel and fertilizer. A token premium should also be collected from the participating workers i.e., a tax rate of Rs. 100- 200 per month, and a premium of Rs.4000-5000 per year should be paid from the funds generated from the proposed cess. Private sector insurance companies (large and responsible ones) should be involved; otherwise the scheme would be wasted either by inefficiencies and corruption of the public sector or fraudulent practices of the small insurance companies ala third party vehicle insurance.

Voluntary schemes could also be promoted especially for the domestic workers. They should be 30-40 population clusters in Pakistan of well to do and rich families which employ bulk of the domestic workers, as maids, cooks, chowkidars, gardeners, drivers, and cleaners. At least 1 million domestic workers should be working for the well to do, who may be encouraged to pay insurance premium of Rs. 200 – 300 per month per employee. It could even be made a legal requirement as well. NGOs and large insurance companies should be employed to enlist participants-employers and employees. A token premium could also be charged to the insured workers as mentioned earlier.

Fortunately there are government plans on the anvil to introduce health insurance scheme for the workers in the informal sector. A NGO with financial support from the Clinton Foundation has also started working to promote and establish workers health insurance. More of such voluntary efforts should be encouraged along with the required initiatives in this respect.

Is beggary a menace to be curtailed?

No. I don't think so. It is the only institution in the unorganized and poor countries especially Muslim societies, which links the needy with the well-to-do. If a person is hungry or needs help, all he has to do is to come out of home and ask from the ones who can help. What is wrong with it, which is called beggary? Anti-beggary baggage in our countries has come from the west, although there Christianity encourages charity and alms giving. In most poor Muslim countries, unemployment is endemic and earnings are barely enough. Governments are poor and resource-less, partly due to corruption and partly due to poor taxation systems; hence, no social security systems. Only lately direct payment programs like Benazir Income Support Programme has been launched .Obviously the outreach and effectiveness would not meet the demand.

Most Western countries have some kind of social security and reasonable job opportunities for all, men, women, boys, girls and even old and handicapped. In Pakistan many otherwise healthy and active workers slide into old age without family support and have to ultimately come out in the open and beg. The stigma from begging should be reduced if not curtailed altogether. There used to be thriving Langars in older times which are no more. Only Shahbaz Sharif's Sasta Tandoor survives-much reviled and criticized by Late Salman Taseer.

Those who think begging does not involve any effort or labor, should try it some day or at least imagine doing it. Coming out on the road, with suitable attire and roaming around, looking for possible alms-givers and applying all kind of creativity in getting a dime or so involves a lot of effort. They are a kind of financial worker, just below the rank of a teller in a regular bank. And I am not joking at all.

There is a law against beggary which used to be implemented toughly in Ayub Khan's reign. Mercifully as with every other law this law is scantily implemented. Infact the law is only abused by Police in extracting bribe and sexual services. The Law on beggary must be suitably amended; if not done away altogether. Only Mafiosi and forcing beggary on the part of non-relatives for commercial purposes should be banned.

There are people who are in perpetual need of help. The term professional beggary is out of context. Islam permits alms and begging and encourages well to do to give alms and treat the beggar with respect and dignity. There should not be any taboo, social or legal, against begging or even beggary. In the given circumstances, this is the only recourse for the helpless people. Recently many needy people have committed suicide due to their poor financial circumstances. The taboo on begging must go. People are committing suicide but do not prefer to come out on the roads and ask for some help which is the most ready and direct solution to their needs. And now there is additional scourge of the Floods. It is not ideal but still better than suffering hunger and committing suicide.

3   Reducing the Budget Deficit

The Ten Point Agenda: reducing government expenditures

The tenth point in the ten point agenda is about reducing the government expenditure by 30%.Pakistan's budgetary deficit is galloping and may cross 7% of the GDP, crossing the agreed target with the IMF or the threshold required by the law ,which was passed by the last assembly. The law is still valid. However, one is not sure what is exactly meant by the demand. Is it the reduction in total expenditure which includes debt servicing, which cannot be possibly done in a span of a few years, and not to talk of the time available under the gun over PPP's head, 45 days which perhaps have already passed. It appears that the PML (N) did not mean to include debt servicing. It certainly may not mean the inclusion of Development Budget in the reduction demand, which is already so low. What then the demand seem to have meant is the government consumption, which also includes a vital component of spending on running the social sector. Then what remains is the government administrative expenditure? I am not finding enough courage to bring into discussion the military expenditure, and so seems to have been done by the powerful politicians of PML(N),who although are the products of Military plantations and nurseries but have proved there mettle against the Military dictator Musharraf.

There is no doubt waste and profligacy on the administrative side amply demonstrated by day-to-day observations. The long security squads and large entourage in foreign travels are the most obvious ones. The less obvious are over employment and duplication. Fortunately, some steps have already been taken in the wake of the 18th amendment and some under ten- point negotiations. For example, Textile ministry is no more. It is sincerely hoped that the provinces would absorb the surplus manpower and not insist on their own. After all they would need the experienced staff. Provincial departments, as it is, are much less equipped with trained manpower than the federal government. Much more departmental and ministerial consolidation is required than has been done. The most important one is the consolidation of a unified Ministry of Energy.

Table 3.1: Government of Pakistan Budget (2009-10)

(Rs in Billion)

Receipts		Expenditure	
(a) Tax Revenue*	1493.6	**(A) CURRENT**	**1699.2**
(b) Non-Tax Revenue	513.6	General Public Service	1189.1
Gross Revenue Receipts	2007.2	Defence Affairs & Services	342.9
Less Provincial Share	655.2	Public Order Safety Affairs	34.6
Net Revenue Receipts	1352	Economic Affairs	84.9
Net Capital Receipts	190.5	Environment Protection	0.4
External Receipts	510.4	Housing and Community	1.5
Self Financing of PSDP by Provinces	173	Health Affairs and Services	6.5
Change in Provincial Cash Balance	72.9	Recreational, Culture Services	3.7
Privatization Proceeds	19.4	Education Affairs Service	31.6
Bank Borrowing	144.1	Social Protection	3.9
		B) DEVELOPMENT	763.1
		PSDP	646
		Federal Government	446
		Provincial Government	200
		Est. Operational Shortfall	40
		Other Dev. Expenditure	157.1
TOTAL RESOURCES	**2462.3**	**TOTAL EXPENDITURE (A+B)**	**2462.3**

Note: Out of which FBR collection has been estimated at Rs 1380 billion.

Source: Pakistan Budget Documents

There is a proliferation of regulatory agencies, one each per subject or sub-subject, providing plum jobs to the retired bureaucrats. There is no possible case of separate NEPRA and OGRA which infact is affecting functional efficiency due to the unnecessary compartmentalization. Similarly AEDB, the Alternative Energy Development Board could have been a cell of Private Power and Infrastructure Board (PPIB) instead of being an expensive full-fledged organization, and may have produced better results. PPIB was, founded in 1982 to implement the private power policy, it has become stale and outmoded .Disliked by the stake-holders and it is just another stop in the process with no facilitating contribution. Similarly due to the march of the technology, there is a strong unification of television, computers and communications, making a strong case for the merger of PEMRA and PTA .Even the moral and censor issues are common and of similar nature. The list could be long which may not only result in reducing expenditure but also may reduce duplication and enhance operational efficiency.

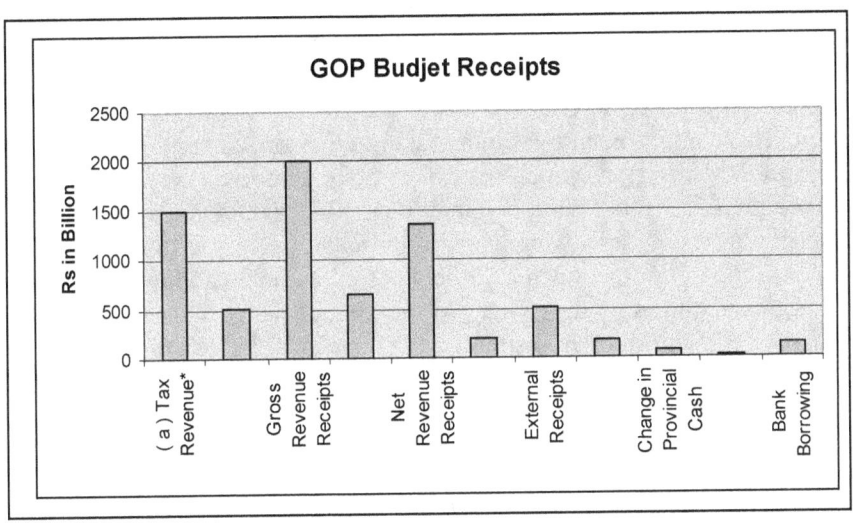

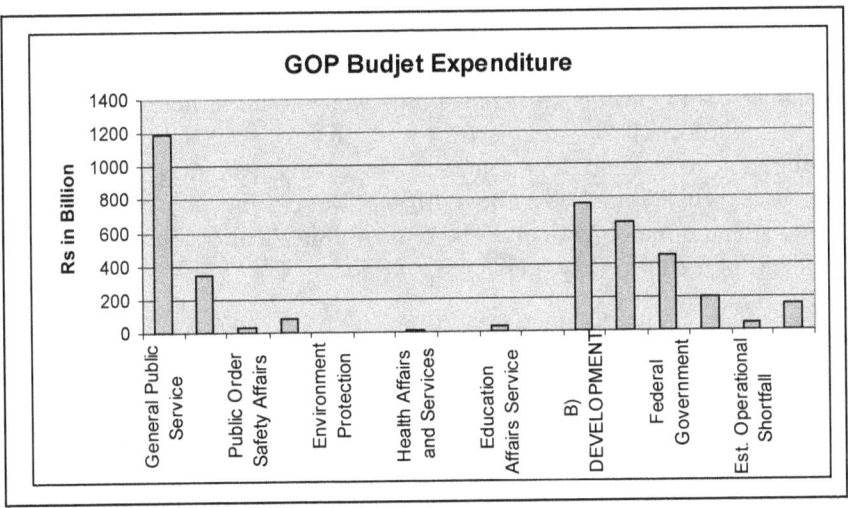

Prime Minister's secretariat is another wasteful invention. It is no more a mere secretariat these days. It houses a full and parallel bureaucracy, who has its own views, interests and cronies, adding not only to cost but compromising merit and efficiency .There are all kinds of Commissions housed in it, including the Human Development Commission, mere words and no output; an outfit to reward relatives and cronies. The democratic government could have done well with undoing this commission as a vestige of the military dictatorship. It can do it now, if it could not do it earlier. There used to be times when Chief Ministers had offices in the secretariats which saved time and money spent in transport and separate facilities and promoted better communication. Today, there are elaborate offices, with advisors and bureaucracy. Is all this talk of frugality meant for the poor and beleaguered federal government? As reported recently, the Chief Minister Punjab has three camp offices as well. There might be similar hide-outs in other provinces. There used to be an O&M division, which may have done some work in this respect, although it is highly unlikely that it would have. One may discover remarkable examples of duplication and even useless institutions. Take an example of the Institute of Strategic Studies and an additional institute of regional studies along with a proliferation of many other similar ones. There are many similar examples that one could cite ad-nauseum. A careful study of government departments ,both in the centre and in the provinces ,along with the employees and expenditure details and their functions may yield useful results, on which action can be taken with a view to reduce expenditure

Reforms and restructuring along with cost reduction are not easy subjects. It is not liked by its objects and victims' .It is opposed by rank and final in many ways. It can be defeated and may be counter-productive if not accompanied by a broad agreement, if not consensus, of the stake-holder. It has to be swift to be effective. But these are counter acting objectives and requirements. Any body who has tried to cut expenses in his home knows how difficult these things are. Yet, it has to be done and done objectively. The cost of doing it is much less than not doing it. In the end every body comes in line.

Military Expenditure

Military expenditure in Pakistan today stands at 5.2 Billion USD, despite many recent accounting adjustments, if not manipulations. The total of military manpower has gradually but surely reached a mark of one million. When Pakistan's nuclear programme was being launched and implemented, the main argument and consolation was that it would result in reduction in conventional defence. We do not know, if it has. The one million of manpower does not indicate it. Admittedly all security forces are probably included in these figures. Our military expenditure in 1980 was 1.4 Billion USD and has been quadrupled in a period of thirty years, along with almost doubling the military manpower. We have become both, nuclear intensive and conventional intensive.

A comparative analysis of MILEX is, however, offering some consolation. India has jacked its MILEX to 36 Billion USD in 2011, from slightly less than 5 billion USD in 1980.In terms of percentage of GDP, Pakistan reduced its MILEX from 7% of GDP to around 3.1 % of GDP, almost equal to that of corresponding percentage of India. In 1980, the ratio of Pakistan-India MILEX used to be 1 to 3 as opposed to 1 to 6 now. Pakistan per capita MILEX stands at 34.12 USD, while that of India around 30 USD, almost equal. In early days Pakistan used to spend twice on defence than India in per capita terms. If there was or is some understatement, it is on both sides and comparable over time. China has maintained its MILEX at 2 % of GDP level over the last three decades, which is much lower than the post cultural revolution period and earlier and has earned the dividend of growth in its economy. Nuclear weapons seem to have made an impact in lowering the MILEX and enhancing Pakistani confidence and psyche. Perhaps more needs to be done and can be done.

High military expenditures did practically break the Soviet Empire, among other factors. Today, Saudi Arabia, an oil rich country suffers under high military expenditure, militating against the much required people friendly budgetary effort. We know what is happening in the Middle East .It may be for freedom and liberty, but also has its economic dimensions. We have 25-30% of our population suffering under abject poverty as defined by the international measure of USD 1.25 per day income. The others left may be under 2 USD except for a tiny prosperous and rentiers class. The much awaited anarchy has already set in. Terrorism and suicidal attacks should be enough of an indicator. We cannot hide behind foreign hands, which can only exploit the prevailing social conditions. Nor can the religious extremism be held solely responsible. The youngster who commits a suicidal attack is also motivating by the suffering in his home.

Does all this manpower of one million contribute to military effectiveness in a nuclear age? The question should be pondered over by the stake-holders with grave attention. General Aslam Beg, in a private conversation with me in a seminar, justified large militaries as solving unemployment problem. He cited NWFP, where in his view there were no jobs except the defence sector. Perhaps he had a point, but only partially. There is a limit to government or defence sector's ability to give employment, beyond its genuine requirements. We should be able to do with half as much manpower. What then to do is not an easy question? Its answer requires deliberations and creative thinking for taking short term and long term measures for downsizing without compromising the genuine needs and the military effectiveness?

In addition to a reasonably sized military force, we badly need perhaps a crack force of 10,000 commandos and an equal number of informers to be able to deal with the menace of terrorism, and not a huge number consisting of low paid menial workers and foot soldiers. A good portion of the manpower ends up in the service of an elitist set up, serving as menial and house-hold workers, cooks and malis and what not.. A frugal, simple and motivated military force in the days of Caliph Omar broke the columns of well loaded Iranian forces, which trampled upon its own men and equipment and ran away or were captured. A worn out social system made their surrender easier and was probably hailed inside. It was true then, it is true now. Indians are getting increasingly aggressive and hostile due to our mounting social tension and problems: be it building dams and diverting water or the refusal to initiate dialogues on issues. We have to put our house in order and solve the grave social and economic problems.

Eminent retired patriotic generals have spoken against the trend and there is a consensus that 25% reduction in military expenditure is possible without sacrificing the genuine needs and effectiveness. All of this may not be done in one go. At this moment of national suffering, some sacrifice may be in order. I wish India could be involved in the same process, making it easier for both the sides. Our defence establishment should be engaged in an amiable, constructive and meaningful dialogue towards this end. Any talk of frugality or reduction has to, however, be accompanied by corresponding reductions on the civilian side otherwise it would be a non-starter.

The revenue side

There are possible solutions on the income side for reducing the budget deficit, other than the RGST and reducing expenditure; taxing the agricultural income or any other incomes that come under income tax schedule, irrespective of the source. There is no escape to income tax on agriculture and eventually some reasonable land reform, at least releasing the unutilized land that continues to be occupied by the very large land owners.(That by the way is not a small number; More on this in some later issues). There is a strong case now than ever before, when there is a dire national funds shortage, to meet the subsidies requirements, especially if oil price continue to grow. Agriculture is no more a deprived sector, with heavy subsidies for inputs and good support prices.

Moreover, it is not the sector that is paying. It is the earner who is being required to pay. One could make a beginning from the large farms or irrigated regions and exclude Barani, for a start. This perhaps PML (N) can do in Punjab on its own and spend the income on social sector. PML (N) supposedly has business origin and orientation and not of big land lords, as seems to be the case with the PPP. It could have been more forth right in at least bringing it on the table. The reckoning time has come. It is, damned if you do, and damned if you don't, situation. On the one side are powerful agricultural interests and pressure groups and on the other side is the general public. The hard choice is to be made, or?

Concluding, these are not the easy issues, except some showy reductions and frugality , like but not limited to bicycling to the office ,as Ziaul - Haque once did , diverting the whole security apparatus to manage the show ,which resulted in the attack on the US embassy for which we had to pay full compensation. Things take time. Forty five days are not enough. The deliberations, negotiations and monitoring may continue and would be fruitful. Perhaps forty five weeks may provide a better time frame. If the present government manages to achieve this in this period, it would have better credentials to win the elections .Does it suit PML (N)? The Ten Point agenda negotiations could have generated the required focus in developing self-reliant policy options, instead of coming out and reporting that some glasses are full and some are not. One would have liked to know the details and quality of discussion that took place. Unfortunately, it appears that there was more eagerness to report failure than to discover solutions to the some of the acute problems. The problems are not financial alone. They runs deeper.

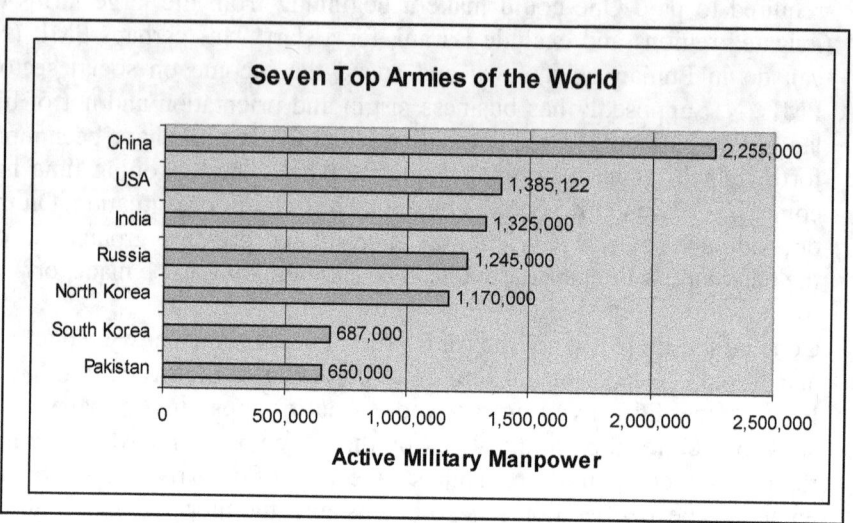

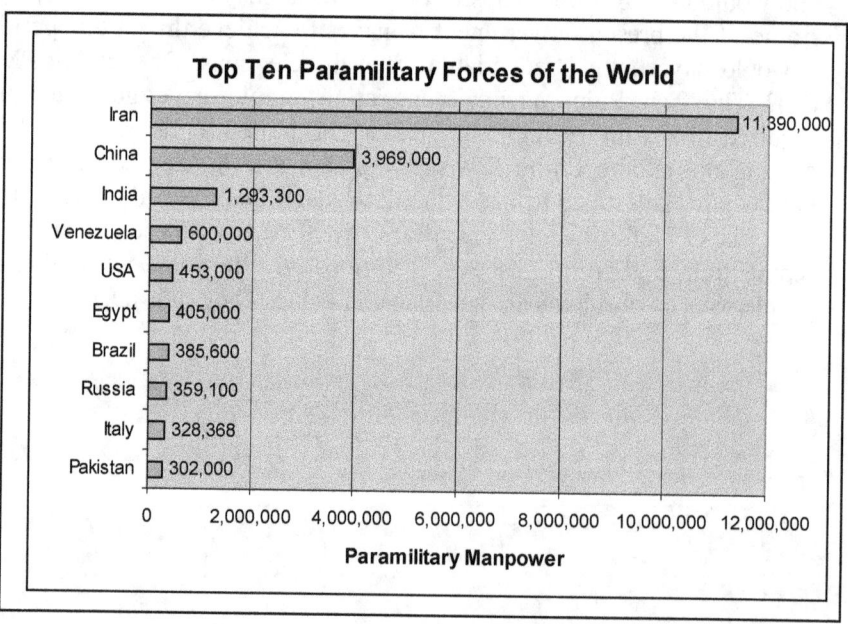

Table 3.2: Comparative Military Strength Pakistan, India and China

	Pakistan	India	China
Total Population	172,800,048	1,147,995,904	1,330,044,544
Total Labor Force	48,230,000	516,400,000	800,700,000
Military Manpower Available	82,747,782	584,141,225	729,323,673
Fit for Military Service	63,822,970	467,795,073	609,273,077
Reaching Military Age Yearly	3,998,981	22,229,373	20,470,412
Active Military Personnel	650,000	1,325,000	2,255,000
Active Military Reserves	528,000	1,155,000	800,000
Active Paramilitary	302,000	1,293,300	3,969,000
Total Air-Based Weapons	710	1,007	1,900
Total Land-Based Weapons	3,919	10,340	31,300
Total Naval Units	33	143	760
Towed Artillery Systems	3,952	4,175	14,000
Merchant Marine Strength	14	501	1,822
Major Ports and Terminals	2	9	8
Aircraft Carriers	0	1	1
Destroyers	0	8	21
Frigates	9	16	42
Submarines	11	18	68
Patrol Coastal Craft	8	43	368
Mine Warfare Craft	3	12	39
Amphibious Operations Craft	0	7	121
Major Serviceable Airports	146	346	467
Square Land Area	803,940 km	3,287,590 km	9,596,960 km

Source: Global Fire Power

The loss making public enterprises & poor performance

We still have a large public sector despite a considerable privatization effort of the 1990s. According to some estimates; there are still 255 public enterprises on the roll in a wide variety of sectors ranging from airlines, railways and road-building to banking, insurance, engineering industries and a steel mill. Most of which are good at losing money and digesting government bailouts and subsidies. The managements of these enterprises are normally selected on political bases and influences than merit. The successive managements have been more adept at polishing balance sheets than introducing efficiency. It is not easy to privatize most of these enterprises. Most employees would resist it, powerful unions and employees from the elite families. Sometimes strategic interests are involved based on misconception or are brought in simply to defend these enterprises. Nawaz Sharif lost his job as a Prime Minister at the hands of Ghulam Ishaq Khan following differences on PTCL privatization, among other complications.

We keep hearing these days of a large number of trains being shut off by Pakistan Railways. The ostensible reason, probably, is losing money on certain uneconomic passages. Will Pakistan Railways come into profit after such a massive closure and pruning of service coverage and level? It is doubtful that it will. I am no expert on Railways, but it is widely known that massive corruption and leakages are mostly responsible for its predicament.

PR is not expected to run into profit. Instead of earning a profit, the excess revenue of such service organizations should bring down the fares? But PR is in massive red and has to be bailed out through subsidies. Indian Railways, some eight times bigger than PR in almost all respects, suffered from similar and comparable problems. Lalloo Prasad, the same former flamboyant and corrupt Chief Minister of the poor Indian State of Bihar, and now the minister of Indian Railways (IR) for some years, has transformed IR into a profitable entity without increasing the fares and service level. Honesty is not his strength, to say the least. But probably efficiency is. IR is full of bureaucracy, perhaps even more than PR is Lalloo utilized the same people and turned IR around.

This brings some hope. Lalloo's Pakistani counterpart could do the same. It is worth going to India and learns a few lessons from the turn around of IR. There is a big market and need for the poor and highly densely populated countries like India and Pakistan, where massive urbanization has occurred, creating massive markets for cheaper travel services. Air Travel, at least in Pakistan, has become awfully expensive. Not only the poor, but higher economic classes and businessmen and their executive would find it appropriate to travel by cheaper trains.

There does not appear to be a basic unsolvable problem. The concerned minister has to apply his mind and energy. You do not have to be a Railway genius. If Lalloo can do it, our lesser Lalloos can do it as well.

Forget the ministers, even the boards of these public enterprises have not functioned properly in monitoring or guiding the performance of these enterprises. Again most appointments in this respect are either political or monopolized by the bureaucracy for both understandable and un - understandable reasons. Where boards have tried to be pro-active, there have been stalemates and destructive actions. GOP has finally become alive to correct the situation and has reportedly decided to make the enterprise boards pro-active, effective and efficient. It is hoped that the jobs do not again go to the cronies and the powerful. I would like to invite the attention of the readers and the policy makers to some alternatives and models in this respect.

In Germany and some other European countries, there is a 2-boards system for corporate management of companies exceeding a certain size; the rationale being, broader risk management, transparency and accountability and catering to the stake-holders and not just share-holders. There are two boards; one board of directors as we find in Pakistan and elsewhere where Anglo-Saxon model is practiced; the other called Board of Supervisors or Supervisory Board. Board of directors is subordinate to the Board of Supervisors. Supervisory Board (BoS) has a chairman of the Board and several members. At least two of the BOS members are to be independent, not belonging to or associated with the company or share-holders. Normally consumer associations, civil society or university professors are elected in the general meeting as independent members.

BOS and BOD are supposed to act together. BoS is concerned with broad policy guidelines, risk management, major contracts and audit. BoD is responsible for day to day operational management of the company under a chief executive (CEO).Lately both models have been converging; single board's powers being more circumscribed and receiving varying levels of external oversight; and BoS's diffused power system and consultative process shortened in the interest of efficiency and quick management.

My proposal is to try this system of two-boards in Pakistan in large public sector companies .We have seen the results of single board managed companies: mounting losses ,corruption ,falling level and quality of service etc; take PIA, Railways, Pakistan Steel, WAPDA, PEPCO, National Bank of Pakistan, OGDC etc. Under the current style of management, the CEO has unbridled powers of Black and White, who is manipulated from behind by controlling ministries. If CEO manages to keep the ministry happy, he is not asked many questions and is free to do all kind of nepotism, and corruption etc. Some powerful CEOs have direct line with the chief executive, PM or President of the country and are immune from ministry's control either. Board members are only part-time and either have full time jobs elsewhere or are board members of numerous organizations earning fee and other formal and informal advantages such as misuse of official vehicles, travel and leverage in appointments of personnel.

BoS, in case of large public sector corporations can bring external and independent oversight, transparency and control over powerful individuals of the board and the CEO. The stakes involved in organizations like PIA and Railways are too much and too many. It is worth examining the viability of such a system in our circumstances. We need not copy the whole system in toto and can and should make suitable adjustments to the German model. We have seen that in the US and other Anglo-Saxon countries, the supremacy of the CEOs has brought in many problems of recklessness and lack of transparency giving rise to financial crashes. Public sector is going to remain in Pakistan for a long time despite efforts of privatization; hence the need of some innovation in respect of corporate governance.

4   Land Reforms and Poverty Alleviation

Introduction

Land has strange properties and characteristics. It is scarce and abundant at the same time. It starts with literally no value and is thus occupied, both by the needy and as well as Mafiosi and organized interests. Ultimately it becomes so scarce and pricey that it makes other things more expensive as well. Many people believe that land belongs to God, State or Tribe. In urban area mostly poor occupy lands without titles or purchasing it, for they cannot purchase. In rural areas, lands have been bestowed upon as a reward for collusion with occupying external powers or a victorious king in lieu of military and extraction of revenue from the tiller. In short the land ownership suffers from many moral, political, social and even legal problems.

Due to highly skewed distribution of land/agri resources, a number of political, social and economic problems are being faced by the country. Firstly, there is an undue and disproportionately large influence of feudals on Pakistan's politics. Absentee landlordism gives the feudals time and money to indulge in the kind of politics they do. It is impossible for the people to exercise their democratic rights in a situation where a few individuals may have such great leverage on the livelihood of the whole populace in rural districts. Some 67% of Pakistan lives in rural areas. The true and real representation of the majority, the grass root leadership of the working people, never comes into play despite frequent elections which, only legalistically speaking, are fair and impartial.

Secondly, agricultural growth has remained, at best, unstable and erratic. Per acre yields have been stagnating or even going down and are pathetically low; in some cases even less than half those of the developing countries average e.g. compare sugar cane yield in Pakistan with that in Egypt. In classical agriculture, the conditions in which most Pakistani feudal agriculture lies, there is an inverse relationship between, farm size and productivity. This phenomenon has been demonstrated almost every where including Pakistan i.e. smaller the farm/above a minimum threshold greater the output per unit area and vice-versa. Although the fact on ground is that small subsistence farming is much less productive; tenure uncertainties further aggravate the situation, as the farmer does not have any incentive to improve/develop the land he cultivates.

Rising population pressures, increasing agri-mechanization and persistent under-utilization of large farms owned by absentee landlords are creating explosive situation in rural areas due to rising rural unemployment. The ejected peasants and other unemployed agri-workers migrate to urban areas where employment opportunities are still more limited, thanks to the industrialization policies adopted in the country that are increasingly augmenting automation and mechanization. Lately the arguments of self-sufficiency and productivity have been used for making grounds for easing the ejectment of tenants and sharecroppers. The question is who will buy the food. Where would the unemployed buy the food produced by highly mechanized agriculture? The familiar demand side question? Both self-sufficiency and full-employment ought to be achieved simultaneously. One cannot be sacrificed for the other. A happy trade-off is to be arrived at that combines equity and efficiency. The issue of land and tenure reforms is still valid and relevant today, as it ever has been.

Agriculture and Poverty

Agriculture has a share of 26% in Pakistan's GDP and employs   % of the work-force. The sector has a potential of growing at rate of 5% p.a., as it did in 1960s earlier. Low growth rates in the economy in general and in agriculture has significantly contributed to poverty and unemployment. Poverty in Pakistan, as measured in 2007-08, was at 26%, which should have increased in the wake of floods and the economic crisis, and has reportedly returned to the previous high levels of 33-38 % of 2001-2002. Rural poverty has always been high in Pakistan at 40% plus. A major reason for it has been the landlessness and low employment. A good 10.36 % of the rural house-holds are landless peasants and another 57% (35.1 % of total population) are under-employed and under-paid non-farm laborers. Both of these groups could benefit from higher agricultural growth rates, land reforms and land redistribution.

Table 4.1: Headcount by land holding using poverty line official 748.56 per adult in 2001-02

		Urban	Rural	Overall
Punjab	Landless	34.21	45.12	44.45
	Under 1 hectare	24.51	26.25	26.19
	1 to under 2 hectares	0	0	0
	2 to under 3 hectares	0	0	0
	5 & above hectares	0	0	0
	Non agriculture	26.92	47.54	38.99
	Total	26.92	39.27	35.71
Sindh	Landless	56.71	58.67	58.6
	Under 1 hectare	27.7	42.34	41.69
	1 to under 2 hectares	0	0	0
	2 to under 3 hectares	0	0	0
	5 & above hectares	0	0	0
	Non agriculture	22.19	46.82	32.99
	Total	22.73	48.79	38.63
NWFP	Landless	61.27	65.95	65.41
	Under 1 hectare	21.25	41.39	40.82
	1 to under 2 hectares	0	0	0
	2 to under 3 hectares	0	0	0
	5 & above hectares	0	0	0
	Non agriculture	33.23	50.87	46.66
	Total	34.21	48	45.98
Balochistan	Landless	56	69.63	68.73
	Under 1 hectare	35.58	29.77	29.86
	1 to under 2 hectares	0	0	0
	2 to under 3 hectares	0	0	0
	5 & above hectares	0	0	0
	Non agriculture	27.84	45.39	41.18
	Total	28.57	42.07	39.72
Pakistan	Landless	48.79	54.89	54.55
	Under 1 hectare	24.84	32.08	31.83
	1 to under 2 hectares	0	0	0
	2 to under 3 hectares	0	0	0
	5 & above hectares	0	0	0
	Non agriculture	25.69	47.76	38.38
	Total	26.04	42.97	38.07

Source: Talat Anwar, Sarfraz K. Qureshi and Hammad Ali, Landlessness and Rural Poverty in Pakistan, PIDE paper, 2004

Higher growth rates would create employment in farm and non-farm sector and would increase wages and incomes. Both growth and equity policies can be mutually reinforcing. Our argument is that the Livestock sector in Pakistan has a contribution of 47 % in the agricultural output, which has been mostly contributed by small holders or the landless, having 2-5 Buffaloes. If 1-1.5 Acre plots are distributed to this group of the landless and the non-farm workers, under a land reforms scheme, it would contribute to both, output and equity. Similarly, the proposed beneficiary group could also participate in high value horticultural sector, which has been shown to have a growth potential of 5.0% p.a. A reasonable land reform component along with the distribution of state land to the rural and possibly urban poor could go a long way in reducing the endemic poverty in this country. Many recent writings have indicated the destabilizing potential of the rural and urban poverty and disparities. Even the Taliban issue is interpreted as having linkage to poverty and deprivation. This creates a new logic and rationale for land reforms which may not only be restricted to land distribution but should go well beyond towards improving upon the tenure issues. The author would strongly argue against the so-called market efficiency and growth-sans-equity policies for example as in Egypt which have worsened the poverty and inequity conditions.

Share cropping, (as quoted by someone), is, "a deplorable method, daughter of necessity and the mother of misery", could be improved by evolving a market-based and yet just and equitable formula, enhancing the welfare of the share-croppers. A rent ceiling /share of less than the prevailing 50% share to the landlord may be promoted. Public works programme like improvements of irrigation, water harvesting and small dams and irrigation in Barani areas, and road-building and other construction projects could improve unemployment and under-employment conditions among the landless and non-farm workers, which would not only increase wages and incomes of these groups, but would generate the necessary market forces and pressure for equitable improvements in the share-cropping terms and land rentals.

Is Land Reform off the Menu?

Pakistan made two attempts at Land Reforms, once by General Ayub Khan and the other by Z.A.Bhutto. Not much was achieved; hence no further attempts were made in this respect, even by PPP governments. Presently a modest Kutcha land distribution programme is being implemented in the province of Sindh. The rationale for land reforms would remain as long as there is grinding poverty, millions of Landless peasants and under-utilization of the land possessed by the big and super landlords.

Some people argue that between 1970 and 2010, in a period of 40 years, large farms have already been redistributed due to Islamic inheritance law. Many differ with this arguing that this phenomenon may be restricted to Central Punjab only, where average land parcels happen to be small. In Sindh and Southern Punjab, the same does not pertain.

Ironically, USAID and the World Bank have supported land reforms in the past in many strife prone regions. Taliban issue seems to have created a new rationale for land reforms among the donor agencies. It is being argued that Talibans may exploit the issue and would most probably be successful in drawing support from the landless poor farmers and enhance their appeal and domain. There is significant evidence that most of the Talibans and their supporters come from the landless class. A recent USAID papers has recommended encouragement and support to GOP in pursuing land reform.

Conclusions and recommendations of US Aid Study

The World Bank asserts that the current tenure system and the continued concentration of land and power among a very small class of landowners is a barrier to the robust growth of Pakistan's agricultural sector. Even those critical of the means and stated aims of Taliban insurgents note that the government's continued failure to address landlessness and uphold the rights of its most poor citizens provides populist fodder that the Taliban insurgents are effectively using in their propaganda efforts. Programming options for LTPR assistance to the Government of Pakistan should include:

• *Encourage and support the Pakistan government to redesign and implement the tenure reform and land redistribution programs previously attempted in the 1960s and 1970s.*

• *Support the establishment and reform of customary and civil land adjudication and conflict mediation institutions and procedures.*

• *Support nationwide efforts designed specifically to strengthen access to land for the landless, and women headed households in particular. Allocation and provision of access to government-held lands might be an option in the near term.*

• *Strengthen urban land access and tenure security of poor households by recognizing and documenting claims of poor households, and funding local dispute mediation and legal aid programs.*

• *Provide material support for land legislative and administration systems and provide training and sensitization to build a cohort of staff knowledgeable in LTPR concepts and practices.*

• *Encourage and support government divestiture of large farms that rely upon perpetuating inequitable land distribution and exploitive labor practices*

• *Reform forest and water rights to recognize greater community control and management of these resources.*

• *A comprehensive development package aimed at addressing both the immediate and structural causes of rural poverty should focus on LTPR issues. The question is whether there is enough time to bring about profound changes in land policy and practice in the face of the festering social discontent of both rural and urban Pakistan.*

Source: USAID Issue Brief, Land Tenure and Property, Rights in Pakistan, LTPR Issues and Support for the Taliban Property Rights and Resource Governance Briefing Paper 4

A New Land Reform Package

In Pakistan, 28% of the total landmass is being under cultivation, and huge chunks of land remain unutilized. About 6.6 million households own 6.6 million farms over a total farm area of 50 million acres. Only some 80% of this farm area is actually cultivated. The remaining 20% of the farm area remains uncultivated. Small farms utilize up to 95% of the available farm land, while large farms owned by big and powerful landlords remain uncultivated to the extent of almost 50%.A total of 2.66 million acres of farm area remains uncultivated in the large farm category(100 acres plus). Some 30,000 landlord families could benefit one million plus landless families, if uncultivated land is given away to the latter under some Land Distribution Scheme, if not land reforms exactly. In Land Reforms, usually land is forcibly taken away under legislation or revolution without any compensation.

There is also a case for bringing more land under agriculture. Perhaps ten million more acres could be added by new land expansion and development activity probably in the next ten years. This would mean one million acres per year of new land to be transferred to the landless. One would argue, where would the water come from? We are already short of water. We are currently wasting water under existing flood irrigation practices. The new land under the landless families would be from the very beginning on more efficient Drip Irrigation (D.I.), which may be cheap as well as efficient. The landless poor beneficiary would be more inclined and capable to introduce bucket and pipe drip irrigation. He would not have much choice. He does not have many choices in life either.

Thus about 14 million acres of land (10 million new and 4 million existing unutilized) could be distributed among the landless over a period of some ten years, benefitting 5-6 million families, with a farm of 2.5 acres each, practically solving the issue of landlessness, if not of poverty totally. Even after getting 2.5 acres, he would not be totally out of the clutch of the grinding poverty. But he would get hope and the tools, to handle the economic problems of his family.

Pakistan would need more land under cultivation to feed its ever increasing population, as productivity increases are too far and few in between. The diseconomy of scale, if any, of the small farms should be taken care of by an organized Cooperative movement that could take care of the credit and inputs. Land is the only thing that governments can afford to give free, may be charge some development cost in the long run under a concessionary credit scheme. Land remains on earth. It does not evaporate and does not disappear. It is excellent collateral for the poor. After all if a country belongs to its people, they should all own some piece of land, however, small it may be.

Land has been distributed in Pakistan among the rich and powerful and literally given away at dirt prices. Some effort would have to be made to include the poor in this largesse. There is a mass appeal and appetite for land confiscation by the state without compensation. Hence the two attempts at land reforms, even though unsuccessful. Any new land distribution scheme should be careful and respect the federalism requirements and the local and regional rights. It should not import people from the outside, unless in special cases, where demand and supply gaps may exist.

Islam may be respecting and even protecting private property, but perhaps not an oppressive feudalism. Perhaps absentee ownership of uncultivated land does not come under the Islamic provision and protection of private property. Many Islamic Jurists have argued and quoted Quran as affirming that" Land belongs to Allah". Revisiting of the earlier Fatwas is in order and Ijtehad and a new consensus required, especially now that the threat of Godless Communism is gone

On the other hand the big landlords may be induced by the State to do away with their excess unutilized land by imposing a variety of taxes including the much dreaded and opposed Income Tax .Excess land can be acquired by provincial governments under a land bond scheme carrying a reasonable interest rate. The poor land allotee may also be required to pay off a part of the land price under a concessionary credit scheme. Similar schemes have been implemented in Japan, Korea and Germany immediately after the Second World War of 1945.

Land Ownership and Utilization in Pakistan

1) Number of households / population increased by 25% during the two censuses (1990-2000).

2) Number of farms increased from 5.071 million to 6.6 million: 1.549 million farms added: an increase of 30.54%; total Farm area increased by only 6.15 %; 0.6% increase p.a.

3) Number of farms under 1 hectare (ha) remained almost the same; however, farm area under this category increased by 68.47 %, an addition of 483,000 ha. Percentage of these farms in the total number of farms increased from 27 % to 36%.

4) Number of largest farms, 60 ha and more, decreased from 15000 to 14000, a decrease of 1000 farms; area under these farms also decreased from 1.936 million ha to 1.683 million ha a decrease of 15% in area.

5) In 1990, 27% farms had 4% of total farm area, while the largest farms (60 ha and more and, less than 0.5 % of the total number of farms) had 10% of the total farm area .In 2000, 36% farms (under 1 ha) had 6% of the total farm area, while large farms had 8% of the total farm area. Has the skewdness decreased? In 1990, the large farms' total area was 2.75 times higher than the total area of small farms(under 1 ha) area, the same ratio decreased to 1.42 times only ; skewedness and disparity still quite high ,but appears to have been reduced by almost 100%, under this indicator.

6) In Pakistan about, 6.6 Million farming families own 6.6 million farms, over a farm area of 50 million Acres (average size 8 Acres), of which 20% farm area remains uncultivated. 58% Farms or farm house- holds

have only 10% of the total farm area, call them very small farmers(under 5 acres); 37% small farmers (5-25 acres) own 47% of the farm area; 5% larger farmers (25-100 acres) own 26% and 0.5% (30,000 families) of super land lords (100 acres plus) own 11% of the total farm areas.

7) Some 19% of the total farm area remains uncultivated. In small farms up to 93% of farm land remains cultivated. This percentage goes down with the increase in farm size. At 100 acres plus, roughly one-half (50%) of the land area remains uncultivated and unutilized.

8) About 2.6 million acres of farm area in large farm size category remains unutilized, which is under the control of 30,000 super land lord families. Another 1.5 million acres remain uncultivated in 50-100 Acres plot size. Potentially about 2.6-4 million acres (50%) of unutilized farm lands is "distributable". Two million landless could benefit.

Source: Author's Estimates; basic data 1) Agricultural Census 1998. 2) FBS Statistical Yearbooks, various years.

Table 4.2: Farms size and cultivated area distribution in Pakistan – 1998

Farms		Farm Area	Cultivated Area
% of total farms	Category	% of farm area	% of total cultivated area
58%	0-5 Acre	16%	90-93%
37%	5-25 Acre	47%	83-91%
5	25-100 Acre	26%	69-78%
0.5% (30,000)	100 Acres plus	11%	52-61%
Average	8 Acre	100%	81%
Total 6.6 M Farms	All included	50 M Acre	40- M Acre

Source: Federal Bureau of Statistics

Landless peasants can be given a 1-2 Acre farm each, at 50% of the purchase cost under 4% p.a. and 20 yrs repayment. Alternatively GOP and provincial governments could develop 2-4 million acres over a period of 7-10 yrs, possibly under budgetary outlay than the procurement of private land. Government of Sindh is already implementing such a programme at a modest scale by converting kutcha forest land but without forest, to agricultural land and distributing among landless. This can be done with much ease in Balochistan, where large tracts of land remain unutilized. For political and possibly good reasons, land in Balochistan can only go to Baloch and hence only 1.0 million families could benefit .Almost all the house holds in Balochistan could get a reasonably sized farm. In Punjab, the problem is difficult due to large population and in NWFP the land is limited, although in both the cases there are less populated areas tribal belt in NWFP and southern Punjab. Instead of giving lands to reward Generals and bureaucrats and large real state investors, the scarce land should go to the landless.

Land is the only thing governments, mostly provincial, have. Budgetary resources are limited and cannot almost always be enough, be it BISP or Zakat fund.

The culturable waste land

There was a total of 8.22 million ha of culturable waste land available to be cultivated, perhaps all of it government land, almost half of it (3.97 Million ha) is in Balochistan. There are only 1.163 million households in Balochistan. If this land is distributed, every house-hold in Balochistan gets 3.41 ha (8.5 acres), much more land than most of the household in Punjab. One doesn't have to take it away from some one; The Government and the province of Balochistan have this with themselves. Likewise, KP has 1.21 million ha of cultivable waste land, and only 2.77 million house-holds. KP has a land area problem, and about 0.5 ha (1.25 acres) could be distributed to every family in KP. Some 1.29 million farms in the country are under 0.5 ha. It is better than being totally landless. Some of the allotted lands would be sold, because every one cannot enter into agriculture. Ultimately, if 50% of the house-holds end up selling the allotted land, the average farm size increases to 1 ha, which should be quite sufficient to produce food for a family or produce products of an equivalent value.

Alternatively, GoKP could allot the available wasteland to 50% of the families, to get the same result. In Sindh and Punjab, landless are high in number and the available cultivable wasteland much less. Nevertheless, 1.6 million ha of this land available in Punjab could be distributed among 3 million households. Similarly, in Sindh, 1.44 million ha could go to another 2 million house holds. A total of 6 million households, out of a total of 14 million rural households can thus get land, without resorting to redistribution. There is a big if in it. The land may not have been grabbed already by the powerful. It has come to public light only after the floods that in Sindh; most of the sailabi land had been grabbed by the powerful landlords, and had been put to share-cropping.

Akhtar Ali

Small farms are not any less productive than the large farms

Often a case is made against land reforms, based on an erroneous argument that small farms are less productive. The empirical evidence is to the contrary .It is also intuitionally logical .Kiani(*ibid p.66*) has recently analyzed Pakistan Agricultural Census data ,which is the most authentic source of data in Pakistan on the subject. She establishes that small farms are no less productive than the large farms. Small farms compensate with labor what they have less in capital, almost a text book but correct case of labor and capital substitution. Instead of making a long commentary myself, I take the liberty of reproducing the conclusion of her paper.

Farm size and agricultural productivity in Pakistan: Evidence from agri census - 1980

We conclude that a negative but insignificant correlation was found between output per cultivated acre and farm size. The smallest and largest farm size has the highest land productivities, while the middle size farms have relatively less productivity; the reason is that the middle farm size is using inefficient combinations of inputs that yield lower marginal productivities.

The more interesting aspect of our results is that given the constraints faced by the smallest, subsistence level farmers, these farmers manage to produce outputs per acre equivalent to, if not higher than, those obtained by the largest farmers. This is primarily due to the fact that the small farmers out of a compulsion to maximize output per unit of land maximize their use of variables inputs in some cases up to and beyond the point where their marginal productivity becomes negative. Differentials in inputs use between the small and other farm sizes are more significant for land capacity utilization and labor. The largest farmers compensate for this primarily through the use of capital equipment and higher levels of current investment.

The most immediate implication of the analysis presented above is that since small farms manage to produce a very high output per acre without high levels of capital input use; their potential for improvement is the greatest. This is a strong economic argument both for land reforms and for directing more capital subsidies toward small farms.

67

Secondly the nascent entrepreneurial classes of farmer's does not appear to be emerging from amongst the middle range of farm size since their production behavior seems to be the least efficient More over it is the largest farm sizes that appear to have the highest capital use. However, this is not to infer that all or even a significant proportion of the large farms have been transformed into capitalist farms since such an analysis would require at least some computation of profit and investment function. Here we can only point out that our results imply only the beginnings of the growth of a capitalist class of farmers from amongst the largest farm owners.

Thirdly since the largest farms, with the aid of very high horsepower capital equipment, only manage to produce only as much as the smallest labor-intensive farms, the rationale for capital intensity loses ground. Farm–level decisions about optimum production techniques must be taken on the basis of inputs valued at their actual shadow costs, and not at their subsidized costs. Accordingly, subsidies and tax relief on the import of heavy agricultural capital equipment must be removed and restricted to lighter varieties. Then only will a lower capital/output ratio in the agrarian sector becomes more compatible with the exigencies of a capital–poor country like Pakistan.

Source: Adiqa Kausar Kiani, Farm Size and productivity in Pakistan, European Journal of Social Sciences – Volume 7, Number 2 (2008)

Farm Size: an International perspective

The largest farms are found in Australia, with an average farm size of 3601.7 ha .This is followed by Argentina with average farm size of 469.97 ha, Canada, 349.1 ha, and the U.S., 197.24 ha. In South America, farm sizes tend to be large, with the exception of Peru and Colombia, where average farm size is around 20 ha, elsewhere average farm size exceeds 60-70 ha. In more densely populated Asia, farm size as a whole is the smallest in the world. The largest average farm size is of Turkey with5.76 ha, followed by Iran, 4.29 ha, and then Pakistan, 3.78 ha. In most South-East Asia, average farm size is very low; Bangladesh, 0.57 ha, China 0.67 ha, Indonesia 0.87 ha, and Vietnam 0.52 ha. Slightly larger farm size is found in Japan. Only in Philippines (2.16 ha) and Thailand (3.36 ha), farm size are comparatively larger.

In Europe, farm size appears to be in the medium category, where the average farm size in EU-27 happens to be 13.8 ha. There is, however, a large variation within EU, with UK, Czech Republic, Finland and

Denmark in 50-71 ha category. France and Germany are in between with 30-32 ha; Netherlands and Spain 18-19 ha.

Farm Size and productivity:

Apparently there does not appear to be any link between the farm size and crop productivity; one finds Egypt at 5th high crop productivity (7506 kg per ha) in the world, and a mean farm size of 0.95 ha, of one of the lowest in the world. In the top 22 countries in the range of crop productivity of 5500 to 8500 kg per ha, we have all kinds of countries with widely varying mean farm size; China (0.67 ha) and Japan (1.2 ha); France (31.46 ha) and Germany (32.11 ha) with medium size categories within EU-27; UK (70.21 ha) and Denmark (52.75 ha) have farm size more than 50 % higher than France and Germany. Australia an industrialized country has one of the lowest crop productivity in the world with the largest mean farm size in the world of 3601.7 ha. In the US only one-third of the agricultural land is cropped. Its crop productivity with its higher technology, business and organizational efficiencies, should have put it higher than its present ranking of only 14. The contributor to relatively lower US crop productivity appears to be the large farm size (12 times the average of EU-27) and relative water scarcity. So if there is a link at all, it is the inverse one; higher the mean farm size, lower the crop productivity.

The same can be made true in Pakistan, if the small farms have the required input and technology available. Smaller subsistence farms are less productive because of the lack of access to inputs and technology. Thus, it can be argued that land redistribution under a land reform may not necessarily lower the crop productivity. And the crop productivity in case of the division of farms larger than 100 acres (40 ha), as has been shown elsewhere in this chapter, is going to improve to much higher levels. Intuitively speaking, a smaller family farm would have more unpaid family labor available than otherwise and would be more intensively cultivated, as has probably happened in Egypt, Korea and Japan. Obviously, any land redistribution programme unaccompanied by an assistance programme is bound to falter and can even boomerang. In the existing share-cropping system, the landlord provides the inputs and the working capital either through personal finances or through privileged access to finance due to power linkages and collateral as well. If a public assistance programme is not there, replacing the finances of the landlord, the farmer may even suffer more despite having given a peace of land, free of cost.

Our Land Reforms experience; a review

Although Muslim League Leadership was 'mostly feudal the latter felt and recognized the popular pressure for land and tenancy reform. Hari Report, Daultana Commission, MLR-54 and MLR-115 have been the major milestones in the land and tenancy reform history in Pakistan. The last move in this respect dates back to 1977, when PM Bhutto announced a new package of reforms including lower ceilings on land and allotment of government land to the poor tenants. Freedom movement and the ideological conflict between the East and the West created and sustained pressures for land reforms in the developing world. Ideological period having gone, the futility of the earlier reforms and the entrenchment of feudal interest in Pakistan's body politic are possibly the reasons, why any such move does not get even mentioned these days. There is substantial postwar evidence that the societies which implemented meaningful land reforms, and put an end to feudalism, could transform themselves into the new dynamism required for scientific and industrial growth and development. Taiwan, Korea and Japan are classic examples. Taiwan and Korea utilized the opportunity created by the exit of Japanese landlords to launch deep and effective land reforms. Pakistan lost this opportunity which was available to it after independence, as many non-Muslim land owners fled the country.

The economic rationale for earlier land reforms was based more on optimal considerations and hither-to under-utilization of the lands available with the big land lord. It appears that redistribution impact was much less of a consideration in the view of the planners and decision makers. The political objectives included acquisition of political legitimacy, and shaking and controlling the feudal class through carrot and stick approach and enhancing the political clientele and image among the masses. Ayub Khan's reforms (MLR 64) put the upper ceiling of irrigated land at 500 acres per family and un-irrigated at 1000 acres per family. Compensation is to be paid through inheritable bond which earned 4% p.a. interest and land was to be redistributed at a price. Bhutto's reforms (MLR 115) put the upper ceiling at 150 acres irrigated and 300 acres un-irrigated per member of a family. No compensation was to be paid to owners and the land was to be distributed free. Put together, the two land reforms affected about 4% of the land, only half of which was actually transferred to landless. Only about 100,000 farming households 8% of the total (and even much less if landlessness was included) benefitted.

Table 4.3: Measures of the distribution of farm size and Agricultural Productivity of selected countries

Countries	Mean Farm Size ha.	Gini	%perm pasture	% hlgs <2 ha.	% area <2 ha.	% hlgs <5 ha.	% area <5 ha.	Cereal Yield kg/ha.
China	0.67	-	-	97.9	-	-	-	5535
Egypt	0.95	0.65	-	91.6	45.9	-	-	7506
Japan	1.2	0.59	-	88.5	48.2	97.6	69.9	6017
India	1.55	0.58	-	76.2	29	-	-	2647
Philippines	2.16	0.55	1.3	65.1	23.4	90.6	56.2	3334
Thailand	3.36	0.47	1.2	33.9	7.6	72.9	43.8	3014
Pakistan	3.78	0.57	-	47.4	11.2	80.9	38.6	2674
Iran	4.29	0.7	7.2	50.5	4.8	71.2	17.1	2479
Turkey	5.76	0.61	4.1	36.5	5.6	67.9	22.1	2601
Italy	7.57	0.8	25.8	57.2	6	77.8	14.5	5275
Netherlands	18.63	0.55	49.8	16.7	0.8	32	3.6	8308
Spain	18.79	0.86	34.3	44.2	1.8	65.3	5.4	3584
Mexico	24.58		68.4	-	-	59	3	3454
France	31.46	0.53	35.7	15	0.5	26.6	1.8	7293
Germany	32.11	0.69	30	15.9	0.6	31.4	2.2	7119
UK	70.21	0.67	56.8	5.6	0.1	14.5	0.5	7419
Brazil	73.09	0.85	78	20.3	0.3	36.8	1	3829
Chile	83.74	0.92	84.9	-	-	42.5	0.9	5842
USA	197.2	0.76	47.9	-	-	8	0.1	6624
Canada	349.1	0.64	39.9	-	-	4.9	-	3387
Argentina	469	0.83	82.9	-	-	15.1	0.1	3918
Australia	3602		96.1			2.6		1650

Source: Combined compiled by the author; Data sources following:

i)   FAO Census

ii) Robert Eastwood, Michael Lipton, Andrew Newell, *Farm Size*, University of Sussex, June 2004

iii) Encyclopedia of Nations

Mean Farm size distribution and Agricultural Productivity of selected countries

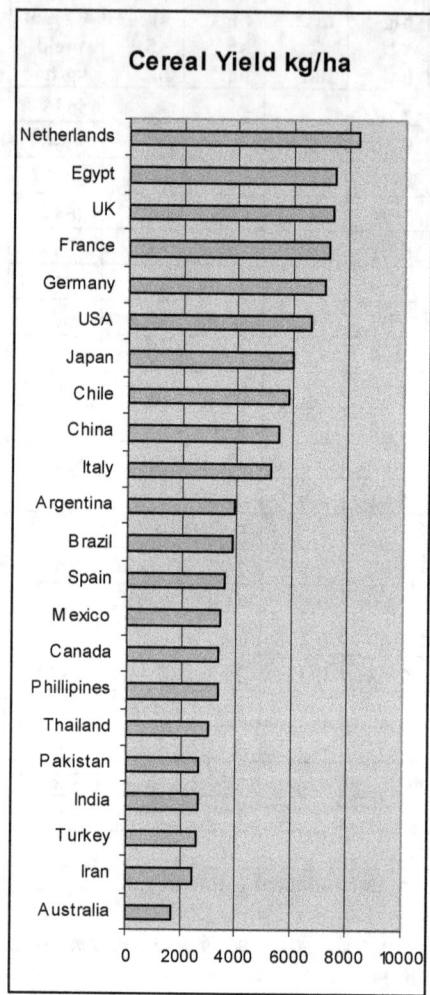

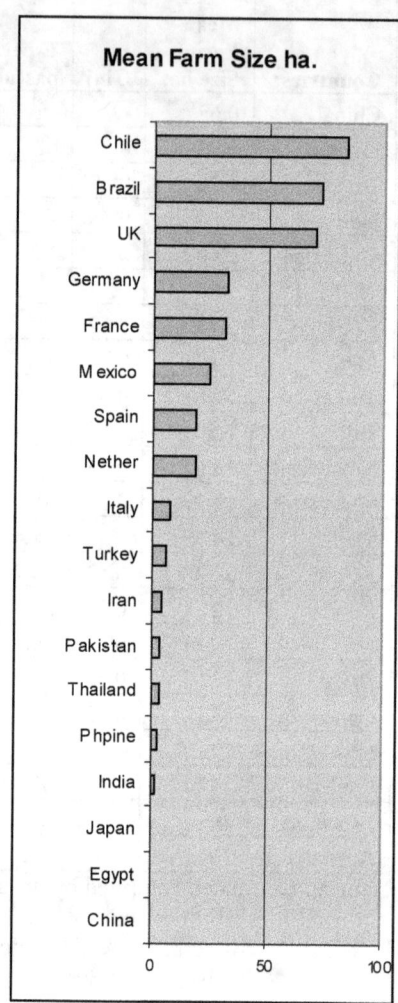

Table 4.4: Scope & Performance of Land Reforms (1952-1972-77)

	General Ayub Land Reforms	PPP Land Reforms (1972)	PPP Land Reforms (1977)
Land Ceiling	500 acres irrigated 1000 Barani (36000 PIUs)	150 acres irrigated 300 acres un-irrigated (28,000) PIU)	100 acres irrigated 200 acres un-irrigated (8000 PIU maximum)
Affected numbers of Zamindars	5,064	1754	
Affected Land Area	5,478,945	1,190,693	
Area actually assumed under land reform	1,903,788	589,499	
Compensation to Zamindars	4% interest bonds	No Compensation	
Number of beneficiaries recipients of land	55,000 - 200,000	50,548	
Area sold to haris	622,199	308,309	
Terms of haris/Landless	on payment	free (5.3-7.9 acres)	free
Land given to non-haris	220,000	N.A.	
Land un-disposed available to land grabbing	951,959	258,974	Not implemented due to the coup of Ziaul-Haq

Source: Mahmood Hassan Khan, Underdevelopment and agrarian structure in Pakistan, Vanguard, 1994

It may be useful here to remind the reader that in the subcontinent the land used to belong to the sovereign the King. Peasants had the cultivation rights which were heritable. Zamindars were appointed by the Mughals for revenue collections for the latter and Jagirdars were awarded revenue collection rights for themselves in lieu of their services such as providing the troops etc. Thus there was no private ownership of land and the so-called Zamindars or Jagirdars were only revenue collectors or intermediaries. With the weakening of Mughal Empire, internal strife and invasion from outside, the intermediary and local interests strengthened themselves and the ownership and revenue collection roles lost their function and meaning. Mughal tax either exceeded or was equal to the rent received from the peasant. It is the British who created private rent interests by fixing revenue demands at rates lower than rent. The British awarded Jagirs to its "friends" and supporters – out of the land that was reclaimed due to the irrigation network built by them. Thus feudals were only intermediaries and did not have historical title to land they control or otherwise it was a reward of collusion with the colonial power. I would not have brought this sordid point to the fore, but for the proponents of sanctity of private property in

73

Islam. Would they still attach sanctity to such property worthy of protection of commandments of Islam? Where the property is not bought and transferred through inheritance and is traceable to such origins, there is a strong case for confiscation. It is rather embarrassing for all of us that most of our political leadership is feudal, whom we have ironically elected. Very few of them can prove or even indicate any resistance to the colonialists, infact opposite is the case for most of them.

Keeping in view the power structure, the history of two or three initiatives in this respect, Islamization of the constitution and a strong emphasis on almost unbridled ownership of private property among orthodox Islamic Jurists, although there is a lot of room for discussion and interpretations in the colonial context of most land ownership, land reforms may remain a Utopia. One may ask; is there any way to dilute feudal structures and influence that predominate in our socio-political life? The answer perhaps lies in gradually persuading the off springs of the old feudal lordship that it is in their own interest, in the interest of the well-to-do sectors of the society, that if feudal structures and underdeveloped Pakistan are transformed into a progressive and prosperous country and society, it is they who are going to benefit also, and even more so. Who is better off-Landlord of Rajanpur and Okara or an owner of an integrated agricultural company marketing processed agricultural products ala-USA? This is rather long term and may be more utopian than the land reform itself.

Implementing the Reform Packages

It can be argued and with a lot of merit that no new reform package is required, in so far as the land ceilings are required. One has to implement truthfully and diligently any of the three reform packages, 1962, 1972 or 1977. If PPP thinks and believes that Mr. Bhutto was deposed unconstitutionally, then they are morally and politically bound to implement the un-implemented reform package of Z.A. Bhutto of 1977. If and when Muslim League comes to power, they could use the agrarian committee, 1948 report as a guidance and basis for reform. Historically there is a bipartisan consensus on the issue, infact it is tripartite as the military regime of Ayub Khan also launched land reforms, but disheartenedly implemented its own proposals.

The packages may have to be revised and updated and the loopholes removed. Furthermore, before announcing such reforms, two preparatory measures would have to be made. Firstly, the potential beneficiaries have to be organized to oversee and monitor the implementation process of the reforms. Earlier in 1960s Kisan committees used to have violent and revolutionary undertones and would have been opposed by the national and international forces. No more. Today even USAID and multilateral agencies are willing to support and even require such mechanisms. Of-course the new bottle is NGO. Conscientious political groups could also chip in such NGOs to support the implementation of the reforms package. In no circumstance, as it has happened before, should it be the sole domain of revenue official or handled in a centralized fashion. Secondly, extension credit and inputs packages should be planned and arranged in advance. Giving only land to the landless without such support would be doomed from the beginning. 5-10 acre plots could be viable in irrigated areas in today's market/technological conditions, and 2-acres for vegetable growing, cattle farming and milk production.

According to, some estimates, one million landless peasants and share croppers may benefit from land reforms, if implemented. Imagine one family's potential, modestly supported, being unleashed to contribute to agricultural/food output. In-order to benefit from scale-economies, services Cooperatives framework as distinct from "ownership" cooperatives, could be organized and encouraged.

It is often argued that land is scarce and no land reform would be able to give land to all peasants. It may be correct. But elimination of two million families from the pool of under-employed rural population would cause labor scarcity and would increase-the wages and terms of labor of agricultural workers. And thus would go a long way towards enhancing the rural welfare and would apply brakes on rural-urbanization.

The Z.A. Bhutto package was not too little but was too late. The reforms could not be implemented as shortly thereafter, Zia-ul-Haque took over. I would not blame the proposed reforms for his ouster. The die had been cast much earlier. But would any well wisher advise his followers to complete his unfinished agenda.

Frankly, democracies with entrenched landlords in the parliament are ill-structured to tackle this issue. In Europe, landlords have survived where there were parliaments; monarchies generally favored land reforms. A prime example is the UK, and to some extent, Sweden. But times have changed both on political and economic front. Communism is no more a threat. Ironically land reforms have been regarded in Pakistan as an off-shoot of the ideological left. As has been discussed earlier, it is the western powers which have supported land reforms. Communism never wanted reform, for it dispelled revolution. They wanted a one-way ticket to the now dismantled iron-curtain. So land reforms could no more be taken to be communist or socialist or anti-Islam. Jamaate Islami has supported land reforms and the chances are that it would not oppose land reforms as to be un-Islamic despite the political inheritance of Zia-ul-Haque which has promoted religious fundamentalism and orthodoxy in religious circles in this country.

The anti-Land Reform argument

From the time of Adam Smith, it has been recognized that with out involving and motivating and improving the tiller's condition, agricultural productivity cannot be increased. Consequently, all developed nations have taken steps in this direction over the last two centuries. Technological development alone, although essential, would not have been sufficient for bringing about the kind of growth and productivity that has been achieved in those countries. Massive land reforms have been conducted reducing the farm sizes and ownership, giving land ownership to tillers, establishing family size farms, controlling and reducing rents, enhancing tenure security and taking measures to assure a comparable living standard.

A strange even perverse notion is taking roots in Pakistan's agricultural establishment, if the recent task force report is taken as an indicator; that agricultural growth has nothing to do with those who till the soil; productivity, yield and production would enhance if a lot of inputs are thrown into the fields and machinery is piled up. Of-course this would require credit, subsidies and even increase in the price of the food crops. This is what the report mainly argues. Ironically, it recommends easing of procedures for ejectment of tenants. It does not say anything about as to what would happen to the tenants. It hardly pays any attention to the plight and living conditions of the tillers and the tenants, but tends to favor international prices.

Had the landlords and managers been so committed, progressive and innovative, perhaps the lacunae of the tiller's motivations and capability would have been partly balanced. Every one knows who is interested in what. The scale economy argument is preposterous in this country when large hand holdings are divided by the absentee landlords into small parcels and are put out to share-coppers, who are de-facto slaves due to perpetual indebtedness to the landlord. The highly iniquitous share-cropping agriculture dominated by the feudal absentee landlord where all roads to the market, society and institutions go through the former, has caused devastating consequence for the growth and development of this country and has mortgaged its future. Without a serious effort towards land reforms, not necessarily restricted to and focused on land confiscations and distributions, neither agri-cultural growth nor democracy, nor larger social development can take place and take root.

Tenure Reforms

If nothing else, tenure reforms must be introduced and vigorously implemented. Despite much adjustments and modifications, PPP still claims its allegiance, affinity and power focus for the poor and the dispossessed. PPP's present leadership owes it to its own history and founders to initiate immediate steps in this regard. The irony is that Shah Mahmood Qureshi's (the 'PPP stalwart from Multan), agricultural task force is asking for easing the tenant ejectment procedures. However, much later in 2011, Qureshi has supported levying income tax on agriculture.

Large land ownerships could also be gradually converted into corporate farms and could operate as a. company with predominantly agricultural labors and leased contracts. Normal book keeping, PLS, audit should be required. Trade Union activity is to be promoted for safeguarding the rights of the peasants and workers. "So surrender land, sell it or go-corporate" could be the message to the absentee landlord. A five years time frame could be provided for complete implementation, whereby minimum wages are implemented, worker/peasant welfare provided through two-year peace agreement and liberal provisions for profit-sharing are to be built-in.

Rents should be controlled and regulated and revised down wards. All tenure contracts should be required to be written and formal and should be based on a model contract developed by the government. A 15 years lease period with a mandatory extension for another term of 15 years should be provided in the law. Ejectment should be made even more difficult and subject to definite and demonstrated bad performance of the tenant in terms of output, property maintenance or regular defaults in rent payments. Recourse to legal reduction in rent should be made available depending on the circumstances of lessees. Neither reasons for self-cultivation nor re-renting are to be entertained for ejectment. Furthermore tenants should have the first right of purchase at standard prices, if and when the owner wants to dispose of his land holding (It is already there, but needs reinforcement).

All kinds of extra and forced labor should be proscribed. The tenant should be paid for extra services, including the improvements of permanent nature that he does on the land i.e. drainage, embankment, water courses etc. He should be entitled for reimbursement of such improvement at the time of leaving. He should also be entitled to disturbance payments once he is asked to quit the land. All these are standard practices and are written into model contracts issued by the governments in most countries.

What ever be the tenure terms agreed between the landlord and the tenant, the tenant should be able to sustain a standard of living to include basic human needs and facilities. Any contractual agreement that results in less than the afore-mentioned for the tenant should be declared void in the statute books.

Land Chambers or chambers of Agriculture should be established with equal participation of peasants and landowners. Professionals, lawyers, citizens and NGO representatives should also be represented in such chambers. These chambers should operate at district level. The chambers should be entrusted with consultative and executive authority to take decisions and hear complaints regarding tenure contracts, water course management, land consolidation matters etc.

Privatization & the Land Bank

On the economic front, a whole new set of possibilities have emerged which may facilitate commercial land reforms if not statutory ones. And this is probably the kind of reform PPP government can implement. That is to facilitate and encourage the sales of large and excess land tracks (say above 100 acres per individual) and assist the purchase by peasants and small land owners. The new possibilities are the development of capital markets in the country and the on-going privatization program. The privatization implemented till now has been only a tip of the ice-berg. Much more of privatizable assets remain in public domain.

A scheme similar to that was implemented by Germans, Swedes and even Americans, involving floatation of Land Bonds, their sale in the secondary markets, and land banks coordinating the whole financial transactions, mortgages and lease payments. Koreans exchanged land bonds with the evacuee industrial property that was left by the former Japanese colonists. We have the public sector assets. Land bonds can be exchanged with the shares of the to-be-privatized public sector assets and undertakings. This may create some incentive to the landlords to dispose of some of their excess land.

One may argue that it would be from fire to frying pan, that the feudal lordship would be replaced by Industrial lordship. Not necessarily. Industrial structures do not lend themselves to the kind of monopolization and social controls as do the land relations. A Land Bank could be created or ADBP could create a division in its present operations. The proposed Land Bank can buy the excess land from landlords, and either issue Land Bonds or issue shares of its capital in lieu. Both shares and bonds would be tradable in stock exchange. The land so acquired may either be leased or sold to the landless, by the way of extending low cost credit. The interest rate subsidy could be financed out of Zakat Fund, through Mudaraba or Musharika, foreign aid, and low cost international funds. The Land Bank could also play a role in land consolidation, as owners of less than 5 acres may be able to also sell/transact their land with it, and new consolidated land patches may be sold or leased out by the bank on the same pattern.

Through this commercial land reform, a limited social transformation could take place. There would be quite a few landowners who may not have political ambitions and may want to change their style, ownership, assets or domicile. If enough land changes hands, it would dilute feudal structures and strangle-hold, would enhance agriculture productivity, improve the lot of rural poor and would promote social and political democracy.

Water Rights

About 75% of Pakistan's agricultural land is irrigated. Under the current dispensation, water rights are associated with land. There is no moral or philosophical base to this linkage. Water is brought to the lands through massive public investments in irrigation projects. Why should the irrigation projects where public money has been spent should exclusively confer rights on those who possess land? Water rights may be accorded equally to the residents of the area, equally and irrespective of land ownership. If water rights are awarded to individuals including tenants, then; there would be a scope for a mutually beneficial cooperation, among land owners and water right owners which would include tenants. It would be on more even footing; if not a totally equal one.

Lest this scheme may be termed too radical to be in implemented, I would argue, that at least: 25% of the existing water rights be awarded to the individuals. In all future .irrigation & reclamation schemes, water rights must be conferred on individuals and not to the lands. Alternatively, private lands which would be, the beneficiary of the irrigation schemes, should be acquired by government at market rates and should later be distributed, among the tenants. It is highly objectionable that scarce financial resumes that are applied on irrigation schemes, may, exclusively benefit the landed, appreciate their land values and enhance-output, most of which is appropriated by them. Equitable access to water, for small farmers and peasants should be made available. Presently a lot of injustice and inequity prevails, in this respect. The proposed NGOs, tenants' unions and land chambers may be given some kind of mandate for adjudication in the matters of water rights and access.

Finally, we all must understand that today. Pakistan's main problem both in industry and as well as in agriculture and elsewhere comes from lagging human development; from a work force that is illiterate, ill-trained, under-fed, weak, and unhealthy, lacking motivation, estranged and even alienated. His commitment to work, routine and procedure is at best wavering. The result is that productivity is low and quality inadequate and inconsistent. There is rampant absenteeism which affects output and delivery schedules. Cheap labor alone is not enough. There are countries where labor is cheaper than it is in Pakistan. A better trained, educated and motivated and satisfied healthy work force is required.

The international market is ready to pay for the human development and the enhancements and investments that one can make to its work force, but it would not accept shoddy output, even though at lower prices. The next slot into which Pakistan's work environment could jump in is of higher quality and still for this, economy wide social transformation and development would be required that could be spurred by effective land and tenure reforms that have been proposed in this chapter. Agri-cultural productivity would be accordingly enhanced. It would not occur by simply throwing in more of subsidized inputs and higher procurement prices at the absentee landlord.

Balochistan; Insurgency and Land Reform

Despite serious attempts by the present PPP government including provincial autonomy as enshrined in the 18th amendment, and Balochistan Aghaze-huqooq package, public apology by President

Zardari and substantial reduction in the role of security agencies, and even background engagement and negotiation with the liberationists, there is apparently no concession by the insurgents and no amelioration in the insurgency. The dialogue and engagement should continue, so that a peaceful and democratic solution is achieved at some point in time. Unfortunately GOPs ability to offer any more carrots as it has recently announced, has been seriously reduced by the recent floods and may not recover from it in a short while. The Taliban terrorism has further compounded the problems. Many interests are converging including India, Taliban, Sipah-e-Sahaba and the nationalists and separatists. GOP and the system are too weak and occupied to take any drastic action. The drastic actions by the military have only exacerbated the problems.

It appears that when ever the opportunity arises some long term measures may have to be taken. Following are the three possible actions that may be examined by the government:

a) Creation of new and counter elite
b) Agricultural land grants to masses
c) Development and colonization of the coastal area by Baloch
   masses and the new elite.

As the colonial Raj did by distributing land in reward for cooperation and bringing about a new elite, in place of freedom fighters and those who did not go and could not go along with their colonial rule and policies. There should be a lot of public land still available in Balochistan. After all, it is only 5% of country's population living in 50% of the land mass of the country. Most of it may be barren land, so most of the distributed land was when it was distributed to the collaborators by the Raj. It is only the later irrigation network that made such land productive. Unfortunately, as it is widely alleged, most of the land grants have been given to military and bureaucracy, who came from outside Balochistan, which painted Pakistan as a colonial power and not a rule of brothers and comrades. Local counter elite could be created by land grants 50-100 acres plus to the educated middle classes, however, little in number they may be in Balochistan. There may be about 50,000 families in this category. Their education, some personal assets and the new land tracts may contribute to the creation of new elite. The possession of land, even if not immediately profitable, may bring a social strength, confidence and consciousness among ordinary people. In rural societies there is no respect and even rights for those who do not have land. So let us bring respect and honor to the ordinary, as a first step towards improvement.

The second component of the reform is, which one may be inclined to dub or term as land reform, but in my view is slightly more than that, to distribute land through smaller land grants among the masses, to about 500,000 families and organize those as cooperatives. Horticultural and rangeland cooperatives may be promoted through credit schemes. Both foreign and local coops may be there. Trilateral JVs of Australian, Middle-eastern and local partners may prove to be feasible and attractive from sourcing and marketing perspectives. Australians sheep industry may find a useful marketing and inventorying point in these set ups. There may be many useful and interesting ideas in this respect. But the focus should be creating economic and social opportunities for the common man of Balochistan away from the strangle-hold of the traditional elite and Sardars. The schemes have to be small and not so lucrative by design so as to prevent creation of interests of landlords, Sardars and the traditional elite.

One may be wondering over the water issue in all this grand drama. More storage dams are being created. All the share of Balochistan in the increase of water supply and the associated irrigation networks should go towards the proposed settlements and the reformed land. It should not benefit the traditional elite but should work for the benefit of new elite and the common man. More over adoption of conservation techniques like drip irrigation may have to be promoted as well. We have also proposed a new system of water rights which benefits the landless and makes them partners in the new irrigation.

Thirdly, urban land clusters and town should be established on the coast, on lands having no Sardar ownership or social and traditional influence. Residential and commercial plots should be allotted to the locals from all over Balochistan, encouraging migration of common man from Sardari strangleholds to these towns where there is rule of law and the Pakistan state. In the past, in Gawadar all urban land went into the ownership of outsiders, although through private commercial purchases. Only landed and traditional local elite may have been benefited. Urban development of Balochistan cannot be done on private sector traditional model. Land development allotments have to be in public sector, while building activities may have private sector component.

GOP does not have resources presently. However, a few years or so may be required in studying and planning such an enterprise. These schemes should be based on bipartisan consensus and include the military also. A strong taboo would have to be created against exploitative interests that may pervert the whole idea in implementation. The goal has to be kept in mind: that is the creation of a new counter elite that is sympathetic to a united Pakistan and creation of socio economic system in Balochistan independent of the traditional elite and Sardars, who often collude and blackmail on anti-Pakistan campaigns.

For the larger issue of country wide Land Reforms, I have already made submissions elsewhere in my earlier blogs. There is a scope, however limited for land reforms throughout Pakistan .Long term planning and sustainable action is required under national consensus to implement the proposed scheme. Impulsive actions, without constructive thoughts and preparation, and only motivated by personal pique has done tremendous disservice to the national unity in the past and has only exacerbated the Baloch issue. But do we have the time?

Land and Housing Reforms: Innovations and opportunities due to the floods.

The destruction of life and property of people in this flood has developed the need and rationale for launching some innovative policies by the government. Some real resource transfer has to take place from the actual or/and potential domain of the rich and the powerful. Roti, Kapra and Makan are the key concept which the ruling party has not abandoned. There are others on the political spectrum that may, even though grudgingly, support non-traditional and innovative actions Classical Land Reforms are out of fashion and out of sync .There is no possibility of forcibly taking away some or all of the land owned by the big land lords. This may be a dream of arch-communists but there are practical, philosophical and ideological issues involved in such confiscation. But there are other possibilities to provide some means or assets to the poor especially in the context of the current floods.

Government does not have the money or the power that comes as a result of a revolution. Whatever flood assistance that the federal and provincial governments would be able to give to the flood victims would be out of the aid and assistance of community. However government has surplus land and the power to change land use, and appreciate its value. It can divert the surplus so generated to the landed aristocracy and the politically or socially powerful elite as has been the case in the past, or divert the surplus to the poor. We shall examine how this can be done.

First of all, there is government land mostly in rural areas, which can be gifted to the landless and also to the flood victims of a certain category. More land could be developed as well. Due to the increased supply of water as a result of new storage dams, more land would come into the irrigation system, which should be passed on to the landless poor. However this is a rather long term measure to be implemented when new dams are built and commissioned. Government is already distributing underutilized forest land among the landless.

Some conditional land leases should be issued to the flood victims of the *Kachcho* land who are cultivating land parcels there and are also living there. Because they do not have titles, they did not leave their places for the fear of *Qabza* by others. There are flood control issues due to which permanent and water restricting structures should not be built. Necessary flood control measures could be built in the land leases and the amendments in the law if required.

Under new irrigation schemes, whenever these come up, trade-able water rights could be awarded to the landless, which he could sell to the willing customer or use it as his collateral or share in the distribution of agricultural output and profits. In this way he becomes partner in place of surf.

In urban land laws, provisions for high -rise building societies could be introduced, where virtual plots in the third dimensions are allot-able. Real state developers could be encouraged to develop multi-purpose projects, where in lieu of subsidized land or free land use conversion, a certain percentage of 3-D plots are allotted to the poor. Currently a lot of money changes hands on conversion of agricultural or residential land to the commercial one. Some fee does go to the local or provincial government but most of the surplus is siphoned away by the builders, landowners and the social and political elite. So the name of the game is to create policy or innovation surplus and divert it to the poor.

There is a lot of government land that is available on the periphery of Karachi near Sohrab Goth (outside Karachi limits) and in district Thatta that could be allotted to the flood victims especially from the inundated towns of Jacobabad, Larkana and Thatta. If Sindh has to develop regional economies are to be established, as has happened around Lahore. Karachi itself would benefit from the regional economic development as Lahore has. Karachi's' economy has been stagnating for many years now. One of the reasons is lack of close geographical interactions and resource reservoirs. Every body would benefit. However the idea would fail if it is used for political and ethnic manipulation and advantage.

I would like to add a caveat here. Last PML (N) government headed by Mr. Nawaz Sharif introduced an innovative housing policy and strategy for urban areas by transferring surplus government land and plots for low-cost public housing projects. A good innovative project was, however, reportedly marred by construction scams. There was no need of involving government in construction by a party which believes so much in private sector. That project perhaps is revived in one form or the other. Some residual land or assets may still be there. Musharraf government quietly put a lid on it. No NAB case has been filed with respect to this project apparently. May be, there is one or a few. I am not sure.

Elsewhere, I have proposed buying surplus land from large landowners of 500 acres plus and creating an economic and tax regime that may facilitate such land transaction between the two. It would be quite feasible to acquire substantial under-utilized land from the large land owners. I would not repeat that here for time and space reasons. But who would bell the cat. Government of the day is forced to face one crisis after the other. Innovative policies require peace of mind and a supportive political regime.

Land Distribution: the joy of the landless in getting a piece of land

Pending a wholesale land reform, whatever land can be distributed under the relevant socio-political constraints, is a praise-worthy and laudable activity, as it brings happiness and prosperity to the poor, as would be evident from an Oxfam report on the subject which has been reproduced at the end of this discussion.

There is a lot of surplus government land which is usually kept safe for projects or vested interest. We have seen how such land has been in the past and would continue to be allotted to the powerful and the civil and military elite. Hiding behind the argument that there are too many landless, and hence no amount of land would be enough to meet their needs and thus withholding land from them is a convoluted logic. This is like as the Holy Quran says: There were two brothers; one had ninety-nine sheep and the other had only one sheep; the one having 99 sheep asked his poor brother to give his lone one sheep to him to make his total add to 100. Quran curses such people promising destruction in this world and hereafter.

Thus there is a lot of merit in the existing government program which should be continued and extended as much as it is possible with transparency and without nepotism. Problematic and useless land should not be given, for the required capital to improve it may not be available with the *hari* and *Kisan*. I am not sure if *Kisan* in Punjab and other provinces are also benefitting under similar land distribution programs. Punjab, especially. Central Punjab is short of uncultivated land. However, southern Punjab should have significant newly developed government land. Although the chance is that quite some of it has been already allotted to the elite and the vested interest. Their needs are never satiated. Older ones die with the lands and the newer progeny springs up every thirty years with new demands of land. There is no dearth of Land in Balochistan where a mere 6 million people are populated in almost half of total Pakistan's area, although developed land may be short there. NWFP is generally short of land but there is unutilized belt in tribal areas and the adjoining settled areas.

Let me reproduce here extracts from an *Oxfam* report, the joys of *haris* in Sindh on getting land. Around 43,000 acres of state-owned land has already been distributed in the first phase of the programme, which had prioritized women landless peasants. But civic groups like PDI had pointed out a number of serious flaws in the scheme. Much of the land allocated was either waterlogged or not level, proved unsuitable for cultivation because it was affected by salinity, or had multiple ownership claims - which led to lengthy legal battles.

The second phase of distribution is now solely targeting landless women. It hopes to iron out many of the flaws in the original process, as well as offering women longer-term packages of agricultural support including providing seeds, fertilizers, pesticides and technical help. "You need to say the glass is half full instead of half-empty," Faisal told me. "When you meet these success stories, women are now making a livelihood for their husbands and families. There is a marked difference. If change is coming in the life of the people for this allotted land and for a fairly large Percentage of people, then it's the start of success."

Mother-of-seven Beebul Hassan's face lights up as she holds up a slip of paper with a signature showing that she's been successful in her application. She is now the proud owner of four acres of land. "The women peasants of Sindh have awakened - and now they will be the landladies; the owners of the land". "We have nothing. We've got by from fishing; but stocks are reduced these days. It is hard to make a good livelihood," she told me. "I have come today to seek land. If we get our own land, we can feed our family and earn more money. Sometimes, we have enough to eat; but often it's not enough".

Her family only receives a quarter of the crops they cultivate - the landlord takes the rest. "We want land of our own to pass on to our children; to have our own house and not live with threats or the fear of having to move. A landlord can ask us to leave at any time," she explained. "Security is a priority for us. If we own land, we will have a safe house; no corrupt people can snatch our crops from us... There are always threats from influential people who can take the land from us." "I still don't believe I am a winner here," she said. "I can't help making plans about how I will now use my land." She says she wants to start growing wheat, chillies, tomatoes and vegetables; and for the very first time, a family home on land that she now can call her own.

Urban Land Reforms - Housing for All

Last PML (N) government launched a housing scheme, whereby it acquired unutilized land from government departments and agencies to build houses for the general public. The mistake they committed was of involving government in construction activity and business. A good initiative turned into a scam and had to be abandoned. The scheme could have been revived after neutralizing the government involvement in construction. It was abandoned altogether, in true Pakistani tradition of disowning, good and bad, of the outgoing and gone governments.

As there are rural landless, there are urban landless also. They live in Katchi-abadis, squatters, and in perpetually rented houses. Some of them may have paid rents that may have eventually far exceeded the total value of the houses they lived in. There is a sizeable population of urbanites who can build their houses through affordable loans, provided a piece of land is made available to them at near-free prices. The right to acquire land or space for living, working and tilling ought to be recognized or at -least promoted. This proposal is restricted to housing although its variants could be developed for developing space for small enterprises and entrepreneurs.

Land is scarce in urban areas. The erstwhile single or two floor housing is uneconomic and infeasible. There is no land for such plotting to meet the huge unkempt demand or it may throw such dwellers so much away from markets and workplaces that their substantial times and incomes would be dissipated in transport cost ; from frying pan into fire, replacing house rents by transport fares and costs. This also puts burden on government's ability to pay the foreign exchange required for the ensuing oil imports.

Plots –in-the –air, or plots in 3-D, call these by whatever names can be a solution. The concept is already there but it comes about when an apartment has been built and recorded as a property with the relevant registrars. The minor yet vital innovation, I am proposing is carving plots in the air and registering these as property. A law may have to be introduced for transaction of such property. Government can acquire unutilized public land for this purpose as was done earlier, or convert adjoining rural lands into public housing schemes. Four to ten storey plotting can be done. Plots can be awarded to the eligible on balloting basis. A plot of 1000 sq yards could be treated as a housing society, that otherwise would require large tracts of unavailable land.

Government need not enter into construction as tried to do vain fully earlier. The allotees can form an elected housing society with powers to borrow and build. Rules can be developed for its working and legal status, registration and transaction. A batch of 100,000 houses/plots could be planned in the first phase of three to five years. If successful, it can be extended into a recurring policy. The proposal has a potential of increasing the house-building rate by several times, may be 4 to 7. The proposal hardly puts burden on government coiffeurs. It is self financing except for the increased housing credit that may have to be allocated or facilitated.

Elections are due in two years time. Political parties may consider this proposal for incorporating this in their manifestoes or the present government can do a beginning in this respect preempting innovation by others and possibly enhancing its chances for re-election.

Conclusion

Land reforms need not be construed or feared as harbinger of a French or Communist revolution. Nor should it be as phony and ineffective as the previous two schemes fared. Landlessness has been ascribed to be the major reason for rural hunger and poverty. Land reforms in Pakistan can have very desirable effects on Pakistan's wellbeing and stability through three simultaneous effects; a) reducing poverty; b)increase in land utilization and productivity ;c)increase in food output ;d) diversity in political power bases and e) promotion of social cohesion having a direct bearing on reduction of terrorism .

There have been several misnomers that have been proved to be incorrect by data and experience ;a) that large farms have higher productivity, and consequently food output would suffer as a result of land redistribution) a minimum plot size of 10-12 acres would be required to be distributed among the landless. It has been found that smaller farms are more productive because of full application of family labor. Large farms do not even cultivate all their land. 20% of the agricultural land remains unutilized in Pakistan, on the average. Out of this, 15000 large farms of 500 acres and more utilize only 50% of their land, resulting in non-utilization of 10-15 million acres .Small farms of under1-3 acres, for obvious reasons, utilize 10% of their land. Also, as mentioned earlier, small plots of 1-2 acre may prove to be very viable, if distributed in clusters of 50-100 acres. Cereal crop agriculture is not the only option. Landless beneficiaries can engage in horticulture (vegetables) and livestock activities. Thus massive redistribution of land may not be required to make a significant impact on landlessness.

There are a number of options, all of which may be employed; a) revival and implementation of the earlier land reform regulations with possible adjustments; b) levying of taxation on unutilized farm areas, encouraging land rentals or /and levying of agricultural income tax on at least the 15000 large land owners; c) development and distribution of government culturable wasteland. Currently most of this land goes to the elite and powerful, as rewards of various types and kinds.

Furthermore, Land reforms are not only land distribution. Tenancy reforms such as stability and security of tenure, written and registered contracts and reasonable land rents and crop-sharing terms ought to be introduced and enforced. Market mechanism can never be of much help, as we have a large and growing population and labor would always be in surplus. Government policy and laws are a must for providing equitable reward for labor and the poor, who do not have any bargaining power. In India and Japan and elsewhere, limitations on land rent have been imposed and enforced. In most countries, a maximum share of 25 % of gross produce is a general norm. In Pakistan, these terms are much harsher. An annual or biennial sample survey needs to be done to monitor these issues, before prescribing any policy or regulation in this respect.

Lately, some neo-market based reforms have been proposed by the international financing institutions. It is argued that unimplemented land reforms have created ambiguous ownership conditions. It is argued by them that the land owner or purported land-owner, neither utilizes the land himself and nor does he give it out on rent, fearing that the land may be expropriated, de-facto by the tenants or de-jure by the government. A clear cut policy in this respect may encourage the land-owners to rent their unutilized or under-utilized land. However, one has to be very careful about these market based reforms. Often, it has resulted in the ejectment of small tenants, and emergence of commercial agriculture, furthering more landlessness and inequity and instability. A perverse market based initiative was recently launched by Hosni Mubarak of Egypt, who almost reversed the Land Reforms of Jamal Abdal-Nasir's era which resulted in eviction and ejectment of hundreds of thousands of small tenants.

Tenancy and Land lordship or Feudalism are archaic institutions signifying old order and subsistence agriculture and personalized power. Modern agriculture is based mostly on owner-farmer who self cultivates and resides on the land, or there is corporate farming on a limited scale that employs well paid agricultural workers. Ultimately, the existing land relations have to go away, if this country has to progress. Both policy and market mechanism should be employed to discourage absentee landlord and effect land distribution among the landless.

Concluding, government should start with developing and distributing culturable waste land in small plots of 1-2 acres, preferably as a part of 50-100 acre contiguous or near contiguous land .Initially 10,000 such schemes involving 1 million acres of culturable wasteland could be distributed. Also a 500 yards plot scheme for permanent residence of the landless could be introduced without causing any fear among the landed class.

Table 4.5: Proposed Distribution of Culturable Waste Land among the Landless based on 1998-2000 census

	Units	Pakistan	KP	Punjab	Sindh	Balochistan
Population	number	132.35	20.92	74.43	30.44	6.57
Urban	number	43.01	3.08	23.57	14.85	1.57
Rural	number	89.34	17.84	50.85	15.59	5.00
Family size	number	6.8	6.8	6.9	6	6.7
Urban %	%	32.50	14.74	31.67	48.80	23.90
Households Total	Million	19.46	3.08	10.79	5.07	0.98
Households urban	Million	6.33	0.45	3.42	2.48	0.23
Households Rural	Million	13.14	2.62	7.37	2.60	0.75
Culturable waste land	Mha	8.22	1.21	1.6	1.44	3.97
Current Fallow	Mha	4.98	0.61	1.6	2.01	0.92
Arable Land Total	Mha	29.42	3.12	14.02	6.32	5.96
Distributed Plot size	ha		1	1	1	5
Number of plots/beneficiary	Million	5.04	1.21	1.60	1.44	0.79
Recipients as % of total Rural H.H	%		46	22	55	106

Source: Compiled by the Author; Basic data from FBS, PCO, ACO Pakistan

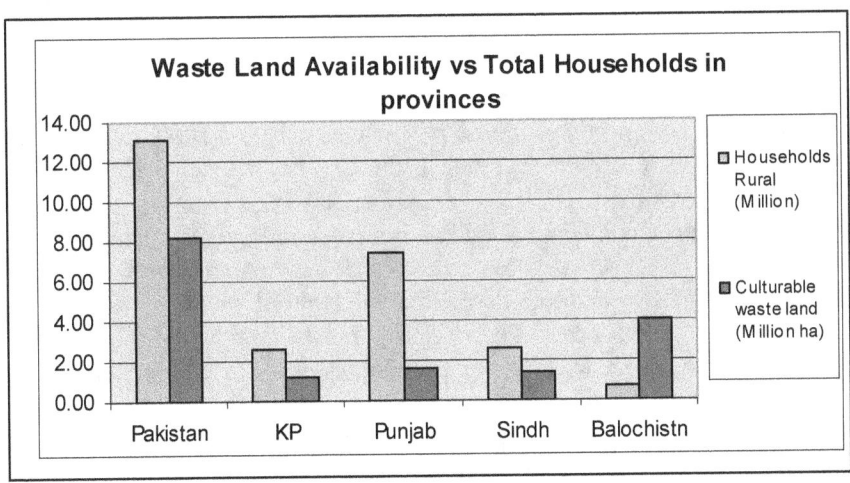

Chapter Appendix

Land Reforms & the Worldwide Experience

Almost all developed nations have implemented one or the other kind of land reform, based on the belief that tiller should own the land and that his position on the farm should be secure. American social idealism still rests on family sized farms, on which the tiller makes his home. In large part of Continental Europe, peasant-proprietor/owner-cultivator is a dominant form of land ownership. Japan and Korea were not deterred from land reforms despite a very small average farm size of 2-4 acres. Let us have a brief resume of the history and status of agricultural ownership and land reforms in some of the major parts of the world.

In ancient China, revolution on land was a recognized right of the people. Every few centuries, the land used to be re-divided and people were set on a new footing of equality. In Eastern Mediterranean, land used to be re-divided among families every seven years.

Great American thinkers and pioneers like Thomas Jefferson, Anderson Jackson, and Abraham Lincoln thought it necessary for democratic strength that the man who tills the land ought to own it and ought to have security in the possession of the land. Therefore, the great majority of farms in the US are family owned, on which the owners live and work. Tenancy and share-cropping has survived in the US largely due to Negroes, slavery and immigrants. As early as the year 1800, three-fourth of the farms were owner operated in the US. For a brief period, during the great depression of 1930s, tenancy increased due to bankruptcies and failures. But previous owners again recovered, and tenancy came back to its low level of 25% by 1947. It is a different matter that family size farm, due to particular socio-economic and technological situation in the US, averages at 160 acres. The reason is not hard to find—the vastness of America. As early as 1831, as per Homestead Act, tillers were given 160 acres per family for living and cultivation. In the early part of the twentieth century, Federal Land Bank was established which financed the land purchases by the peasants and small farmers.

In Europe, Adam Smith (1776) expressed his views on land tenure and ownership in his pioneering book `Wealth of the Nations", and regarded good land tenure as a most valuable and indispensable tool for creating wealth. In the UK, tenancy on large farms has survived but is highly regulated. All tenure contracts are written and formal and iniquitous provisions can be determined to be void by the competent authorities. There is cash rent/lease only and strong protection against eviction. Disturbance is to be paid to the farmer if he has to be removed for whatever reason and he is entitled to reimbursement for whatever improvement he may have done on the land.

Ironically tenant farming has survived in countries where there was democracy and parliaments were manned by landlords. Prime example is the UK, and to some extent Sweden and perhaps Netherlands. Throughout the continental Europe, peasant- proprietorship and owner-cultivator and family sized farms are a norm. Tenancy and share-cropping is severely limited in Denmark, less than 3%, Norway less than 7% and Sweden where tenancy is at its highest at 18%. Land purchase by peasants and small farmers have been financed by land banks in many countries, leading ones being West Germany and Sweden, where redeemable bonds were issued to the land sellers by government or state-funded credit institutions and agricultural land was sold to small farmers on credit. In Germany, farms less than 10 ha are still in majority, although over the past three decades, through land consolidation, farms of less than 1-2 ha have been disappearing, but still number around 800,000.

So is the case in Japan, where average farm size is around 2 acres. In both Japan and Germany, there is a strong cooperative movement which enables them to benefit from scale economies despite small average farm size. 75% of German farms and 90% of the Japanese farms are members of one or more service cooperatives, through which they sell most of their output, make purchases of inputs and keep their deposits and borrow from the cooperative credit institutions.

In France, more than two-third farms are less than 50 ha, half of which are less than 20 ha. Owner-operator is the dominant mode, while a quarter of the farms are tenant operated and there is very little share-cropping. At the beginning of the nineteenth century, sharecropping used to be on 50% of the farmed area. Under French law, share cropper offers only labor, while land and inputs and equipment is provided by the land owner. Still only one-third of the output goes to land, while two- third share goes to the share-cropper. No further service or contributions beyond the agreed payment in cash or kind is permitted under law. The tenure contracts are written and formal. They are for a period of a minimum of nine years, with the possibility of automatic renewal for another nine years, if desired by the tiller. Only failure to pay rent regularly, bad husbandry or damage to the property may be the cause for cancellation or non-renewal. Share-cropping contracts may be converted into farm tenancy. The lease rental remains fixed throughout the period of contract and provisions are there for rent waiver in case of crop failures and acts of God.

Table 4.6: Global extent and characteristics of land reforms

Country	Area		Beneficiary households			
	Total area (1000 ha.)	Share of arable land (%)	Num ber (000)	Share of rural H.H. (%)	Area per household (ha.)	Implementa tion Period
Africa						
Egypt	390	15.4	438	10	0.89	1952–78
Kenya	403	1.6	34	1.6	11.85	1961–70
Zimbabwe	2,371	11.9	40	3.1	59.28	1980–87
Asia						
Japan	2,000	33.3	4,300	60.9	0.47	1946–49
Korea, Rep. of	577	27.3	1,646	45.5	0.35	1948–58
Philippines	1,092	10.8	1,511	24.2	0.72	1940–85
Taiwan, China	235	26.9	383	62.5	0.61	1949–53
Central America						
El Salvador	401	27.9	95	16.8	4.22	1932–89
Mexico	13,375	13.5	3,044	67.5	4.39	1915–76
Nicaragua	3,186	47.1	172	56.7	18.52	1978–87
South America						
Bolivia	9,792	32.3	237	47.5	41.32	1953–70
Brasil	13,100	11.3	266	5.4	49.32	1964–94
Chile	9,517	60.1	58	12.7	164.09	1973
Peru	8,599	28.1	375	30.8	22.93	1969–79

In Japanese Land Reforms, 3 million farmers (50% of total) got land. Before reforms, 30% of the farms were owner-cultivated and after reforms, this percentage went up to 85%. Absentee landlord disappeared.

In Japan, the plight of tenants was almost as worse as here in Pakistan country. Land rents used to be high, as much as 50% of the crop yield, while all inputs were applied by the tenant. Only land tax was payable by the landlord. Government acquired 4.39 M acres of land from landlords.

Redeemable bonds were issued bearing 3.65% interest p.a. with an
annuity of 24 years. Tenants got the land, were required to pay in 30
years at 3.2% p.a.; 30-40 million pieces of land changed hands in 11000
villages. The job was completed in less than 2 years.

Table 4.7: Land reforms in Latin America and West Asia

Where	When	Outcomes: Land transfers	Outcomes: People	Change in distribution
Mexico	1918-68	64m ha, 65% of 1961 farmland	Farmland Gini still high (.68 1991)	Otero 1989: 27; King 1977:93
Ecuador	1964-1983	0.8m ha, 9% of farmland	15% of farm families received land	Share of land in holdings > 100ha fell from 37.1% (1954) to 22.1% (1974)
EI Salvador	after 1980	Land acquired from holdings above 100 ha	22.7% of rural households received land	
Dominican Republic	between 1961 and 1981	83,000 ha (2.7% of 1961 farmland) as private parcels and 30,000ha as collectives	32,275 private parcels created comprising 13% of peasant holdings	
Peru	1969-1980	About 8.6m ha, 40-50% of farmland, acquired	375,000 direct beneficiaries, 24% of rural workforce	Land Gini 0.91 (1972), 0.86 (1994)
Chile	up to 1973	0.9m (basic irrigated) ha acquired (20% of 1973 arable area), 1986: 57% still in reform sector		Land Gini 0.92 in 1996
Iraq	1958-1982	1958, 1970 reforms moved 60% of arable land by 1984	322,000 (56%) of agri-households got land by 1980	Land Gini 0.90 (1958), 0.39 (1982)
Iran	1962-75, in 3 stages	53% villages redistributed	1.9m families got land	

Source: World Bank & FAO Papers

Today, in Japan, less than 5% are pure tenant farmers, 67% are owner-cultivators and the rest are part- owner, part tenants. Sharecropping and rents in kind have been abolished. Rents are to be paid in cash which should not exceed 25% of crop yield for rice and 15% for other crops. All contracts are to be written based on a model contract issued by the government. Ejectment or ejection is not permitted either for re-renting or self- cultivation. Although the land reforms were implemented under orders of occupation forces commanded by Gen. MacArthur, the efficiency with which it was implemented by the Japanese people and government indicated that the Japanese, even the affected landlords discerned benefits and advantage to the society.

In South Korea, in 1945, 70% of all farms were tenant operated, with an average farm size of 4 acre and for rice farms 2 acres. Exorbitant Land rents prevailed i.e., 60% of the crop-yield. Land reforms brought these down to 33%. Govt. acquired land at a price of 150% of the crop yield which amounts to a rent payment of 30% for 5 years. Bonds were issued to the landlords, who could buy the evacuee property left by Japanese colonists, with these bonds. Thus a significant percentage of land lords acquired interest in industrialization.

Praise for Egypt's Jamal Abdul Nasser's Land Reform by the USAID

Nasser-era agrarian reforms starting in 1952 were two-pronged. First, the government redistributed ownership rights to some land by setting a maximum ceiling on land ownership,(50 feddan / acres) expropriating land above the ceiling (300,000 ha), and distributing it in small plots averaging 2.4 feddans (approximately 1 hectare) to about 350,000 families between 1952 and 1970. Second, because not all landless households received ownership rights, the reforms also established rules protecting lessee households, fixing rents at seven times the land tax and granting beneficiary households permanent, heritable tenancy rights. Landlords could not evict tenants unless they did not pay rent, and rent levels became increasingly nominal over time. Furthermore, landlords wishing to sell their land for non-agricultural purposes were required to pay one-half of the sales-price to the tenants. The government registered beneficiaries of the reforms (both lessees and new owners) in records kept at the village level).The land reform was generally considered a success in that it transferred ownership rights and long-term secure leasing rights to a large number of poor households. Ownership rights to more than 300,000 hectares were redistributed, comprising between 12% and 14% of the land under cultivation.

96

Hosni Mubarak's reversal of Land Reforms

In 1992, Law No. 96 reversed key provisions of the 30-year-old pro-tenant reforms by providing for increased rent levels over a 5-year period and removing, by 1997, the permanent, heritable rights of tenant households that were beneficiaries of the earlier reforms. The new law gave landlords the right to evict such tenants for the first time in many decades. The implementation of Law No. 96 led to significant levels of rural unrest and dispossession of approximately 1 million longstanding registered tenant households, representing 30% of all farming households in Egypt. Compensation to evicted tenants amounted to a fraction of the value of their land rights.

Source: USAID LTPR (Land Tenure and Property Rights) Portal

Land Reforms in India

There is a mixed story of success in India. India took the following steps, with varying levels of success:

1) **Abolition of the intermediaries (Zamindar and Jagirdar)** ,who used to collect Land Tax on behalf of the governments , and pocket a margin. There was a lot of fragmentation and hierarchy of large and small Zamindars, who extracted margins at every level.50% of the land, was under this system.20-25 million Zamindars were eased off. They received compensation equal to the 15-30 years of rent. 20-25 million beneficiaries got the ownership rights, who continued to pay rent/land tax, but this time directly to the government. This aspect has been adjudged by various scholars as the most successful one.

2) **Land Ceiling;** Under the Indian constitution, Land and Agriculture issues came under the domain of state/provincial governments, although the larger policy framework came from the Central government. A land ceiling law was passed; land ceiling, however, varied from state to state; ceiling was as low as 9 acres in Jammu and Kashmir, and as high as 54 acres in Gujarat, Haryana, Punjab, Rajasthan, Tamil Nadu and Madhya Pradesh. Excess land was acquired by the excess governments with a very low compensation. It is said that due to a very low compensation, there was a lot of resistance and manipulation. We will provide the data in Table 4.7. Some 12.4 million tenants (12 % of the total agricultural house-holds) got ownership of 15.6 million acres (4.5% of the total cultivated land). 81 % of the beneficiaries were concentrated in West

Bengal, Assam, Gujarat, Kerala, and Maharashtra. Landowners, under the ceiling, were allowed to evict farmers .Resultantly, it is said that more farmers were evicted in the decade following ceiling laws than in one hundred years before.

Table 4.8: Shares of rural households and arable land area affected by different land reforms in Indian States

State	Area (%)	Tenancy legislation		Average age	Ceiling legislation	
		Pop. (%)	No. of laws		Area (%)	Pop. (%)
Andhra Pradesh	3.48	0.75	2	17	8.34	3.81
Bihar	0	0	3	18.3	4.42	4
Gujarat	15	11.2	2	15.5	1.95	0.31
Haryana	0.51	0.01	0	0	1.26	0.26
Himachal Pradesh	0.16	3.19	n.a.	n.a.	0.06	0.05
Karnataka	15.38	5.29	2	14.5	1.71	0.3
Kerala	8.47	12.49	4	10.8	1.3	1.04
Madhya Pradesh	2.15	0.61	1	24	2.69	0.71
Maharashtra	27.01	10.68	1	23	7.74	1.08
Orissa	0.15	1.43	3	9	2.24	1.28
Punjab	1.89	0.04	1	10	1.5	0.25
Rajasthan	0	0.16	0	0	6.63	0.75
Tamil Nadu	3.65	3.23	5	13.6	2.47	1.24
Uttar Pradesh	0	0	2	14.5	5.81	3.68
West Bengal	6.41	10.8	5	8.2	14.91	19.73
Total	5.45	5.35	2.1	13.03	4.41	2.27

Source: Klaus Deiningera, Songqing Jinb and Vandana Yadavb, Impact of Land Reform on Productivity, Land Value and Human Capital Investment Household Level Evidence from West Bengal, DOA, F & R E Michigan State University, U.S.A.

3) **Distribution of government wasteland;** Some 14.7 million acres of government wasteland has been distributed, which is almost equal to the land redistribution under ceiling surplus. Andhra Pradesh, Gujarat, Bihar, Karnataka, Kerala, Maharashtra, Orissa, UP and West Bengal had most of the share in waste land distribution. In many respects, wasteland distribution proved to be more effective than Ceiling surplus redistribution which suffered from several problems, and actual transfers may be less than the records show. Relatively speaking, actual transfer in

case of government wasteland was much higher. There were problems, however, in the development of the barren land.

4) **Tenancy reforms;** Rent ceilings were fixed, although variable from state to state. General rent ceiling varied from $1/5^{th}$ to $1/4^{th}$ of the gross produce, which was almost consistent with Japanese land reforms. In West Bengal, however, rent ceiling is 50%, if the landlord provides the input. Tenants' tenure has been allowed from 5 to 10 years.

The aforementioned reforms are still valid and current and have varying level of implementation. Some thinking, however, is going on to bring in market based reforms which may enhance commercial availability of land to the tillers. There are however many opponents and critics .Market normally goes against the poor. The poor lacks knowledge, capital and power and is in large supply, exceeding the demand.

5   Supervisory Boards for corporate and public sector oversight

We have experienced and observed the performance and often corruption in large public sector organizations. Traditional boards have not been successful in overseeing the performance of the entities under their control. Apart from profitability, there are issues of quality of service, fair prices, resource stewardship and management and other public sector issues. In this space, we would examine the advisability of introducing a supervisory board for protecting the public interest and perhaps for curbing corruption in these enterprises.

The concept of outside control of corporations is not new. The issue has become more important due to the diversity of sources of capital for the companies. A dominant or majority group of shareholders control the management. There are rules and procedures to protect minority interest, and also ways not to follow those rules; hence the need for some sort of outside controls. External auditors do provide some handle on the problem but have been found inadequate even in the West. Company managements and executive have become too powerful. One way to measure this is the exorbitant salaries, they have usually succeeded to justify and often without the corresponding contribution or efficiency. This has started to happen even here in Pakistan; the case of NBP and other banks is an example. Executives and shareholders combine is often capable to maximize individual interest and conduct illegal and immoral activities and get away with it. Supervisory Boards have been introduced in Europe to bring the required outside controls and to supervise the activities and performance of the company management.

Large companies, private or public, affect people and societies far beyond the mundane profitability. Companies' activities outputs or inputs may affect a community or even nations in many different ways. This has given rise to the debate and concepts on Corporate Social Responsibility that ought to be taken care of by companies Board of

Management or Directors, in addition to the pursuit of corporate interests, incomes, profitability and market share etc; easier said than done. Corporate issues are often so demanding and sometimes at cross purpose with community interests, it often is easier to lose sight of the larger interests of the community, society or even a nation or even of its own employees.

German Law of Corporate governance has created an interesting institution called supervisory board of Management, for large and listed companies. This is in addition to the generally known Board of Directors which is chosen by the shareholders and is responsible to control companies' assets and run the companies' commercial activities. There is two-tier system, Supervisory board and Board of Directors, while the former broadly supervises the activities and strategic decisions of the companies' board of management or directors. In Germany, Board of supervisors (BOS) is chosen by Company shareholders and employees in equal numbers; 50% of the members of BOS are chosen by Company management or shareholders and 50% by employees or their unions. Normally employees' representation in addition to the workers interests also promotes larger social responsibilities of the company.

The Dutch Law goes a step forward. The BoS in Netherlands provides for a Board of Supervisors which draws its membership from civil society, profession and the general public. No company interest, owners or employees, are represented in BOS under Dutch Law. In that respect it serves the sole purpose of oversight. All large corporations come under the ambit of this law. BoS assures that the companies operates and abide by the law, promotes corporate social responsibility and serves as a cushion or restraining influence on more controversial activities and decisions. The result is that European large corporations have a softer image than that of the, say, US corporations which concrete evidence is a more cooperative, supportive and compliant attitude of European corporations on global environmental issues than that of the US corporations. US government's opposition to global environmental initiatives largely is based on the pressures of the US corporate interests.

BoS are appointed by the Annual General Meeting and operate under the articles of association. It can have three or more up to ten members depending on the company size. It elects its own chairman. It meets six times a year and operates through committees. There can be 5 or six committees looking after Finance, major contracts, risk management, etc. Companies and BoS can design their own procedures with respect to BOS around model and best practices statements issued by SEC's of the country where they operate. One member in any Board committee and deliberations include one member of the company management, executive or shareholders for coordination purposes. BoS recommends external auditors for the AGM's approval and comments on audit reports requiring explanation of the executive. BoS members' remuneration is decided by AGM also.

Anglo-Saxon countries have not accepted this two-tier model arguing that it dilutes freedom, speed and efficiency of the company management and may also affect companies' confidentialities and legitimate secrets compromising competitive conditions. More countries are following the above example of the BoS. China has also adopted the same convention, perhaps in a bid to have control and oversight of its public sector or having some handle on foreign listed companies. In Pakistan, one is not sure that the time is ripe for introducing the same laws of corporate governance and the institution of BoS. However, there is a scope for examining the possibilities for selective application of the same, like on large public enterprises e.g., PIA, Pakistan Steel, Railways, OGDC,PSO,PEPCO,WAPDA etc. and in private sector such as Banks, insurance companies, stock exchanges and companies dealing with products and services of grave public importance such as Hospitals and educational institutions.

It can be argued that representation of stakeholders through Boards of Supervisors in large corporations like PIA, Pakistan Steel and Railways etc could have averted the continued deterioration in performance of these institutions and allegedly rampant corruption. Also some policy initiatives and decision may be too critical and of larger societal interest like open sky approaches or JV agreement with foreign airlines (as was the case of contentious agreement with Turkish Airlines) or capacity expansion like leasing or buying of aircraft by PIA, or of locomotives and engines by Railways or Mega expansion contracts for expansion or procurement of inputs. Corruption is done in close and cozy quarters. Bringing and expanding the oversight function s may curb such activities, if not tendencies. It may act the other way round as well. Companies may need outside support in fighting internal vested interests of bureaucracies or the unions and oversight institutions may come to support and rescue of sincere and forthright management and executives. The proposal is worth consideration by SECP and other relevant authorities. Political parties should also include this issue in their deliberations on preparing their manifestoes for the forthcoming elections.

6   Pakistan and Muslim countries; a socio-economic overview

In this Chapter, we present a brief socio-economic overview of Muslim countries that is possible within the constraints of space. Sixty one countries with 1.6 billion people cannot be dealt with adequately in a few pages. However, it may serve a useful purpose for the lay reader who may also have time constraints. For a detailed treatment, we have the Muslim World Source Book, for which this paper is a prelude. Life in Muslim countries is varied, full of thrill and can be rich at times and places. Numbers do not capture all this. Besides, there is lack of documentation and coverage. In many Muslim countries, there are large parallel informal economies, as large as the formal documented economies. Let us see how the published numbers look like and compare.

Population

Population of Pakistan is 170 million, the second largest after Indonesia. It is projected that in due course Pakistan's population would exceed that of Indonesia. As per the latest population estimates released for the year 2010, the total Muslim population in the world is 1.6 billion, 23.4 % of the world population. It was 19% twenty years ago, and is projected to be 26.4% twenty years hence that is by 2030. 18% Muslims live as minorities in non-Muslim countries as well.

There are 61 Muslim countries with a total population of 1.50 Billion people, with a share of 22.94% in total world population. There is much diversity among Muslim countries ranging fro tiny-super-rich Brunei to the large and poor countries of Indonesia, Pakistan and Bangladesh. Majority of Muslims and their countries are in MENA and Asia- Pacific. A large number of countries with relatively small populations lie in West African region. Turkey, Albania, Kosovo and Bosnia are in Europe. Azerbaijan, Turkmenistan, Tajikistan and Kazakhstan and Kyrgyz

Republic are in Central Asia. More precisely following is the regional distribution of Muslim population;

Asia-Pacific	1,005,507,000(62.1%)
Middle East-North Africa (MENA)	321,869,000 (19.9%)
Sub-Saharan Africa	242,544,000(15.0%)
Europe & Americas	5,256,000(3%)

Classification of Muslim Economies

For the purpose of this publication, we have classified the Muslim countries as per their size of the economies as measured by their GDPs. These are; 17 countries with *large economies (LMEs)* led by Turkey with a GDP of 734 Billion USD to Qatar with a GDP of 71 Billion USD; another 18 countries with *medium sized economies (MMEs)* in the range of 12-66 billion USD of their GDPs; the rest are *small economies (SMEs)* with under 10 billion USD GDPs.26 countries are SMEs. *LMEs* have a share of 72.3 % in the total population *(AMEs)* and a share of 86.65 % in the total output of Muslim countries. *MMEs* have a share of 15.7 % in population and 11 % in output. *SMEs* have a share of 1.17% in population and a share of 2.25% in output.

Economies; growth and structure

Pakistan size of the economy (GDP) is ranked at ninth among Muslim countries closely equal to the economies of UAE, Algeria, Egypt and Kuwait. By comparison, Bangladesh economy comes 16th in terms of GDP. Turkey and Indonesia have crossed the barrier of 1 trillion USD GDP economies in terms of PPP dollars, which infact is a more comparable yardstick .Turkey and Indonesia have rankings respectively of 15th and 16th largest economies of the world only next to South Korea, Canada and Spain. Turkey spearheads the Muslim community by its size of the economy, high per capita income and probably the highest level of achievements in the area of Science, Technology and industrial and broad-based economic development. This has naturally resulted in better living conditions for its people. Turkey could achieve all this without oil or other natural resources. Fortunately Turkey is trying to come closer to its roots and is establishing more active political and economic linkages with other Muslim countries. We welcome this, as it would be to mutual advantage. Malaysia, Indonesia, Saudi Arabia, UAE and Iran have achieved significant economic development Political and economic conditions have worsened in Afghanistan, Pakistan, Iraq and Sudan.

Muslim countries have a share of 7.31% in the world output, significantly much less than their share in world population of 22.94%. Average per capita GDP stands at 1536 USD which includes the highs of around 50,000 USD for countries like Qatar, Kuwait and the UAE which are a few exceptions to many countries mostly in West Africa having per capita GDP of well under 1000 USD. Poverty and Inequality is quite visible in most Muslim countries.

Surprisingly double-digit growth in the economies of Azerbaijan, Turkmenistan, Afghanistan and Chad has been recorded for most of the period of the last decade. Next big performers are the oil rich Qatar, Kuwait and UAE with GDP growths of 8-9%.Median growth in LMEs has been at 5-6% which appears to be a good achievement on the part of these countries. In most other economies the median growth rate has been around 4%. Iraq for understandable reasons had a negative growth rate of -11.4%. Only five countries mostly of Western Africa had very low growth of 0.5-2.4 %.

Food and Agriculture

Over the years, Pakistan Food imports have come down from 18% of total Pakistan imports to 12% of the total. Agricultural raw materials are another 5%.Pakistan's agricultural output is 33 Billion USD, 20 % of its GDP. By comparison, Turkey's agricultural output is around 80 Billion USD, 9% of its GDP. Nigeria's agri-output is 70 Billion USD, one-third of its GDP. I hope the data is correct .Indonesia's agricultural output is around 40 Billion USD, 14% of its GDP. Surprisingly, Malaysia, a small country both in terms of geography and population, has a sizeable agricultural output of 22 Billion USD, closely following Iran with 22 Billion USD. Thus Pakistan's agricultural sector comes out to be 4th in order, in terms of output.

In Small Economies (SMEs), agricultural sectors' have relatively high shares i.e. 30% or more, most of which is subsistence agriculture. In Yemen, Niger, Mauritania and Gambia, food imports account for 25-30% of total imports. While these percentage averages 13 % for Low Income countries at world level, and 18% for SMEs on the average. This is despite abundance of water in most West African SMEs. In Large Economies (LMEs) Algeria and Bangladesh have high food imports, respectively 20% and 225 of the total imports. Agriculture fares highly in the overall economic structure and outputs of most Muslim countries, except some Oil rich countries of MENA. Nigeria has the highest share of all of 33% for agriculture in its GDP, and in absolute terms as well has high agricultural output, higher than agriculturally prominent Pakistan. Turkey, Indonesia and (surprisingly) Iran are the three highest agricultural producers as measured in terms of value added in agriculture. Both Turkey and Iran produce high value added items and have large food processing industries. The food imports of Turkey and Iran countries are the lowest respectively i.e., 45 and 2% of total imports. Food imports of the two large countries Egypt and Pakistan are alarmingly high, 17% for Egypt and 12% for Pakistan. Both of these countries have myriads of problems like large population, water scarcity and poverty etc. Despite being the largest agri-producer in the group, Turkey's share of agricultural production in GDP is one of the lowest i.e. 9% as opposed to 33% of Nigeria, 20% of Pakistan and 19% for Bangladesh.

Industry and services

In most large economies (LMEs), share of industrial output is relatively high, except for Pakistan with 27% and Bangladesh 29% of GDP. Most MENA countries seem to have high industrial share due to the large oil sector and the associated processing; 75% for Saudi Arabia, and 61% for UAE. Malaysia and Indonesia both have a 48% share for industrial sector, more than 50% of which is from manufacturing, signifying the importance of their large manufacturing sectors. Turkey's economic structure seems to be coming closer to the relatively more advanced and industrialized countries of the world with high per capita income, efficient industry and agriculture and increasing share of service sector in the total national output. Between 1995 and 2008, Turkey increased its share of service sector from 50% to a high 64%, matching closely with the averages of advanced economies.

Trade and deficits

Due to the influence of oil exports, exports occupy an average of 50% or more in the GDPs of most LMEs. A figure of more than 101% for Malaysia is probably mostly non-oil. Exceptions are Pakistan, Iran, Indonesia, and Bangladesh and surprisingly Turkey with low exports to GDP ratios of (13-30%).Pakistan has been the worst performer (13%), while Bangladesh (20%) fared much better comparatively. Although oil bill played a major role in Pakistan's negative trade balance, interestingly in Pakistan there is a debate going on as to the claims of economic performance in the last decade. However, the large current account deficits are shown by Lebanon, (-13.9%) followed by Jordan of (-10.1%).A number of non-oil producing countries have had large import bills due to lowered tariffs and non-development of domestic resource base.

Poverty & Inequality

In large economies *(LMEs)*, poverty is much less than in other Muslim countries with the exception of Nigeria (64.4% population below 1.25 USD daily income), Bangladesh (49.6%), Indonesia 29.4% and 22.6% in Pakistan. Other countries in LMEs have either no reported poverty like in oil rich Saudi Arabia, UAE and Qatar etc. or very small poverty prevalence of around 2%. This is under a USD 1.5 per day daily income measure. *National Poverty Measure (NPM)* which may reflect a more realistic situation report much higher poverty prevalence of 16-27 % in more prosperous countries. Turkey reports 27% poverty as per NPM vis-à-vis 2.6% in terms of 1.25 dollar measure. Similarly Egypt has a surprisingly low 1.25 USD poverty of only 2% vis-à-vis a poverty prevalence of 16.7% as per NPM. Admittedly 1.25 USD poverty measure represents very stark poverty conditions. SMEs poverty levels are much higher: 74.4% in Mozambique, Malawi and Guinea to 34% in Gambia. Fortunately the total population incidence in the last category, as mentioned earlier is much smaller (1.17%).More difficult issues are of large country poverty such as Indonesia, Nigeria, Pakistan and Bangladesh.

Data on Inequality such as Gini Coefficient is not available for most Muslim economies. However, one is surprised by the relative egalitarianism as revealed by the data. We divide the countries ranking in Gini Coefficient in four categories: 1.very highly unequal 2.highly unequal 3.significantly unequal and 4.the least unequal. In the first category of *The Least Unequal* come countries like Sweden, Denmark, Norway ,Austria , Germany, Italy, Spain and Finland and infact most of the EU countries except the UK .Pakistan comes in this category as well largely due to a very small rich population and perhaps negligible number of super rich families. Eight Muslim countries fall in the category, with Egypt being there alongside with democratic India. Sixteen Muslim counties fall in the third category of highly unequal countries with such heavy weights as Indonesia, Malaysia, Turkey and Iran. Surprising Iran (ranking 47) is closer to the US (ranking 44) in this respect. A large super rich community and a generally pro-rich and pro-profit US understandably earn it this rather undesirable ranking in the company of most Muslim countries. Among the countries of *very highly unequal*, only 3 Muslim countries (Mozambique, Gambia, Niger) merited their inclusion among a total of 34.Mostly Latin American

(Bolivia, Brazil, Argentina and Chile etc) and African countries fall in this unfortunate situation.

Inflation

As to the inflation, surprisingly Turkey heads the list with a CPI growth rate of 18.6% p.a., followed by Iran of 15.1% and 12.9% for Nigeria. Trade embargoes may be behind Iran's inflation and in case of Nigeria governance issues may have resulted in a high figure. Inflation of 6.7-7.2% for countries like Pakistan, Egypt and Bangladesh is to be understood in the perspective of their traditional budgetary and current account deficit. Most oil exporters have had very low inflation or none at all, except Qatar with a CPI growth of 8.3% which either is surprising or seems to be an error. Most other Muslim countries had an inflation of fewer than 4%, which in itself appears to be quite a comfortable figure. In some countries, this may also be due to sluggish growth.

Education and Human Development

HDI (Human Development Index) has been widely accepted as an indicator of human development and conditions. Life expectancy, Education Index and Per capita GDP are the constituents of HDI. Within Muslim countries Pakistan's rank on HDI scale is 30th out of 55 countries in the good company of only Afghanistan, Bangladesh and very poor and underdeveloped African countries.

Pakistan ranks 125 in world order on HDI scale. 12 Muslim countries are classified among the High HDI (rank 1-70) countries, with a total population of 163.4 Million (11.01 % of the total Muslim countries population). Notable in this group are Saudi Arabia, Malaysia, Iran and Kazakhstan, and Azerbaijan. Others are mostly smaller countries of the gulf, namely UAE, Qatar, Bahrain and Kuwait. Albania and Bosnia from Europe are also in this select group. Bulk of the Muslim countries (34) with a population of 82.72%, are classified as Medium HDI (rank 71-155) countries. Surprisingly, Tunisia heads this group, with a world ranking of 81, followed closely by Jordan (rank 82), and Turkey (rank 83), the latter one would have expected to be among High HDI list. Afghanistan is at the bottom of this group with a ranking of 155.8

Muslim countries (population share 6.26 %), all belonging to sub-Saharan Africa are grouped as Low HDI countries. There are 7 other countries which HDI has not been reported, out of which 3 may be Low HDI countries and 4 medium ones. These are small population countries as well. Uplifting these countries to at least a higher ranking of 100-150 may not be such a big issue, if the richer community members extend a hand of assistance to these rather blighted countries. Similarly Oil rich countries are capable to enhance their HDI rating to even higher levels on their own. The real issue is the transformation of the predominantly large population countries with lower HDI achievements.

Over the years considerable achievements have been made with respect to literacy and education. Except for Pakistan, Egypt, Nigeria and Senegal, where literacy is relatively low, in Large(LMEs) and as well as medium sized economies (MMEs) literacy is in the range of 80-90%.This is a major improvement since 1960s when literacy levels used to average around 20% , as was the case with many other developing countries. In small economies of West Africa, the literacy is very poor, in the range of around 30%.In all the Central Asian Muslim countries ,irrespective of size or others, the literacy is 100% , one of the good legacies of early communism in these countries. One of the main contributors to low overall literacy levels are, problems and difficulties in the area of female literacy which is particularly low, in low literacy countries. Contrary to popular notions, female literacy in most Arab countries, particularly oil rich countries is high, trailing only a few percentage points behind the male literacy. A noteworthy figure is of 80% female literacy in conservative Saudi Arabia vs 81% for a liberal and modern Turkey. In addition to retrogression and conservatism, poverty, lack of resources and even lesser public expenditure on education, give rise to falling Gross Enrollment Ratio (GER) in most low literacy countries, giving rise to literacy deficits. Child labor has also contributed to lesser achievements in education and literacy.

Health

In the health sector, similar situation as it exists in education is there for almost identical reasons. Poverty, lack of adequate sanitation and hygiene, lesser country resources and a trend of even lesser public expenditures seem to be the reasons for under-achievement in countries where health conditions are particularly low. Afghanistan has probably the highest infant mortality in the world (165 per 1000) followed by Nigeria (96 per), Pakistan (72 per) and Sudan (70 per) against a world average of 50.On the other hand Malaysia has the lowest infant mortality of 6%, equal to the average of high income developed countries of the world. Most other LMEs have an infant mortality ratio in the range of 20-30% for the world middle income countries. Oil rich countries except Nigeria spend much higher percentages of their public expenditure on education and health with relatively much ease. Poor health conditions in most under-achievers are due to lesser public spending on health .Private sector in these countries provides bulk of the health services (as indicated by two-third or more of the health expenditure coming from private sector) which is often unaffordable and inaccessible by the poor and even the middle classes. Fortunately in many such countries Philanthropy comes to the rescue and has been playing a very significant role in health sector providing free or near-free service.

Governments Revenue and Finances

In oil rich countries such as Saudi Arabia and UAE and others there is no income tax. Most revenues come from oil and trade. In Afghanistan, government tax revenues are perhaps the lowest in the non-oil world i.e., 5.8% of GDP, to be followed by Bangladesh 8.8% and Pakistan 9.8%, resulting in high dependence on foreign assistance. In most other countries taxation revenues average 15-17 % of GDP.

As to the central government financial resources, in the LMEs largest budgetary deficit is displayed by Pakistan; figures of -7.4 % to be followed by Egypt with a corresponding figure of -6.4%.Turkey too has had a deficit of -1.9%. Pakistan's large deficit is explained by its highest incidence of interest payments (34.8%) and Military Expenditure (MILEX) of 17.6% and lower tax receipts of 9.8% of its GDP. In terms of GDP, Saudi Arabia seems to have the highest spending at 8% as opposed to 3.3% of Pakistan. Highest incidence of salaries and compensation of government and public sector employees accounted for 45% of national budget in Jordan, followed by 43% for Morocco, 38% for Iran, 35 % for Tunisia and 33% for Qatar. Figures of 21-28% are median figures for other countries. Pakistan's low figure of 4% seems to be either an error or most probably explained by its federal structure of governance, whereby a considerable employment cost is borne by provinces, the latter being excluded from the total.

Foreign Aid dependence

Of the 91 billion USD of total ODA, Muslim countries took a share of 43 billion USD. Understandably Iraq and Afghanistan are the largest recipients of Overseas Development Assistance (ODA) ,which reached the levels of 9.87 billion USD for Iraq and 4.865 billion USD for Afghanistan in the year 2008.For both of these countries, ODA used to be only 100-136 million USD in 1995.Surprisingly, Turkey remained as one of the large recipient of ODA with 2.024 billion USD , which however constituted as only 1.2% of its budget. Sudan, Bangladesh and Mozambique got around 2.0 billion USD each, resulting in high dependence, as much as 23.9% of the central government budget of that country. In small economies mostly of Western Africa, Aid dependence can be as high as 50-75%, with modest amounts of aid money of a few hundred million USD per year. In medium economies, dependence is also significantly high; Jordan 9.6% and Lebanon 12.1%.In large economies , moderate dependence is there ; 5.7% for Pakistan and 2.7 % for Egypt . Against a publicized notion of being large recipients of ODA (Overseas Development Assistance) due to the political and strategic roles of the two countries, Egypt received 1.348 billion USD and Pakistan 1.539 billion USD in 2008. Pakistan has usually more problem with its balance of payment and trade deficits which became graver in 2008 due to the rise in oil and other commodity prices.

Natural Resources

As for natural resources, there is a mixed situation. While most of MENA countries falling in the category of LMEs with some exceptions like Egypt, Morocco and Sudan, are rich in oil and mineral resources; Saudi Arabia has the largest oil reserves and Iran and Qatar have among the world's largest natural gas reserves. Even when fossil fuels run out, MENA countries are looking forward to a good solar energy future. Already there are plans and projects such as *Desertec* to export solar power to Europe. The SMEs of West Africa are generally rich in natural mineral resources. Indonesia exports coal, while Pakistan which is currently passing through a major energy crisis hosts a very large coal deposit with more energy content than the oil wealth of Iran and Saudi Arabia combined. SMEs of Western Africa tend to have suffered from what the Economists term as," Resource Curse". Mineral resources instead of having benefitted their economies have harmed them.

Most large economies except MENA countries are significant fuel, mostly oil, importers. Pakistan's fuel imports are the highest constituting 33% of its annual total import bill. Similarly Indonesia's oil imports are as high as 24%, Morocco at 20% and Turkey at 17%. In the case of all other Muslim countries, fuel imports are significant, constituting 20-36 % of their respective total annual imports. Surprisingly, Iran also imports oil to the tune of 4% of its total imports, which, however, seem to stem from the shortage of refining capacity.

Richness in natural resources is measured primarily by land area and water, and secondly by energy and mineral resources. Except for water, many Muslim countries especially of MENA are quite rich. Eleven countries have land area in access of 1.0 million square kms, out of which four countries are above 2.0 million sq. kms. Consequently these countries are quite sparsely populated , having population density as low as 3.58 person per sq.kms for Libya , 12.3 for Saudi Arabia , 14.40 for Algeria, and 5.82 for Kazakhstan.

The most densely populated and congested is Bangladesh with 1229 person per sq. kms, with a population of 149 million or so in only 130,000 sq.kms. Significantly dense and large population countries are Indonesia, Nigeria, and Pakistan (215 persons per sq.kms) with population densities in the range of 100-225 sq.kms. The other densely populated countries are very small countries, although rich in terms of natural wealth, namely Lebanon, Kuwait, Qatar, UAE, Bahrain, Kosovo, Albania, Togo and Gambia. Otherwise poor and underdeveloped countries of mostly Sub-Saharan Africa are not dense and have large areas e.g. Mali and Chad and Niger with areas respectively of 1.2 million sq. kms , 1.259 million sq.kms and 1.266 million Sq.kms. Consequently they are relatively rich in mineral resources. However average may hide acute congestions due to skewed distribution of populations. Almost all big cities are dense and congested. In the case of Pakistan, 97% of the population lives in 50% of the area in its three provinces, while the smallest province of Balochistan with a population of 3% of the total has an area of 50%.Within Punjab, the most populous province and probably the densest as well, central Punjab is even denser within.

All land may not be Arable. In terms of Arable land, Niger and Kazakhstan top the list with arable land in excess of 100 hectares per 100 persons i.e., with more than 1 person per ha of arable land. Most countries have median values lying in the region of 20-30 ha per 100 persons. This compares well with the Middle and High income developed countries of the world. Countries with low availability of arable area are Bangladesh 5.1 ha per 100 persons, Egypt 3.8, Indonesia 9.9, Pakistan 13.4 and Saudi Arabia 14.6.Iran otherwise identified as oil and gas country has a significantly higher arable area at 23.8 ha per 100 persons. Similar are Nigeria and Algeria with corresponding figures respectively of 24.8 and 22.4.

Muslim countries especially of Sub-Saharan Africa are rich in mineral resources. For example, Niger is famous for Uranium. Pakistan, Iran and Saudi Arabia, Nigeria, Algeria and Sudan have reportedly many explored and under-explored mineral resources. Finally and most importantly, seven of the top ten oil reserves countries are Muslim countries, namely, Saudi Arabia, Iran, Iraq, Kuwait, Kazakhstan, UAE and Nigeria, while five of the top ten Natural Gas reserve countries are Muslim ones as well, namely; Iran, Qatar, Saudi Arabia, UAE and Nigeria.

In terms of per capita energy consumption, only a few countries have a lower figure than the average for low income countries, namely Bangladesh, Sudan, Yemen, Cameroon, Senegal Benin and Togo which need not, however, be a point of consolation. Among other low per capita consumers are Pakistan, Indonesia, Morocco, Syria, Tunisia, Albania, Mozambique and Tajikistan and Kyrgyzstan. Elsewhere energy consumption is as high as mid-income countries of the world. Naturally, oil producing countries of MENA are quite profligate consumers.

Water

Generally MENA countries have very low fresh water availability typically well under 100 Cu. meters per capita per year. Particularly water stressed countries with large populations are Pakistan and Egypt who have large agricultural base requiring water. Water is generally scarce in most MENA countries and in a few cases fresh water availability is as low as 22-34 cubic meters per capita as in Egypt and UAE. Oil rich MENA countries have tackled the problem by installing water desalination plants. Water situation is also bad in South Asia with Pakistan having only 338 cubic meter of fresh water per capita and having a large population to support which in large measure is dependent on Agriculture. Elsewhere, Water is relatively abundant. In Indonesia and Malaysia and West Africa, water availability is not an issue, although there may be problems in the supplies of safe drinking water in the generally poor countries of Western Africa.

Table 6.1: **Muslims in all Muslim Countries**

Large Economies (LME)		Medium Economies (MME)		Small Economies (SME)	
Turkey	73.9	Sudan	41.3	Afghanistan	29.0
Indonesia	227.3	Syria	20.6	Mozambique	22.4
Saudi Arabia	24.6	Azerbaijan	8.7	Mali	12.7
Iran	72.0	Oman	2.8	Chad	10.9
Malaysia	27.0	Tunisia	10.3	Burkina Faso	15.2
Nigeria	151.2	Lebanon	4.2	Benin	8.7
U.A.E.	31.7	Uzbekistan	27.3	Kosovo	1.8
Algeria	34.4	Yemen Republic	22.9	Niger	14.7
Pakistan	166.1	Côte d'Ivoire	20.6	Tajikistan	6.8
Egypt	81.5	Cameroon	19.1	Kyrgyz Republic	5.3
Kuwait	2.7	Jordan	5.9	Brunei	0.211
Kazakhstan	15.7	Bosnia-Herzegovina	3.8	Malawi	14.8
Iraq	30.7	Turkmenistan	5.0	Guinea	9.8
Libya	6.3	Gabon	1.4	Togo	6.5
Morocco	31.6	Uganda	4.5	Mauritania	3.2
Bangladesh	160.0	Senegal	12.2	Sierra Leone	5.6
Qatar	1.3	Albania	3.1	Eriteria	4.9
Sub-Total LME	**1138.0**	Bahrain	0.65	Suriname	0.084
		Sub-Total MME	**214.4**	Maldives	0.309
				Gambia	1.7
				Djibouti	0.853
				Guinea-Bissau	1.6
				Comoros	0.679
				Guyana	0.055
				Palestine	
				Somalia	8.9
				Sub-Total SME	**187.0**

Source: World Bank development Indicator (WDI 2009)

Table 6.2: Population Sample Countries 2008

Countries	MENA	Sub-Saharan Africa	South & South East Asia	Central Asia	Europe	Total
Turkey	73.9					
Indonesia			227.3			
Saudi Arabia	24.6					
Iran	72.0					
Malaysia			27.0			
Nigeria		151.2				
Pakistan			166.1			
Egypt	81.5					
Kazakhstan				15.7		
Bangladesh			160.0			
LME	391	151	580	16	0	1138
MME	108	58	0	41	7	214
SME	0	142	29	12	2	185
Total (AME)	499	351	609	69	9	1536

Table 6.3: Employment Sample Countries 2008

Countries	Population		Labor force			Poverty	
	Million	ROG % p.a.	Total Millions	Female % of labor force	unemployment %	National Measure	Population below $1.25 a day
	Million 2008	1990-2008	2008	2008	2005-2008	%	%
Turkey	73.9	1.5	25.8	26.2	9.4	27.0	2.6
Indonesia	227.3	1.4	112.8	38.4	8.4	16.7	29.4
Saudi Arabia	24.6	2.3	9.0	16.3	5.6		
Iran	72.0	1.6	27.8	30.1	10.5	14.2	2
Malaysia	27.0	2.2	11.7	35.2	3.2	..	2
Nigeria	151.2	2.4	48.6	34.9	..	34.1	64.4
Pakistan	166.1	2.4	55.8	19.2	5.1	32.6	22.6
Egypt	81.5	1.9	26.3	23.9	8.7	16.7	2
Kazakhstan	15.7	−0.2	8.5	50.0	..	15.4	2
Bangladesh	160.0	1.8	76.8	40.9	4.3	40.0	49.6
LME	1110.80	2.32	444	27	7.4	23.8	16.90
MME	199.60	2.38	91	36	14.7	26.9	17.64
SME	62.30	2.33	73	43	8.4	51.3	46.02
Total (AME)	1372.70	2.30	608	35	10.2	34.0	26.85
World	6,697.3s	1.3	3,102.8t	40.4w	..w		
Low income	976.20	2.20	441.40	44.50	..		
Middle income	4652.30	1.30	2159.80	38.80	..		
High income	1068.70	0.70	501.50	43.30	5.90		

Source: World Bank development Indicator (WDI 2009)

Table 6.4: Economy Sample Countries 2008

Countries	GDP 2008 Million US$	Per Capita GDP US $	GDP (PPP) Million US$	Per Capita GDP (PPP) US $	GDP Growth % p.a. 2000-08	Exports of goods and services % GDP 2008	Imports of goods and services % of GDP 2008
Turkey	734,853	9944	1040275	14077	5.7	24	28
Indonesia	510,730	2247	966956	4254	5.2	30	29
Saudi Arabia	468,800	19057	594886	24182	4.1	69	38
Iran	286,058	3973	843860	11720	5.9	32	22
Malaysia	221,773	8214	384043	14224	5.5	110	90
Nigeria	207,118	1370	332681	2200	6.6	42	25
Pakistan	164,539	991	445549	2682	5.4	13	24
Egypt	162,283	1991	471475	5785	4.7	33	39
Kazakhstan	133,442	8499	183132	11664	9.5	57	37
Bangladesh	79,554	497	230395	1440	5.8	20	29
LME	3,836,904	3454				50	37.1
MME	491,408	2040				44	45.3
SME	100152	543				28	47.3
Total (AME)	4428464	2883				41	43.2
world	60,521,000	9037				28w	28w
Low income	564,572	578				34	47
Middle income	16,722,126	3594				31	30
High income	43,273,506	40492				27	28

Table 6.5: Education

Countries	Education							
	% of GDP 2008	% of total gov. exp 2008	pupils per teacher 2008	Gross Enrol ment Ratio	Male litrcy % 2005-08	Fem litrcy % 2005-08	Total litrcy % 2005-08	HDI Ranking 2010
Turkey	..	..	..	98	96	81	89	83.0
Indonesia	3.5	17.5	19	121	95	89	92	108.0
Saudi Arabia	..	..	11	98	90	80	85	55
Iran	4.8	20.0	20	128	87	77	82	70
Malaysia	4.7	..	16	98	94	90	92	57
Nigeria	..	..	46	93	72	49	61	142
Pakistan	2.9	11.2	41	85	67	40	54	125
Egypt	3.7	12.1	27	100	75	58	67	101.0
Kazakhstan	2.8	..	16	109	100	100	100	66.0
Bangladesh	2.4	14.0	44	94	60	50	55	129.0
LME	3.79	16.26	23.50	103.81	85	73	79.1	
MME	4.17	18.78	27.55	98.07	87	76	77.1	
SME	3.87	18.36	47.06	98.71	64	45	31.3	
Total (AME)	3.94	17.80	32.70	100.20	79	65	62.5	

Source: World Bank development Indicator (WDI 2009)

Table 6.6: Health

Countries	Total Expend % of GDP	Public Expenditure % of total	Physicians	Maternal mortality per 100,000	Infnt mortality per 1,000	Life expect at birth	Undernourishment % of Population
	2007	2007	2003-08	2000-08	2008	2008	2004-06
Turkey	5.0	69.0	1.5	29	20	72	<5
Indonesia	2.2	54.5	0.1	228	31	71	16
Saudi Arabia	3.4	79.5	1.6	10	18	73	<5
Iran	6.4	46.8	0.9	25	27	71	<5
Malaysia	4.4	44.4	..	30	6	74	<5
Nigeria	6.6	25.3	0.4	..	96	48	8
Pakistan	2.7	30.0	0.8	276	72	67	23
Egypt	6.3	38.1	2.4	84	20	70	<5
Kazakhstan	3.7	66.1	3.9	31	27	66	<5
Bangladesh	3.4	33.6	0.3	351	43	66	26
LME	4.00	57.24	1.40	125.00	30	70	
MME	5.35	45.67	1.31	301.29	41	66	
SME	5.55	44.15	0.40	688.40	88	55	
Total (AME)	5.00	49.02	1.01	371.56	53	64	
world	9.7w	59.6w	..w				14w
Low income	5.4	42.7	..	0	76	59	30
Middle income	5.4	50.2	1.3	0	41	69	13
High income	11.2	61.3	..	0	6	80	5

Table 6.7: Government Budgets

Countries	Revenue	Tax revenue	Cash surplus or deficit	Interest payment	Compensation of employees	Military expenditures	
	% of GDP	% of GDP	% of GDP	% of Revenue	% of expense	% of expense	% of GDP
	2008	2008	2008	2008	2008	2008	2008
Turkey	22.6	18.6	−1.9	24.2	26	9.5	2.2
Indonesia	..	..	..	..	..	..	1.0
Iran	34.8	7.3	7.9	0.8	38	12.6	2.9
Pakistan	13.4	9.8	−7.4	34.8	4	17.6	3.3
Egypt	27.7	15.4	−6.4	16.5	23	7.6	2.3
Kazakhstan	13.4	12.7	4.3	1.9	7	6.7	1.0
Bangladesh	11	8.8	−1.0	21.8	21	10.4	1.1
LME		17			25.50	11	2
MME		15			28.29	11	3
SME		15			35.57	12	2
Total (AME)		16			29.79	12	2
Middle income	20.2	14.2	−0.6	4	23	12.9	2
High income	27.9	17.8	−1.0	5	15	10.2	2.6

Source: World Bank development Indicator (WDI 2009)

Table 6.8: Natural Resources

Countries	Land Area	Arable Land	Population Density	freshwater resources	Energy Consumption Per Capita	International Reserves Ranking from top	
	thousnd sq. km	hacter per 100 people	Persons per Sq.km	Per capita cu.m	Kilogram oil per year	Oil	Gas
	2008	2005-07	2008	2007	2007	2008	2008
Turkey	769.6	31.8	96.02	3,109	1,370	53	83
Indonesia	1,811.6	9.9	125.47	12,578	845	26	12
Saudi Arabia	2,000.0	14.6	12.30	99	6,223	1	5
Iran	1,628.6	23.8	44.21	1,809	2,604	3	2
Malaysia	328.6	6.9	82.17	21,841	2,733	30	15
Nigeria	910.8	24.8	166.01	1,496	722	10	8
Pakistan	770.9	13.4	215.46	338	512	52	26
Egypt	995.5	3.8	81.87	22	840	25	20
Kazakhstan	2,699.7	148.1	5.82	4,871	4,292	11	
Bangladesh	130.2	5.1	1228.88	666	163	80	49
LME	1011	23	1098.71	3218	4096		
MME	361	21	552.91	9437	1364		
SME	430	29	144.88	5970	406		
Total (AME)	601	24	2284.03	6208	1955		
world	1296113	21.7w	5.17	6,616w	1819w		
Low income	18731.9	17.3	52.11	5004	423		
Middle income	77325.4	19.6	60.17	6350	1242		
High income	33,554	35	31.85	9305	5321		

Source: World Bank development Indicator (WDI 2009)

SECTION-II

Resource Development

7   Mineral Policy

Resource Curse

Natural resource is a curse, especially the mineral resources particularly when these are exploited by large foreign mining interests for export purposes without any linkage to the local host economy. Royalties of 2-4% are a mere pittance, as compared to the environmental degradation that is caused to local lands often depriving the poor communities of their livelihood. Resources have typically invited occupations, invasions and colonialism. Mineral resources generate local conflict and instability by promoting unrealistic dreams and ideologies bordering secession from other federating political entities. The empirical evidence is abundant. Only a few countries have positively benefited from mineral resources; which are Chile, Botswana and Malaysia etc. On the other hand, there is a long list of failed states and near-failed states that have mineral based economies. Do countries like Angola, Bolivia, Congo, Zaire, Mali, Chad and Sudan have an image of prosperity, growth and development; far from it?

A resource rich Kuwait invited aggression from greedy Saddam of Iraq, which many argue was done to keep oil supplies intact. Iraq is on course to dismemberment, as oil rich Kurdish areas want to go it alone with their oil and have already started exporting oil without central government's concurrence. Late Mujibur-Rehman laid the foundations of Bengali nationalism on "jute" once considered golden fiber and now forgotten as a dirty and coarse item, resulting in much repressive and retrogressive regimes of Major Zia as similar to Zia-ul-Haque of the parent country Pakistan. Nigeria was divided under factional fights. Almost all African mineral countries are suffering from one or the other kind of factional fight largely originated by quarrels over the exaggerated perceptions of mineral incomes and benefits.

Europe benefited from its coal, because it utilized its coal and fired its industry and power plants on it. Had they exported coal and depended on its export revenue, the face of Europe would have been different. Similar is the story of Australia and the USA. China and India consumed their iron and coal in an integrated industry with forward and back ward linkages. In the colonial period, the two countries were commodity exporters.

Economists have discovered many other side-effects of the resource-disease. One of it is Dutch effect. The steady stream of commodity exports, strengthen the currency and thus discourages exports of competitive local products, which require a continuously depreciating and competing currency. The non-resource sector suffers and does not develop. Based on new found wealth, in the form of oil price increase in 1973, Shah of Iran entered into a hasty and unprecedented militarization consuming petrodollars in weapons purchase. His lopsided economic policies and accompanied repression resulted in a revolution which again pursued un-economic policies due to resource abundance with the result of a bad economy, high inflation, stunted growth and persisting poverty. Similar is the case of other oil rich states of Arabia.

In Pakistan, people think that Pakistan is a resource abundant country. In hay days of communism, the popular myth was that the foreign countries were stealing our wealth. In the more enlightened period that followed and now, the myth is that Pakistan is a rich country but its rulers have looted it and do not let the country benefit from its resource richness. Far from truth, Pakistan is a poor country in terms of resource endowment. Water and land two basic resources are highly limited. Half the area is covered by troubled Balochistan where only8 million people live, and on the remaining half bulk of the population of 180 million is cramped. Baloch nationalists harp the mantra of exploitation, when Pakistan has not emerged on the map as a mineral country. There is very little mineral activity. Only Sui gas has been produced. In Saindak Copper project where GOP lost a lot of money and had to beg Chinese to take it over.

Balochistan resources would benefit Balochistan and rest of Pakistan due to the utilization of these resources in Pakistan economy creating jobs and skills for both Balochies and other Pakistanis. Other wise it would be the same as happened to rich Africa. I would strongly urge the GOP to arrange trips and visits of our nationalists leaders to Bolivia, Angola, Zaire, Congo and other mineral rich countries so that they can see vividly the worth of so called natural or mineral resources.

The perception of income from resource is ill founded. As mentioned earlier 2-4% royalty is a pittance. The market is structured around this pittance; you cannot insist on more, in view of prevailing competitive price and the over eagerness of host countries and their leadership, tribal and national, for easy money and the loot that usually follows.

However there is a pending case of correcting the gas royalty situation of Balochistan and paying the royalty arrears due to unrealistically low well head prices that were applied to Sui gas. I have made a strong case in favor of Balochistan in a separate particle.

National Mineral Policy-1995

NMP-1995 had been a good omen and a start for Pakistan's mineral sector. The policy recognized eminent provincial domain in minerals, and has therefore not faltered at the door of provincial autonomy drive that culminated in the 18th amendment. The policy has been welcomed and accepted by the provinces and the provincial governments have made rule under the policy to give it a formal and legal cover. Hence we have Balochistan Mining Rules 2002.

The policy recognizes the role of DFI and aims to encourage it. It calls for efficiency, transparency and promptness in dealing with investors and in the award of exploration licenses and mining leases. However, as has been made apparent in the Rekodeq controversy, there seem to be some grey areas that need to be clarified.

There is a genuine case of encouraging and requesting the higher bureaucracy and national scientists to read the policy carefully and abide by it. If it is not considered to be correct, then propose and effect changes in it or revoke it altogether with a due process and without retrospectivity. No where the policy requires do-it-yourself- approach, so as to warrant or justify the preparation and approval of ECNEC PC-I that we have discussed and elaborated upon elsewhere. If at all, the policy discourages the involvement of public sector and refers to the privatization of existing mineral development corporations that are engaged in the business of mining. Despite the failures and losses of SAINDAK, it requires obduracy of the highest order to make the claims of local capability. NMP must be revised, and should discourage DFI, in favor of do-it-yourself-approach, if that be the preference of the elected representatives. The approval granted to ECNEC project should be withdrawn at the very least, if not to suggest action against the proposers and approvers.

Secondly, more clarity may be built in the award of Mining Leases and the security of tenure thereof. An explicit statement with respect to a seamless transition of Exploration License into Mining Lease is brought in, in case of DFI. A secure and hassle free process, as opposed to what is happening in Rekodeq, may go a long way , towards attracting mining investments. Separate treatment provided to, Exploration License's conversion, direct lease and deferred lease. The role of bidding, obviously not in the case of exploration done by the investor, needs to be elaborated upon. There are some difficult issues though in the ideal of seamless conversion. The question is that do we award a carte-blanche to the investor in proposing whatever he may deem fit, simply because he has undertaken the exploration. One may consider compensation. But the investors work for profits and not the compensations. Some creative thinking has to be done to bring more structure and detail in this grey area.

Provinces may be encouraged to launch a mineral development fund or the same could be organized at federal level with provincial participation and representation in it. The MDF could be financed through royalty earnings of the provinces, donor funds and a Mineral cess on mineral exports, as has been done in the case of textile sector. Exploration activities could be funded out of MDF. Also some money is to be spent in organizing the Exploration Licensing divisions at provincial level. Bidding could be encouraged for the award of Exploration Licenses or for free acreage Mine licensing on which no exploration investment may have been done by some investors. Infact a balance may be maintained between bidding and non-bidding approaches and licensing activities thereof.

NMP-95 does provide for a transaction advisor, and even for an arbitrator and eventual recourse to the International Centre of Settlement of Investment Disputes (ICSID).However, one requires input into project design. In most countries where Laissez-fare investor friendly regime works, there is freedom of choice to the investor to design a commercial project, keeping in view his own business interests and strengths and strategies. Raw exports of Copper concentrate can be done and is done from the USA without discussion, in India it may be an affront; and perhaps with us as well. Sometimes, a good policy is not to have a policy, which is roundly opposed by conservative economic thinkers.

Thirdly, royalty clauses may be improved and made more comprehensive. It is no use, building in attractive and competitive royalty conditions that are not finally implementable and acceptable politically at home, being opposed and dubbed as looting, as the case of Rekodeq seems to indicate. There is a case for adequate royalty provisions, with an upward revision of rates, and providing for incentives for local processing and disincentives for raw exports (export duty on raw exports or higher royalty). It has been found in most rules and laws in Pakistan which falter in implementation and do more damage than a seemingly inferior law would have. Such a gap between what ought to be done and what is feasible, ultimately results in breakdown of the law and encourages nepotism and corruption , giving a long and flexing stick in the hands of those who are to oversee the execution of the law.

Fourthly, no law or policy is absolutely correct and efficient and inclusive enough to be able to work in all times and spaces. There is a role of implementation as well. Small provinces where the minerals really are lack the capacity in dealing with massive DFI projects. They can at best handle the local mining companies, and that may be in question as well.NMP-95 provided for Mineral Investment Facilitation Board, which has not been brought into being. It may be, however, an over-kill and be wasteful to have a full time set-up for this. A committee, serviced by a cell in the Foreign Investment Board may be helpful. Similarly, MIFA has been recommended by NMP-95 at the provincial level.

The idea is to provide a forum for having a broad control of mineral licensing processes and provide a grievance handling mechanism at the provincial level. Again a full scale authority and a full-time organization would be an over-kill and in today's environment of at least talking about frugality, it is totally out of fashion. Mineral regulatory function, however, could be organized at Federal level, as are other regulatory agencies. These could serve as tribunals for hearing complaints against provincial licensing authorities, especially where DFI is involved. Government organization and functionaries ought to respect government policy. And to close it with some humor, let me reproduce as somebody once said; our policy is to have no policy.

Fifthly, and finally, the issue of balancing the provincial and federal take (income) in the mineral sector has to be examined, creatively and sympathetically. Often the royalty income (which goes to the producing province) may be less, than the corporate Tax (which goes to the Federal government).This does breed discontent and may be exploited by the secessionists and the vested interest, feeding on conspiracy theories and megalomanias of varying kind. Market for the latter is very hot these days in our country.

There are two aspects to it. In the US and possibly some other federations, states and provinces are also eligible to impose and collect corporate and personal income tax. In the US, the most dominant rate is 15% Corporate Income Tax rate for the state/province. This is deductable, in most cases, from the income tax filing of the federal government of USA. This also solves the mineral sector issue as well, as it is inclusive. The second aspect is of our own system. Eminent domain of the provinces has been recognized in Agriculture, although the case is weaker for the latter than minerals. Agriculture depends on many more inputs than just land and draws upon more varied inputs which may have a common domain. Agricultural income tax has been passed on to the provinces, although for passing the buck, than being the real intention. Theoretically, this generates a case for sharing corporate Income Tax coming from mining with the provinces.

Sixthly and similarly, there is a tendency to centralize within the provinces. Provinces demand devolution and decentralization of powers and functions away from the centre and deny the same downwards to the local bodies. What is opposed and taken by the provinces from the centre is denied down to the local body. Decentralization is not ethnic or linguistic; it is for freedom, liberty and efficiency. Mining generates quite some nuisance to the host districts and Tehsils. Their land is almost permanently damaged and land use permanently altered. Some mineral revenue should be formally shared with the local bodies under statutes. Land rent and property taxes must directly go to the locals. Current rules deny the locals with any such provisions and largely depend on the largesse and arbitrary determination of the provincial administrations. The mineral policy does provide for some modest contribution to the social sector of the host local population, to be made by the mining company. That may not be enough or judicious at all and even may not be respectable, if one goes by the haranguing of some lawyers in the SC on the subject.

Table 7.1: Mining Company Ranking of Investment Decision Criteria

Exploration stage	Mining stage	Investment decision criteria
1	n.a.	Geological potential for target mineral
n.a.	**3**	**Measure of profitability**
2	1	Security of tenure
3	2	Ability to repatriate profits
4	9	Consistency and constancy of mineral policies
5	7	Company has management control
6	11	Mineral ownership
7	6	Realistic foreign exchange regulations
8	4	Stability of exploration and mining terms
9	**5**	**Ability to predetermine tax liability**
10	8	Ability to predetermine environmental obligations
11	**10**	**Stability of fiscal regime**
12	12	Ability to raise external financing
13	16	Long-term national stability
14	17	Established mineral titles system
15	n.a.	Ability to apply geologic assessment techniques
16	**13**	**Method and level of tax levies**
17	15	Import-export policies
18	18	Majority equity ownership held by company
19	21	Right to transfer ownership
20	20	Internal (armed) conflicts
21	14	Permitted external accounts
22	19	Modern mineral legislation

Source: James Otto, et al, Mining Royalties – World Bank, 2006.

Table 7.2: Foreign Investor Internal Rate of Return and Total Effective Tax Rate for a Model Copper Mine in Selected Countries and States

Country	Foreign investor IRR (%)	Total effective tax rate (%)
Lowest taxing quartile		
Sweden	15.7	28.6
Chile	15.0	36.6
Argentina	13.9	40.0
Papua New Guinea (2003)	**13.8**	**42.7**
Zimbabwe	13.5	39.8
Philippines	13.5	45.3
2nd lowest taxing quartile		
South Africa	13.5	45.0
Greenland	13.0	50.2
Kazakhstan	12.9	46.1
Western Australia	12.7	36.4
China	12.7	41.7
United States (Arizona)	12.6	49.9
2nd highest taxing quartile		
Indonesia (7th, COW)	12.5	46.1
Tanzania	12.4	47.8
Ghana	11.9	54.4
Peru	11.7	46.5
Bolivia	11.4	43.1
Mexico	11.3	49.9
Highest taxing quartile		
Indonesia (non-COW 2002)	11.2	52.2
Poland	11.0	49.6
Papua New Guinea (1999)	10.8	57.8
Ontario, Canada	10.1	63.8
Uzbekistan	9.3	62.9
Côte d'Ivoire	8.9	62.4
Burkina Faso	3.3	83.9

Source: James Otto, et al, Mining Royalties – World Bank, 2006.

130

8   Rekodeq Copper and Gold Project

There has been a lot of controversy these days over the Rekodeq Copper and Gold project. A foreign company Tethyan   has completed exploration of the resource located in Chaghi, the famous place where Pakistan's first nuclear explosion was carried out, and has prepared and submitted a feasibility study for consideration and approval of the government of Balochistan. The company claims, and perhaps rightly so that it has spent some 200 million US dollar on the project studies and exploration over the past several years. The company expects that it is given mining rights pursuant to its exploratory efforts and investments. The company proposes to bring a foreign investment of 3.2 billion USD and has provided for spending 50% of the investment on local procurement of goods and services. For seemingly archaic confidentiality reasons, the company has refrained from revealing its feasibility study, which has created doubts and controversy among the mind of general public. The project is being opposed by many quarters. This article takes account of the debate and the arguments, attempts to build a picture of the project in terms of real numbers, develops proposals on royalty issue based on international practices and in conclusion broadly supports the project, while advising Government of Balochistan to avail the services of third party experts in contract negotiations with the company.

Project Data

We do not have access to the feasibility study of the project and its numbers. The company has been releasing vague and variable global statements regarding potential income and revenues to Governments of Balochistan and the federation. It would have been in its own enlightened interest to release figures on important issues like royalty rates and mineral prices. However based on the project data released by the company on expected production volumes, a back-of-the-envelope calculation can be made, which provides the following projections based on currently prevailing prices.

Based on an annual production as proposed by the company of 200,000 tons of copper and 250,000 ounces of Gold in concentrate form, an annual sales turnover of 2.345 Billion US dollars could be expected. At a 5% royalty on sales and 25% share in Equity of the Government of Balochistan would generate 158 Million US dollars, while GOP would be netting 95 Million USD in corporate taxes, if tax exemption is not extended to the project. Foreign investor would be earning an after tax profit of 200 Million USD per year. In this configuration, Pakistan side earns 244 Million US Dollars, 44 Million USD more than the company. The proposed royalty offer should be a subject of negotiation and may be brought in line with the standard and usual royalty rate of 5% on sales value. In that case Pakistan revenue would total to a good 256 million USD. Over the project's life time, Pakistan Earns 12.2 billion USD and the company earns 10.0 billion USD. With this small proviso, one would like to support the project. Probably, the biggest impact of the project would be on the balance of payment with exports and foreign exchange earnings of more than two billion USD.

Let us take the example of Australian mining industry which is known for its size and profitability. In the year 2008-9, the profitability of mining industry remained highest, higher than any other sector of Australian economy, with a 37.1% pre-tax gross margin. However, nearly half the firms, usually smaller firms, remained in loss. This also means that large mining companies made even a higher than 37.1% margin. This is in a period when mineral prices are exceptionally high. More realistic and conservative estimates of profitability (before tax) in Australian mining sector put it at 15-16%.

Many argue that there is significant price manipulation especially in Copper. We must not be afraid of high profits, as GOB is going to have a 25% share in equity. There may be downturns also, with low demand and low price which can go down below the cost of production.

Table 8.1: Rekodeq profits, royalties and Revenue projections (guess-estimates)

Assumptions		USD	%	50 year Revenue
		One year revenue	Percent	
Total deposit Tonnage	billion tons	5.9		
Economic Deposit	billion tons	2.5		
Ore composition				
Ore copper	%	0.53		
Ore Gold content	gms per ton	0.30		
Ore concentrate				
Copper output	Tons per year	200,000		
Gold output	Oz per yr	250,000		
Average selling price CU	USD per lb	2.2		
Avg. selling price gold	USD per Oz	1,200		
Royalty rate	% of sales	5		
Before Tax Profit	% of sales	30		
Tax rate	% of profit	30		
GOB Equity	%	25		
Estimates & Projections				
Sales Total o/w		1,268,000,000	100.00	63,400,000,000
Sales Copper		968,000,000	76.34	48,400,000,000
Sales Gold		300,000,000	23.66	15,000,000,000
Annual Royalties		63,400,000	5.00	3,170,000,000
Estimated Profit o/w		380,400,000	30.00	19,020,000,000
GOB share		95,100,000	7.50	4,755,000,000
Tethyan Profit b. Tax		285,300,000	22.50	14,265,000,000
Tax Rev. GOP		85,590,000	6.75	4,279,500,000
After tax Profit Tethyan		199,710,000	15.75	9,985,500,000
Total GOB Revenue		158,500,000	12.50	7,925,000,000
Total Pakistan Rev		244,090,000	19.25	12,204,500,000
Asset value				
Ore Copper Value	Billion USD	64.13		
Ore Gold Value	Billion USD	31.68		
Total	Billion USD	95.81		
Asset value(@royalty rate)		4.79		

Source: Authors Estimate: Based on Tethyan website data

Table 8.2: Top Twelve of world's 250 copper mines

Project	Company	Cu (tpa)
Escondida Chile	BHPB/Rio	1,400,000
Grasberg Indonesia	Freeport	600,000
Chunquicomale Chile	Codelco	550,000
Norlisk	MMC/Norlisk	425,000
El-Temiente Chile?	Codelco	400,000
Antamine (underground)	BHB Xatra Tech	390,000
Molenci	Phelps	380,000
Toqepola + Cuenzane Peru	S.Pem Copper	370,000
Batu Hiju	New Mont	325,000
Los pelambres Chile	Anto fagosta	320,000

Table 8.3: Major Producing countries of Copper

Countries	Concentrate	Electro-win	Total
Peru	1,107,789	160,078	1,267,867
USA	801,000	507,000	1,310,000
Zambia	383,000	163,000	546,000
Australia	833,000	53,000	886,000
Brazil	206,000	-	206,000
Canada	606,999	-	606,999
Chile	3,356,600	1,973,700	5,330,300
China	940,000	20,000	960,000
Congo (knishst)	189,000	46,000	235,000
India	648,000	-	648,000
Indonesia	632,600		632,600
Iran	241,000	8000	249,000
Kazakhstan	420,000	-	420,000
Mexico	172,093	74,500	246,593
Leos	24929	64075	89,007
Mongolia	129,500	-	129,500
Papa New Genuea	159,650	-	159,650
Others	-	-	-
Grand Total	**12,400,000**	**3,040,000**	**15,400,000**

Valuation of the Rekodeq deposit

Let us have an appreciation of the realistic valuation of the Rekodeq deposit. It all depends on what price of copper is assumed. At this moment Copper is being quoted at 4.35 USD per lb. It had gone to as high as 5 USD in 2007-8 and it was only 1.00 USD per lb in1996 to 2003.It was only 0.5 USD per lb only in 1980s, which made Saindak project unfeasible for many years and later went into losses for the same reason. These prices may come down again from the present day high. Tethyan has revealed its calculation basis at 2.2 USD per lb as a long term average price, which may be taken as reasonable. Gold can be expected to continue to go high and a price of 1200 USD per Oz appears to be a reasonable assumption.

Table 8.4: Top Ten Mining companies

Company	Mining output (Cu)
Co- delco	1,840,000
Phelps Dodge	1,389,600
BHP Billiton	1,028,000
Groupo Mexico	874,000
Anglo America PLC	766,000
Rio-Tinto Group	753,100
KGHM Polska SA	550,066
Falcon Bridge	491,000
Xastra PLC	460,643
Free Port-McmoRan	452,000

Source: Various

As revealed by the company on its website, the total Rekodeq deposit is of 5.9 billion tons, out of which 2.2 billion tons has been declared as economically feasible. Ore composition averages at 0.41% of copper and .22 Gms per ton, which is rather low grade. The company proposes to mine the richer parts with an average of 0.53% of Copper and 0.3 Gms per ton of gold. At these prices, the total surface value of the deposit comes out to be 96 Billion USD out of which one-third would be Gold and two-third would be Copper. It must be borne in mind that, it is the surface value which is obtained by putting in some two-third of this figure as a production cost. To realize the 100 billion USD of the asset value, 70 billion USD has to go towards production costs. Its valuation in buried form as it is today may be computed as the present value of earning streams to the parties involved. As a rough measure, it can be valued at the royalty rate for Pakistan which comes out to be only 4.79 billion USD.

Samar Mubarakmand (SMM) proposal

Dr. Samar Mubarakmand ,formerly Chairman NESCOM and currently Member Science & Technology Planning Commission of Pakistan , has got a Project for Rekodeq mining approved from ECNEC , while it is not known on whose behalf it is .His project ,hereinafter called SMM project ,proposes a Mining and Mineral processing facility to produce Electrolytic/Electro-won copper. It's claimed output is 15000 of ore per day and 45000 tons of Electrolytic copper per annum. The project cost (CAPEX) proposed are only 54.3 Million USD and an operating cost component of 90 million USD per annum. Please see Table 7.5   for details. Apparently no major mining equipment has been included and the reliance is made on the output and capabilities of local private sector mining companies and labor force.

Yet, there is another variant of the project, with only 5000 tons per day of ore, which means an annual Copper output of only 6-7000 tons per year, with identical capital cost. Perhaps these are the original figures of the ECNEC approved project, from which later extrapolations have been made. This later one is too small to have any value. Although the project has been championed by big names, as has been mentioned earlier, we have a number of questions about the project structure and strategy.

Firstly, it is highly doubtful, if the local mining companies can provide the require output on a daily basis. Secondly, the mining out put provided cannot give the required output of 45000 tons. Based on an ore concentration of 41% Copper, the Copper output would be around 20000 tons per annum .If this output is taken as a base, then the variable cash cost comes out to be 4500 USD per ton, which is more than three times the cash cost of TCC, which although may be compensated by low capital cost, appears to be still too high to be economic. This is in line with the international and national mining cost data which indicates that low capital small scale mining is uneconomic. Most of the Copper projects today are in the range of 110,000 tons per day as proposed by TCC .Even if we take into account the higher prices of finished copper of SMM option, it hardly break evens, and generates a meager Gross profit of 10.57 million USD per year. Adding the contribution of Gold, the SMM project yields a gross profit of 2.959 billion USD which may not be able to pay even the royalty, and not to talk of any profits or taxes to the Federal government. Infact with such a low margin , the risk is that it may go into down right losses, as most public sectors do .The common theme in public sector projects is under-estimation of costs and over-estimates of revenues .On the revenue side also , the most optimistic prices of 9350 USD per ton have been assumed. It is this factor which has led the ECNEC proponents to suggest that their Cost to price ratio is 30:70 as opposed to 70:30 for TCC, argued by them. Current prices these days are all time high prices and may not sustain very long over the project life cycle of 56 years. TCC has taken a more conservative figure of 2.2 USD per lb or 4840 USD per ton. This may have been advised to TCC by expensive market studies that may not be in public domain. Our projections for SMM have provided for another 500 USD per ton higher for SMM for its finished product out put.

Table 8.5: SMM vs Tethyan Proposals Compared

	Units	SMM		Tethyan	
		Total Value	USD/ton	Total Value	USD per ton
Product		Electrolytic Copper		Cu Concentrate	
Output Mine	Tons per day	15000		1100000	
Output Product Real Claimed	Tons per day	45000			
Output Product Real	Tons per Year	20000		220000	
Cash cost	Million USD	90	4500	220	1200
Revenue/Selling price	Million USD	106	5300	1064.8	4840
project cost(Capex)	Million USD	54.3		3200	
Financial cost	Million USD	5.43	271.5	320	1454.54 5455
Production Cost			4771.5		2654.54 5455
Gross Profit	Million USD	10.57	528.5	480.8	2185.45 4545
Gross Profit 56 years	Million USD	591.92		26924.8	
Add 25% for Gold	Million USD	147.98		6731.2	
Total Life cycle Gross Profit	Million USD	739.9		33656	
On Capacity Expansion	Million USD	2959.6			
Govt. Share (52%)	Million USD				

Source: Basic Data from ECNEC project report 2009 & TCC website

It is rather obvious that 5000 tons per day ore capacity project is a toy project, as compared to the TCC project of 110,000 tons per day. By no sense of imagination, it can graduate, in some near or even distant future, to internationally competitive scale. And certainly, the projections of delivering 132 Billion USD to Balochistan government's coffers are grossly unrealistic. It is rather unfortunate that overnight, ECNEC project capacity has been tripled for public consumption purposes, without making any upward revision in capital costs and erroneous, if not false, claims of an output of 45,000 tons per year of Finished Copper have been made.

Table 8.6: SMM ECNEC Project

Description	Units		Mn. USD
Copper Ore Output	Tons per day	5000	
Finished Copper Output	Tons per day	20.5	
	Tons per yr	6765	
Capital Cost	Million Rs	4619	54.3412
Cash Cost (annual)	Million Rs	1816	21.3647
O/W Raw Material Cost (local)	Million Rs	338	
Cash Cost per Ton	Rs per Ton	268440.503	3158.12
O/W R.M. Cost(local) per Ton		204.848485	

Source: ECNEC PC-1, 2009

Concluding, it appears that SMM project has not been prepared without adequate care , neither in terms of basic parameters and nor in other project data. As we will see later, this scribe has much more fundamental reasons not to support SMM hypothesis than the accuracy of its figures, as we shall

The arguments against

The foreign company led investment project involving three billion US Dollars is being opposed by various quarters. Firstly, there is a general and usual argument of Baloch exploitation with generalities and statement of lot of generally known grievances, which are not specific to this project alone. Their specific complaint is that they get very little out of the exploitation of their natural resources. They have very little say or control on such projects and that most Baloch cannot even enter those project   areas, as those are declared as "sensitive" installations. Secondly, there are those who think that government of Balochistan is not getting a fair deal from the company and that it should get more than what has been offered. They believe that international tendering would have resulted in a better deal.

Thirdly, there are objections on project structure whereby refining and smelting has been proposed by Tethyan to be done abroad by third parties. The objectors argue that refining and smelting must be done locally to have higher component of local value added .Fourthly, there is a section of a very powerful scientific community belonging to the nuclear programme that argues that such a valuable project should not be handed over to foreign companies at all and that the government of Balochistan stands to get much more income if their proposition and approach is accepted. They claim that having built the BOMB, they have acquired practical expertise over a number of minerals and its value chain and that they can do it and should be involved. They have made similar claims with respect to Thar Coal and have been provided the resources to prove their point on a small scale.

Let us examine the merit of these arguments one by one. The Baloch question and the point of view of nationalist circles is too broad an issue and have many facets. Most readers would be familiar with it. It requires a separate space to elucidate on it; hence we drop the very first objection as mentioned earlier. However, we would keep in view the genuine issues as pertaining to this project. Let me bring in some facts and back ground data.

The Resource Curse and the political economy

Many economists dislike mineral sector and have coined the term of Resource Curse. They question the rationale and impact of mineral sector on the welfare of the host countries. The evidence is divided, of the countries who have lost and who have prospered as a result of mineral production and exports. They cite that except for small population oil producing countries and a few other mineral countries in developing countries, most others are basket case poor countries despite their large mineral resources and their extraction and exploitation.

This scribe is not very fond of mineral exports either and often has sided with the "resource curse" argument. The mineral resource has often caused dissension among the sections of the mineral countries and has resulted in much political instability and in-fighting. However, Pakistan is today passing through a critical period and is in great need of exports, foreign exchange and investments and priming of employment generating economic activity. And these arguments can be postponed for better times. We have to evaluate the project not only in long term but also in its short to medium run impact, which seems to be positive and value-enhancing in the light of the afore-mentioned data.

The real contention may, however, lie within Pakistan, as Baloch nationalists, if not the government may argue that federal government makes more money than the royalty of the owners of the resource. This is a usual problem with mineral industries. The problem can be resolved with an appropriate sharing of corporate income tax from mineral resources among federal and provincial government. In several democracies including the US, provinces do collect or share in income taxes as well.

Table 8.7: Comparison – Copper projects in pipeline (next 4-8 years)

Project	Owner	Plant	Cu ktpa	Gold koz pa	Capex US$
Olym pic Dam expansion	BHPB	60 Mtpa All Leach	515	700	+20B
Oyu Tolgoi – Mongolia	Rio / Ivanhoe	48 Mtpa	450	320	+5B?
Pebble – Alaska	Rio/ Anglo	73 Mtpa	400	680	+4B?
Tampakan – Philippines	Xstrata / Indophil	44-66 Mtpa	340	360	5.2B
La Granja – Peru	Rio Tinto	84 Mtpa All Leach	300	n/a	3.38
Toromocho – Peru	Codelco	55 Mtpa + 8 Mtpa Leach	228	n/a	3.28
Frieda – PNG	HIG/Xstrata	+40-50 Mtpa	200-250	260-320	4.4 B
Las Bambas – Peru	Xstrata	18 Mtpa	200	48	2.8B
El Pachon – Argentina	Xstrata	40 Mtpa	150	n/a	2.9B
Reko Diq - Pakistan	Antafagosta Barrick	26 Mtpa + 7Mtpa Leach	150	212	2.8B
Other Recent New Projects					
Lumwana-Zambia	Equinox	20 Mtpa	120	n/a	US$ 841M
Promonent Hill	OZ Minerals	8 Mtpa	100	60	A$1.1 5B

Source: Highlands Pacific Group Brochure

A review of world mineral sector

There are more than thirty countries where Copper is mined and more than ten countries where abundant Copper resources are there. It may be appropriate to mention here that China has recently acquired Copper deposits in Afghanistan ignoring Pakistan understandably, inter -alia, to avoid an acrimonious debate that usually follows in Pakistan on such projects. There is no shortage of mineral deposits in the world especially of copper. International mining companies have options and usually they select easier and receptive locations. This however does not mean that we need not work for a better deal. Our demands and negotiations should be in line with the international practices and be competitive with other host countries. I have suggested elsewhere that foreign experts from multilateral agencies be inducted to assist in these negotiations so that reasonably maximum terms are negotiated and adequate protection and provisions are built in the long term contract of this nature.

Mineral sector is one of the most difficult areas of business. Metals are known to have a highly variable and cyclical price behavior. For several years there may be a glut resulting in depressed prices to be followed by a period of high demand and very high prices. International mining companies balance out the peaks and troughs through various business devices such as long term contracts, diversifying investments across metals, region and timings of investments to be able to take care of such difficulties. So it is not just the technical ability and the initial investment requirements but having the infrastructure and wherewithal that enables them to stay in business and make profit for their share-holders. There should also be an objective and realistic appreciation of the valuation of mineral resources. A mineral buried in earth hardly has a value share of 3-5% of the selling price of the mined ore .More than ninety-five percent of value comes through expenditure and investment of the mining company, whether it is local or foreign. There are three income streams; royalty goes to the owner of the resource, which as per our constitution is the provincial government of Balochistan; profits go to the share-holders in proportion to their equity investments; and the corporate and personal taxes go to the federal government.

Economics of Copper mining and Processing

Profitability of Copper mining companies has been very high for the last five years due to high copper prices. Against Cash costs of 100-140 cents per lb, the selling price of copper is around 400 cents per lb. EPS(earning per share) over the last five years has been varying between 67 cents and 170 cents per share of many copper mining companies including Antafagosta. Copper mines are also shut down, and not infrequently, when copper prices come down to the level of cash costs. Copper is sold at Exchange prices (LME, NYSE, and Chinghai) and also under long term price and supply contracts. Price Hedging through Futures is a routine practice both in buying and selling inputs and outputs respectively. This makes the life of small parties and newcomers very difficult, a factor that the proponents of self reliance should be mindful of. We have also noted it in the case of Saindak. Modern large scale mining and processing are capital intensive operations. In the adjoining Table , we provide the CAPEX details of some of the Copper mining projects that are in the pipe-line. We find that most projects are in the range of 3-5 Billion USD. Two-third of the Cash (variable) costs are consumed by Energy (12%), Administration (11%), Equipment Rental(11%), Labor (11%), Maintenance (11%) and Explosives(19%).The adjoining pie chart provides the detailed break-down of Cash costs.

Table 8.8: Cost Structure of Copper Mining

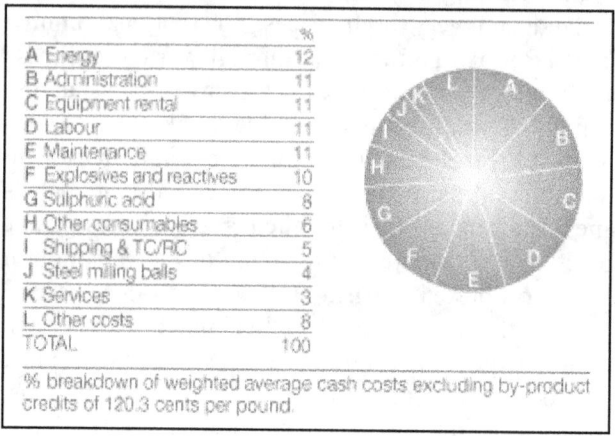

	%
A Energy	12
B Administration	11
C Equipment rental	11
D Labour	11
E Maintenance	11
F Explosives and reactives	10
G Sulphuric acid	8
H Other consumables	6
I Shipping & TC/RC	5
J Steel milling balls	4
K Services	3
L Other costs	8
TOTAL	100

% breakdown of weighted average cash costs excluding by-product credits of 120.3 cents per pound.

The adjoining table gives a break-down of Cash costs of Antafagosta, whereby 56% of the expense goes towards defraying prime costs of Energy, labor, maintenance etc., and 26% goes towards consumables.

Royalty rates and practices

Royalty rates and practices vary a great deal among mineral producing countries; most fall within a range of 3-5% of sales value of the produce. (Pls see the table)Federal US charges 5% flat rate, while states like Arizona. Michigan charges 2-7% on adjusted sales values. China charges 2% on sales for Copper and 4% for Gold, in both cases with an additional 0.4-30 Yuan per ton depending on price conditions which may total up to 3% for copper and 5% for Gold. Arizona (US) provides for a minimum slab of 2%. Some countries allow a variable rate depending on the price variation of the minerals and some allow upward or downwards adjustments of sales value. In a few cases, royalty is linked to profits, which may be highly contentious and unfeasible in countries like ours.

India charges 3.2% on sales, with the sales price objectively determined by LME prices.

There is quite some scope of understatement and transfer-pricing if India-like precise criteria are not applied. In Western Australia (in federal countries, there is variation of royalty practices across the states and provinces), an interesting royalty practice is there, which may be relevant to the current debate in Pakistan with respect to the local processing of ore. In that country, 5 % royalty is charged on concentrates and 2.5% on processed metal. GOB could negotiate something on these lines. In slumps and recessions when metals demand is low, mineral producing governments allow discounts on contracted royalties in order to remain competitive and earn foreign exchange ,if nothing else. Thus a royalty of 5% on sales gross or net is the maximum that can be reasonably expected, and one should not go down below 3%. A variable rate within this range could provide for price variations and local processing incentives.

Table 8.9: Royalty Rates and practices in various countries (% of sales unless, otherwise specified)

	Copper	Gold
Queens land	2.7% + plus	2.7% + plus
Arizona (USA)	2% (Min)	2% (Min)
Michigan (USA)	2-7%	2-7% of adjusted value
China	2% + 0.4-30 Yuan per tonne	4% + 0.4-30 Yuan per tonne
Brazil	2%	1%
Venezuela	3%	3%
Argentina	3%	3%
Botswana	3%	5%
India	3.20%	
New South Wales Australia	4%	4% less AD
Nevada	5% of net proceeds	
Western Australia	5% on concentrate 2.5% or processed	
USA (federal)	5%	5%
Saskatchewan	5-10% of profit	5 - 10% of profit
Zambia	5%	5%
Namibia	5%	5%
Canada (North)	5-14% on profit	5-14%
Ontario Canada	10% of profit	10% of profit
Philippine	2%	

Source: Mining Royalties: The World Bank

The Aynak Counterpart project in Afghanistan

Aynak deposit is located in Aynak valley, situated only 20 kms from Kabul in the South West. It used to be an Al-Qaida training camp. The copper deposit was extensively explored by the Soviets and later evaluated by the British Geological survey. Aynak has been termed as the second largest undeveloped copper deposit in the world. Its copper resource has been assessed as 240Mt at an ore concentration of 2.4%.

Aynak is reportedly much more profitable resource due to its high ore concentration of 1.95-2.4% as opposed to 0.41 % of Rekodeq. At an assumed price of 7100 USD per tonne , a constant revenue stream of 400 million USD per year for 30 years project life have been contracted for among the parties, perhaps slightly less than twice that offered in case of Rekodeq for an equal production volume. The proponent argues that the difference is due to the richness of Aynak deposit. Five times lesser earth has to be dug and processed in Aynak, than is required in the case of Rekodeq. These claims can be verified. But surprisingly and more importantly , the distribution arrangements are identical, i.e. 52% of the gross profit goes to the governments in both the projects. There is an exception, however. Government of Balochistan has to put in 25% in equity which comes out to be 250 million US dollars. The proponent has offered to sweeten the deal for arranging the equity finance for the government of Balochistan as an interest free loan.

Let us have a look at the figures of Aynak deposit which may be comparable in the sense that the production volume of both the projects is identical; 220,000 tons per year for Aynak and 200,000 tons per year for Rekodeq. Aynak project was fully explored by the Soviet Union under its occupation terms. However, the Afghan Aynak deposit is reportedly much richer than Rekodeq; 1.85 % metal content than 0.41 % of Rekodeq. This would mean that 3.7 times more earth in the case of Rekodeq may have to be dug and processed than Aynak. This may result in a proportionate increase in operating costs, with the variable differences due to technological choices. Reportedly, this has resulted in much lesser project yield of 10-12% ,which is on the lower side of the returns as compared to the other projects elsewhere.. Please see the adjoining table reproduced from World Bank sources. No wonder Chinese did not take interest in Rekodeq and opted for more profitable fixed price arrangement In Aynak deposit. Otherwise Chinese presence in Balochistan and Pakistan is much more entrenched and welcome. They are involved in Saindak project and are receiving muted criticism from the same quarters which are opposing Rekodeq/Tethyan project. Chinese perhaps realized the potential of bickering and wrangling, innuendos and down right embarrassment as is being currently witnessed.

The Fixed Price formula in case of Aynak

According to the unconfirmed reports, CMG has offered a fixed price deal to the Afghan government guaranteeing a fixed amount per year irrespective of the ups and down in prices. It has been estimated that the cumulative revenue impact of both the deals, Rekodeq/Tethyan and Aynak/CMG, are almost identical and equivalent under certain price conditions i.e.13 Billion USD over the projects life period to the host governments. Variable offers, as offered by Tethyan proposal, links royalties, profits and taxation income to the host government with the prevailing copper prices in the international market. Host government shares in the wind fall profits and revenues and loses when the prices are low. Fixed price offers are easier for Chinese state companies which are less sensitive to the long term risks. Fixed price offer would have been much more unacceptable in Pakistan politically under an atmosphere full of conspiracy theories, hyperbole and mistrust. On the other hand the variable offer as made by Tethyan has not been fully comprehended by the general public.

What ever are the perceptions, real or imaginary, regarding the value and preciousness of the Rekodeq deposit, the host governments of Balochistan and Pakistan get their share under the formula. Under fixed price conditions, the scope for mis-understanding would have been much higher and would have been termed much more scandalous than it is being perceived currently. A fixed price contract would have been riskier entailing higher risk laden interest rates for project finance.

On the other hand the yearly proceeds and the present value of earnings in the case of Aynak project, would be almost double that of Rekodeq/Tethyan due to the shorter project life of the Aynak , concentrating the revenues of 13 billion in half the period. This probably is the reward of higher ore concentration of Aynak, and partly perhaps the frugality of Chinese.

Why can't the same competitive process be adopted in case of Rekodeq?

Recently, a contract to develop and exploit the Aynak deposit has been awarded to a Chinese company, named China Metallurgical Group (CMG).Initially, out of a list of 14 international mining companies, 9 were shortlisted and invited to bid. 5 companies submitted their bids, and CMG was finally selected and was awarded a thirty year lease. World Bank has been providing technical support and a consulting company acted as transaction advisor .World renowned NGOs are monitoring the contract implementation and the environmental issues. The whole process has been handled in a highly transparent, structured and technically sound manner, amidst grumbling by the losers that CMG has bribed the Afghan government.

Soviets had done all the exploratory work for Afghanistan on the basis of which international bids were invited. In Pakistan, despite the claims of, "we can do it on our own" ,this preparatory exploration was lacking. By spending on exploration, the proponent secured an implicit right to get the lease, and perhaps consequent to the agreement between the proponent company and the government of Balochistan, which details are not available in the open. Does this mean that Tethyan has got the right to unilaterally impose project terms and the results of its feasibility study? Not really. Negotiations should take place based on the announced Mineral Policy and Balochistan Mining rules and the generally accepted good practices and instances of comparable projects. Third party neutral services on which both the parties have confidence can be acquired to facilitate an amicable resolution and agreement.

The choice of Technology

The traditional processing route is crushing-Milling-grinding-Floatation-smelting-refining-electrorefining.The proponents proposes to stop after floatation and export the ore concentrate usually carrying 27-33% copper metal ,along with Gold etc and the rest being gangue ,sulfur, iron etc. This is not unusual. Copper is traded in international market as concentrate as well. The local processing argument would like to go further in the processing chain to at least semi-refined copper and ideally to the electro-refining stage that produces Copper rod for making Copper wire.

There is another route, shorter and cheaper, that is called the leaching-Extraction–electro winning (SX_EW) route that directly produces electrical grade Copper rod or Cathode on site (without going into the need of making concentrate, smelting and cleaning).It has become quite popular lately. There are some 64 Leach-SX-EW plants in the world to date, making more than 3 Million tons of Copper, which comes out to be 20% of the total production. SX-EW plants come in all types and sizes. A plant of 80,000 tons per year output has cost 400 Million US dollars, while MINTEK/Enami have offered small plants costing 3.1 Million US dollars for a small plant of an output capacity of 200 tons per month. We will discuss elsewhere the potential of this technology in the promotion of SMEs in the mineral processing sector.

Leaching is done by percolating acidic solution (sulfuric) through ore heaps and thus dissolving copper from the ore. Originally this route was used in Uranium ore processing, which explains the possible stress on this route by our retired nuclear bureaucrats. This route was later used in Copper Oxides and Carbonates processing. More recently even CuS ores are also being processed through this cheaper, shorter and environmentally more acceptable route. Even bacteria have been used for leaching purposes. Chemical composition details of the ore have not been released, but it is understood that this route can also be adopted. Antafagosta (parent company of the proponent) has implemented the leaching route one its Copper-Oxides mine at El-Tesoro. Antafagosta does not possibly have exposure to copper smelting and refining, a position that they have perhaps adopted to answer criticism of restricting Rekodeq project to concentrate exports only.

The case for local processing?

Ore exports in the concentrated form has been derided and disapproved by some development experts as sign of gross under-development. This is not necessarily so. Significant amount of Cu concentrate is shopped to Japan from the US, while in some African countries total local processing has been employed. A lot of factors depending on current business environment and strategies ,local risks, self-owned or contractor smelting facilities elsewhere etc determine the scope of local processing , although transport logistics and costs dictate in favor of local processing. Thus there may be a strong case for a part of the mineral output to be at least partially locally processed.

The proponent argues that, it has no experience in smelting and refining and cannot handle this difficult area. One is inclined to take this assertion with a pinch of salt, to say the least. They argue that if refining is feasible and attractive, other investors can be attracted and given the responsibility. In this scribes' view, a variable royalty rate formula ala-Western Australia, as mentioned elsewhere, could also be adopted in this respect to encourage local processing in time. We have also recommended in the following that the proponent consider and study the economics of local copper smelting , possibly in place of the proposed slurry pipe line of 689 kms for transporting 600,000 tons of concentrate from the Mine site to the Gawadar port. And the pipeline investment can be diverted to the smelting or other processing facilities. These proposals may, however, need not stall the project. There are other possibilities of installing alternative processing technologies like SX-EW (Solvent Extraction-Electro winning), on a portion of mine output or on the mineral waste and tailings. All options would require large scale open pit mining. We would explore this further under the head of a compromise solution.

Direct Foreign Investment and the issues of Government Policy

And perhaps most critical of the argument and a legalistic question is whether Government of Balochistan is obliged to award the mining contract to the investor Tethyan. There is a simple and reasonable question, as to why should a foreign company invest in exploration and bring the project to an implementation stage. They are not a foreign government or a donor agency. We did not hire them as contractors. They are to bring a foreign investment of 3.3 billion US dollars, largest in Pakistan history, in a highly discouraging security environment. LNG companies are dragging their feet on coming to Pakistan like many others who even do not consider Pakistan at all .There is a mineral policy and there are mining rules , under which the project has been designed as clarified by the Ministry of Petroleum officials. For years, Government of Pakistan and Balochistan have been lobbying such companies hard to come in and invest. There is hardly any appreciable foreign investment in mineral sector, although there is significant potential.

Successive governments including the present one have shunned the policies of launching public sector enterprises and privatization is being pursued. There is almost a national consensus around it. Even profitable enterprises like PTCL have been privatized and more are on the list including very profitable ones .It is one of the key options in reducing foreign debt and improving balance of payments. Attracting direct foreign investments is a declared government policy. It is ironic that some of the public servants have been allowed to speak openly against a project that has been cleared by responsible officials of relevant ministries. These persons should have been disciplined by GOP.

Can we do it on our own?

The most difficult question is of development of these resources by our local scientists and technologists as mentioned before. This is a cherishable goal and the aspirations of our local scientist are laudable. But let us be slightly more realistic and objective. Firstly, it is not simply a technical issue; it is a business issue as well as has been noted earlier. It is one thing to handle something on a small scale in a non-commercial context, it is quite another to be able to handle large mining business and enterprise. And then where is the money. GOP does not have money at all, and the government of Balochistan has asked the foreign company to finance its share of equity through interest free loan; so much for the financial capability. And no matter how respectable, our scientists may be, would they have credibility before international lending agencies to finance the debt portion of more than 2.0 billion US dollars and where would the collateral come from.

There are other projects where they can demonstrate their capabilities. There are other minerals lying unexploited. Why throw spanner so late in the day, when a project is to start its implementation. Mineral policies and rules should have been lobbied in favor of local development much earlier and should be reserved for future projects, if at all. And if they insist despite all these arguments, 10 % of area could be allocated for them through negotiations with the company.

As to the local capability, it took the then Resource Development Corporation and its successors several decades to implement a much smaller Saindak project and we had to literally beg the Chinese to take over. Neither could we produce, nor finance and even could not sell the product. The country is under energy crisis and major large public sector projects are running under losses and subsidies. Among the few profitable ones, the national company ODGC could not increase its exploration activities despite considerable oil and gas potential. So where is the collateral to claims other than the non-commercial nuclear program?

The mindset

Unfortunately having been under colonial rule for long, we seem to look into these things in the context of British East India Company. In an international economic climate when exports led growth and Direct Foreign Investment is being encouraged and widely practiced, such anti-foreign company attitude may be counter productive and untenable. This attitude has discouraged many foreign companies in the past and has prevented possible influx of foreign investment. The most recent case is of Senhua of China, which spent two years in Thar and made a reasonable offer. Bickering and uncooperative attitude sent them away, with the result that we are sitting on one of the largest coal deposits and are suffering under a persistent energy crisis. It is highly doubtful that any other mining company would make the offer for Rekodeq, if the present project fails to materialize. It would send the kind of wrong signals among investors abroad, that we can least afford.

Normally explorer has a preemptive or preferred right to develop and operate a mineral deposit, subject to the announced policies of the host country. Admittedly it is a large unprecedented project and many issues may not be spelled out by the broad policies. Neither should the Government of Balochistan try to find legal loopholes to deny the foreign investors of their due, nor should the foreign company assume an unlimited license to demand unreasonable terms. A negotiated settlement can be reached on the basis of usual international practices.

Potential fall-out of the contract cancellation

What if the government of Balochistan unilaterally terminates the agreement? In that case, complicated international Chamber of Commerce proceedings may be invoked by the aggrieved party and make huge claims not only for recouping its investment but also for the loss of potential profit valuing in excess of 13 billion USD. Whether ICC would grant it, is an open question. Would GOB be subsequently able to call international tenders? Litigation may stall international tendering and international companies may not adequately respond due to the insecure legal situation.

Would Government of Balochistan be able to implement the project, financially and technically?

It says it will and states that it has provided for 2 billion rupees for the project in the budget against a requirement of 250 billion Rupees .In terms of technical capability they have the support of some glib talkers who know and can do every thing from Thar Coal to Copper mining to nuclear weapons and missiles.

One may be inclined to ask them ,as to why didn't they applied their knowledge and skills in much simpler and less expensive exploration activity in the first place , to preclude any preemptory claims of foreign mining companies. And in that case, international tendering could have been done; easier said than done. Results equivalent to international tendering can be obtained, as suggested earlier, through hiring third party services and the services of multilateral agencies such as the World Bank, IFC etc.

Conclusions

Present mineral sector output in Pakistan is a paltry o.4% of GDP, way below its potential variously estimated at 2-3% of GDP, which would mean an annual output and exports of 5000 Million US dollars. By comparison, IMF contribution to foreign exchange deficit is slightly more than 1000 million USD. However, mineral sector has been stagnating due to low technology and small scale mining and that mostly in non-metal sector. Except for Saindak with an output of 16000 tons of blister Copper, there is no sign of large scale mining, benefiting from foreign capital and technology.

TCC-Rekodeq is a good window of opportunity; Pakistan has been waiting for years. With a foreign investment of 3.2 Billion USD and an annual output of 220,000 tons of Copper and 16 tons Gold ,resulting in annual exports of more than one Billion USD, it is a project of international scale in every respect.

The project has been opposed on many counts, the most significant ones are as follows; a) the monetary terms offered by the foreign JV TCC are not adequate; b)we can do it on our own and make more money; c)there should be local processing done within the country instead of the export of raw concentrate. The alternative cited is a ECNEC approved project.

The ECNEC project, as proposed by Dr. Samar Mubarakmand is very small with a daily ore output of just 5000 tons, as opposed to 110,000 tons per day of ore output of TCC proposal. It is even smaller than the existing Saindak. ECNEC proposal relies on small scale mining of the local mining companies. It is doubtful, if even 5000 tons of ore can be mined by the local sub-contractors. Understandably, its cash cost per ton are very high, i.e.3158 USD per ton, several times higher than international cost including those of TCC. It is widely known that small scale mining operations are uneconomic and the ECNEC project only supports that. There is a high probability that this project runs into snags, cost over-runs and lack of output. There may be a good chance of success, however, if the ECNEC project restricts itself to mineral processing, a point that we are going to take up later in these passages. ECNEC project does not make the kind of claims that have been attributed to the project. There is no possibility that it can give an output of 45000 tons per annum of finished Copper. The claims of the ability to give profits of 133 Billion USD can only be termed too exaggerated, unrealistic and grotesque, if not out rightly false. Apart from a poor economics, the premise of relying on local mining contractors to provide the raw materials output for such high through-put rates so as to generate 133 billion USD of Gross Profit , does not stand up to robust calculations and judgments. It cannot be done. Hence no profit or outputs in those scales are to be expected.

If there is a compulsive need for demonstrating capability, excellence and utilization of S&T manpower, it can be done on many unexplored and unexploited resources lying dormant in **Kohistan, Waziristan** and in **Chagai** itself. The ECNEC project, as small as it is, may be implemented on those resources. These areas badly need investment and employment opportunities. ROZ funds of the USAID could be mobilized there as well.

On the other hand, TCC proposal has been prepared by world renowned consultants and overseen by two big JV partners Antafagosta of Chile, where the latter operates several copper mines including Leach-Electro win operations. The other minority partner, Gold Barrick specializes in Gold project. The project structure and numbers are in broad conformity with similar international projects. t is quite likely that the proponents would make a success of the project and would be able to produce and export in the quantities planned.

This, however, does not mean that TCC proposal cannot be improved and altered, keeping in view some of the reasonable aspirations and requirements. Local processing component could be added, for a portion of the output. Local processing can be done by TCC itself based on its operations in Chile or give it to a local or foreign JV or to the proponents of ECNEC project. Other financial terms offered can be negotiated as well. It should be discussed in a business like setting in a transparent environment, avoiding legal battles and claims on both the sides.

ECNEC approval of a Copper project is rather strange in the wake of a consensus on FDI and privatization and in the light of a bad experience in Saindak. GOP has privatized many profitable ventures in the past and many strategic projects like HMC and KSEW have been put on privatization list. Some explaining of the rationale is in order.

TCC could have followed a better project politics and communication policy which would have prevented hostility and debate against the project. It has taken the classical view that the ore being Sulphide cannot permit the much economic and viable route of Leaching. There is abundant evidence to the contrary. Many projects have been launched recently by such big names like Phelps Dodge, BHP, Codelco etc. Infact earlier data available on the internet about Rekodeq as released by TCC included a leaching component for a percentage of output. We have included a table to substantiate this. Local processing is an important political issue, if not an economic one. It should have received much more serious attention. Secondly, it is the archaic attitude to secrecy contending that its feasibility studies contain technical secrets. This is untenable. TCC cannot possibly teach its competitors any thing new. A more open communication policy would have been in its own interest generating public confidence and support.

TCC project can be a start of a new chapter in Pakistan's mineral sector offering technology, capital and exports and can be a good example to attract investments in other minerals. The reverse can also happen, if this opportunity is vitiated and wasted in hostility and delay.

No looting is involved in the project proposal, neither is the Rekodeq project out of this world and not certainly worth trillions of dollars. Infact, its Cu content is lower than elsewhere and matches only the US deposits which are generally considered inferior. Its on-surface valuation of 100 billion USD is realistic, and the proponent company may not be able to net over more than 3-4 billion USD over the entire project life cycle of 56 years, as is the case with other comparative projects.

A 50% share in gross profit is a good formula and matches with competitive offerings elsewhere. Contract framework must ensure that the promised terms actually result in the expected income. Contracting for such high value projects is a highly complicated business.

153

Government of Balochistan should establish a transparent negotiating structure and process under the guidance of a *transaction adviser* seconded or selected by multi-lateral agencies and their processes.

Government of Pakistan may do well by launching an information campaign disseminating true and realistic data and information to correct public opinion and perceptions mired in conspiracy theories and unrealistic presumptions regarding uniqueness of mineral deposits in Balochistan and Pakistan. The reality is that there are abundant mineral resources in the world vying and competing for the investment of foreign capital and technology. The uniformed public opinion in Pakistan creates mistrust and unrealistic romanticism and folklore which in turn feed separatist tendencies.

Recommendations

1) The proposed Rekodeq project is in national interest and it should be allowed without stalling it in unnecessary argumentation. It would bring in much needed foreign investment and would contribute in a meaningful way in energizing Pakistan's economy.

2) Government of Balochistan should adopt a transparent process in negotiations with the company with suitable advice and over sight. Government of Balochistan should engage the services of an independent professional transaction advisor to facilitate a reasonable agreement maximizing national and provincial interests in the framework of adequate profitability and international good practice. International tendering is not the only feasible option always.

3) Environmental aspects should be investigated adequately and requisite remediation provided for within the established rule and good practices.

4) The company is expected to adopt a more open policy towards releasing adequate information out of the feasibility study conducted by it. Trying to hide facts does not create confidence in the minds of the general public, either in Balochistan or elsewhere in the country. It would be in every body's interest if all aspects of the projects are out in the open. TCC should at the very least issue a JORC or NI43-101 statement.

5) Consideration should be given to provide for producing blister Copper. The company has proposed a very capital intensive and risky transport system of installing a 682 kms long slurry pipeline. The same investment could be diverted to installing Blister copper facilities. Recognizing that copper smelting is an energy intensive operation, flash smelting based on electric arc furnaces based on cheap electrical power from Iran could be considered as a technical option. Alternatively the Bio-leaching SX-EW route could be implemented on mineral waste and tailings and as well as the virgin Sulphide ore as has been done elsewhere in the world (pls see appendix for details). The company has already offered a fund of one million US dollars for undertaking the relevant feasibility study, which is a welcome step. A separate JV can be formed for this purpose, with a possible participation of Pakistan's private sector. The mining contract should provide for local sales, if and when such projects come up.

6) A railway track linking Rekodeq mine site with Gawadar airport would have been a more advisable option for concentrate transport. Reportedly that aspect was investigated and dropped in the least-cost perspective. GOP may be asked to fund the additional finance, if required.

7) A 189 MW power project has been proposed based on furnace oil based Internal Combustion Engines in a combined cycle mode. Pakistan is already burdened under very large unsustainable oil imports. Rekodeq has Good Wind and Solar Thermal resource. It may also make a good commercial sense to have a wind-cum solar thermal based power generation, whereby the mines process heat requirements may be met through the wind-solar combine. Possibilities of imports of cheap electrical power from Iran may also be looked into, if nothing else, than to add to the projects energy –mix and security.

8) There is almost a national consensus on pursuing open economic policies encouraging FDI and privatization. It is in this spirit that even profitable companies like PTCL have been privatized. It would be highly unadvisable for government to venture into the risky and capital intensive business of Copper mining. Government is already facing problems in meeting the deficits of large public sector corporations. The claims of self-doing do not meet up to our robust enquiry and consideration. There are other Copper deposits in the area where local excellence and expertise can be adequately demonstrated. These would

become more feasible, once the proposed project is implemented which may provide a pool of trained manpower.

9) The project deserves much more conscientious attention of all the stake-holders in the interest of the best outcome in the form of the earliest implementation maximizing national gains, without recourse to a possible international litigation that may not be in Pakistan's best of interests.

10) Recent confusion and litigation has indicated that there are grey areas in the Mineral policies framework and Balochistan Mining rules. Such areas need to be looked into. Also the royalty schedule and rates may be revisited and brought in line with the provincial aspirations of earning higher revenues. There is a scope for royalty enhancement from the present rate of 2% to a higher rate of 3%, providing for a fixed and variable component; variable component being linked to the prices of the mineral. It is much more damaging to a host country's reputation not to honor the written policies offering lower rates, than to have slightly more stringent rule.

11) Government of Balochistan may consider creating a ***provincial mineral corporation*** to deal with the mineral sector policies, projects and exploration and development activities. Saindak project, if and when it is handed over to the province may be handed over to the proposed corporation. A mineral development fund may be created out of the royalty proceeds of Saindak and Rekodeq etc for funding exploration and development activities. It would be politically much more acceptable and economically more expedient to invest some money in exploration in promising areas (and low hanging fruits) , and prepare projects for international bidding than to get entangled in prior and premature claims for mining lease of the explorer company. The price is worth paying. In more risky areas, mining companies may be invited for exploration and be prepared for awarding mining leases without acrimony to the successful explorers.

12) Publishing and advertising convenient information is not enough. The proponent should not try to hide behind its intellectual property rights. It should make its feasibility study public and may omit some technical details that it considers to be a trade secret. After all, it would have to submit feasibility study for financing agencies. And copper mining is no rocket science, unless it wants to hide some mineral finds, it ought not to conceal. It would be in the interest of every body that the foreign company does not adopt a secretive policy. In particular ,it

should release the capital expenditure details and break-down, the chemical composition of the ore, proposed process and environmental remediation and projected PLS and balance-sheet. In the absence of which, an informed public discussion cannot take place. I wonder, how, has an EIA been conducted without making the necessary details public. In short, it appears that the proponent has adopted an ill-advised Communication policy, which it should reconsider in its own enlightened interest, if nothing else.

There have been wide allegations of corruption, under-reporting , accounting manipulation and many leakages on the part of multi-national mining companies around the world. Often host government officials and mining companies engage in collusive corruption depriving the host country of its share in revenue, royalties, profit and foreign exchange. Under the cloak of business confidentiality, under-hand transactions are made .Many mineral countries are in perpetual bade shape, while the mineral companies have prospered along with the collaborating host government bureaucracy and politicians. A number of initiatives have been launched under which the following measures have been provided for;

1) EITI (Extractive Industry Transparency Initiative), whereby substantial transparency requirements have been laid out.
2) PWYP (Publish What You Pay), whereby companies undertake to publish details of every significant transaction either on websites or periodic reports.
3) Companies are required to abstain from regions where violent conflict may be going on, to avoid getting involved in such conflicts.

Many Western countries having sizeable mining industry operating abroad have joined these initiatives. Smaller provinces, especially Balochistan would be more susceptible to leakages and collusion due to the special political problems there. It may be advisable that GOP/GOB join these initiatives to ward off or ameliorate potential threats in this respect.

Chapter Appendix

Table 8.10: Antafagosta Five year Summary of Financial Performance Mn US$

	2009	2008	2007	2006	2005
GMP Turnover	2962.6	3372.6	3826.7	3870	2445.3
EBITDA	1680.70	1899.8	2824	2957.3	1674
Profit B.Tax	1437.6	2609.5	2750.2	2859	1536.3
Income Tax	(317.7)	(519.7)	(638.4)	(664.9)	(308.1)
Minority Interests	(452.2)	(383.3)	(729.7)	(839.8)	(502.4)
Net Earning	667.7	1706.5	1382.1	1354.3	725.8
Basic EPS (cents)	67.7	175.1	140.2	137.4	73.6
Cash Cost per 1b	96.3	87.3	31.6	40.2	13.5
Production cost(conc.+ cathodes) (000 tons)	442.5	477.7	428.1	465.5	467.3

Source: Antafagosta web-site

Table 8.11: Antafagosta Mines details

Name	Los Pelambres	Eltessoro	Michilla
Location	240 lass NE Santiago	1350 kms North Santiago	1500 less north of Santiago
Share holders	60% Antafagosta 40% Jap consortia	70% Antafagosta 30% Marubeni	74% Antafagosta 26% local Chile
Ore Reserves	1502 Mn tons @ 0.64% Cu, 0.018% Mo, 0.03 gms/ton Au	211.6 Mn tons @ 0.57% Cu	9.5 Million Tons @ 1.35% copper
Mineral Resouce	6164.9 Mn tons @ 0.52%, 0.11% Mo, 0.03 gms/t gold	270 Mn tonnes @ 0.56%	42.8 million tons @ 2.27% copper
Cash Cost	80.4 USc /lb	123.4 USc/lb	157.6 USc/lb
Production	407,000 tons	96,000 tons/yr	45,100 tons/yr 99.95% Cu
Ore grade	0.52-0.69%		
Product	concentrate	Cu Cathode	Cu Cathode
Transport	Pipeline		
Mining Method		Heap leach, solvent- extraction & Electro winning SX-EW	Heap leach SX-EW

Source: Antafagosta web-site

Table 8.12: Friede Copper Gold Capex Breakdown

Item	Amount
Location	Papa New Guinea
Capex	US$ 4.4B, CI cash cost = USc 22 / 1b
Mining & Processing	1.2 B USD
Infrastructure (incl. 140 MW hydro)	1.4 B USD
EPCM, Indirect, Owns Cost	900 M USD
Contingencies	900
Total	4.4 B USD
Copper (Resource)	17.9 Billion 1bs (8.1 M tones)
Gold	13.4 million 02
Copper output	160,000 tpa / 246,000 tpa
Gold output	240,000 02/379,000 oz
Gross Revenue	US$968 Million (US$ 2.2/1b Cu, 800 $ / oz)
Annual Cash Flow	US$ 700 Mn (--- do ---)
Annual Cash Flow	US$ 1028Mn(US$3.00, US$1000 (oz)

Table 8.13: Occurrence of Copper in Pakistan

Hundreds of Copper occurrences have been reported form Pakistan in all four provinces associated with porphyries, skarn, hydrothermal veins, replacement of breccias, volcanogenic sedimentary including massive sulphide. Major copper deposits, the world over, are mainly concentrated to subduction plate margins and spreading centers.

Copper deposits of significance in Pakistan are related to above two environments i.e. porphyry type and volcanogenic. Copper occurs extensively at several localities particularly in ophiolite Thurst Belt and suture zones, Kohistan Island arc, Karakoram block and Chagai magmatic arc.

In all afore mentioned areas copper mineralization is found intimately associated with igneous intrusions and volcanic rocks, hydrothermal veins with gold and silver, Kuroko and Cyprus type massive sulphide deposits at Makki (Chagai) / Ann Dhora, Las Bela and Shinkai, Waziristan respectively.

Associated with magmatic and volcanogenic sequences in Bela Ophiolite belt, Waziristan ophiolite belt, chagai magmatic arc, kohistan arc and Tirich Mir zone of the Karakoram block there are numerous gossans and associated hydrothermal alteration ones where detailed exploration work may prove copper deposits of significant economic worth.

Chagai magmatic arc is the most important district where more than 27 significant occurrences dominantly of porphyry type have been reported.

These include, Makki Chah, Talruk, Saindak, Max G White, Reko Dik (Koh-e-Dalil), Mashki Chah, Darban Chah, Amuri, Kangard, Ziarat Pir Sultan, Kabul Koh, Dasht-e-Kain. Cyprus type massive sulphide deposit of Shinkai, Wazirsitan has also been explored.

Source: Mundi

9 A Case Study of Saindak Metals

Saindak Metals is located in the District Chaghai, close to the mine site of the proposed Rekodeq Copper and Gold Project. Useful policy lessons and conclusion can be drawn from the project experience and performance. After many studies and stumbling blocks, the project was approved in 1987 in its present form .Resource Development Corporation, predecessor of Saindak Metals Limited, was disbanded with the emergence of SML. Chinese metallurgical giant, Metallurgical Corporation of China (MCC) was awarded the contract in 1990 to implement the mine construction. The project was commissioned in 1996 and handed over to SML on 8th January 1996. The mine and the production were shut within a short period of time of six months for a variety of reasons including lack of finances and expertise. The project remained shut for 7 years and MMC had to be invited to run it under a management contract. The operations began in 2003.

Substantial investments have been made in SML. Initially, a sum of USD 412 Million in the period 1990-1996, was invested and an additional BMRE of 236 Million USD in the period 2003-2008, taking the total project outlay to 648 Million USD. The project has since been running in loss, and has only recently acquired profitability and full capacity utilization, although carried forward losses are still on the books. MCC had to finance the working capital needs, through its lending of 120 Million USD, which is to be paid for and adjusted through Copper sales to China. MCC is to pay a rent of 0.5 Million USD and 50% of the surplus (Profit before Tax).The details of the contract are not known.

Since 2003, SML has earned a Profit before tax (PBTAX) of Rs.7.283 Billion (by the end of 2008), and an annual PBTAX of 2.5 Billion Rs. (before adjustments of accumulated losses) since 2008.Therefore the project has only been able to pay a presumptive tax of 0.5% of sales, which comes out to be Rs 157 Million only. The project would run till 2022, for a period of 19 years, as the Copper resource is to be exhausted by then. If the project continues, as it has started to do under MCC management, a PBTAX of 12 Billion Rs would be generated over the entire project life cycle. One has to do precise IRR calculations, based on the availability of reliable and complete data, to be sure. One is not sure whether there is the required technical and management resource base to run the project, despite the claims of some eminent scientists to the contrary. One is not sure, if MCC would be willing to renew the contract, whenever the terminal date comes. MCC does not have financial stakes by the way of capital investments. Here in comes the merit of Direct Foreign Investment. The project's future seems to be in doldrums.

The Way Forward

Following steps may be considered;

1. The project may be privatized, preferably to a foreign mining company. TCC may show interest in buying at some stage, if its main project of Rekodeq comes on stream. There are a number of synergies, as we shall see.

2. The projects life may be extended by procuring ore from Rekodeq or other deposits in the vicinity.

3. Bio-Leaching or Heap leaching facilities may be installed along with SX-EW plant, to work on the waste dump and tailings that may be accumulated already or will be eventually in a few years.

4. The claimants of local processing and know-how may be invited to assume this project and prove their point, which would be much easier in SML. The risk is to be though, to be carried away by the egotism of those who have more than completed their professional lives and careers.

5. Concluding, the best option lies in privatization, once the present contractor refuses to run it or starts demanding un- acceptable conditions. It would be easier once TCC project starts to show promise to both the sides and the present difficulties removed. Negotiations with TCC may include the disposal of SML as well or planned synergies between the two projects.

Project Data (as extracted from the information memorandum of SML privatization)

There were other economic studies carried out between 1980 and 1986 towards development of Saindak Project in 1987. Metallurgical Construction Corporation (MCC) of China offered to develop mine and construct concentrator, smelter and auxiliary facilities on turnkey basis with supplier credit of US$ 84 million for supply of machinery/equipment for the plant with 78 million tons minable ore and life period of 19 years. Total construction cost was Rs 13.6 billion (roughly US$412 million).

Contract for turnkey construction of mine, plant and auxiliary facilities were signed in September, 1990 between SML & MCC in Beijing. The contract became effective in October, 1990. MCC completed the construction including performance test of equipment and trial production and handed over to SML on 08.01.1996. The mine and plant stopped the entire production activities within 6 months of completion due to non-availability of financial resources and trained manpower. In addition to mine and plant construction by Chinese infrastructural facilities i.e. Residential Quarters, 50 MW Power Plant, Bulk Water Supply System, 37km Broad Gauge Rail track, Metalled Road, 20 Bed Hospital, School, Water Treatment Plant were constructed/arranged by SML.

The mine operation was put up for tender in May 2000. The lease was awarded to MMC in 2003 and has been operated since that time. Recently (mining news 14/4/2005) Jiangxi Copper Co announced spending US$120 million to secure 20,000 metrics tons of copper and 2 tons of gold, presumably this money is being used to upgrade the concentrator which was a bottle neck previously to getting better utilization from the smelter.

Description of Project

Mineralization

North	28 million ton	0.441% Cu
South	111 million ton	0.426% Cu
East	273 million ton	0.336% Cu

Significant quantities of magnetite, molybdenum, gold and silver were found associated with copper are contained in the south and north ore bodies and molybdenum in the east ore body.

Ore Mineralogy

Pyrite, Chalcopyrite, Bornite (minor), magnetite, Molybdnite, Minor Chalcocite has been determined at place in all three ore bodies. Malachite, azurite and other forms of copper oxide minerals are found at places and confined to Oxidized parts of the deposit.

Design Capacity and Product Output

The Concentrator capacity is 12,500 t/d of ore. The products are gold bearing copper concentrate, pyrite concentrate and magnetite concentrate. The run-of-mine ore contains very little molybdenum; it is technically difficult and uneconomic to produce the qualified concentrate. Therefore, recovery of molybdenum is not considered in this design.

The smelter capacity is 20,000 tons of blister copper per year, but the blister copper output obtained from utilization of the copper ore from Saindak open pits is about 15,500 t/year; the shortfall part of the copper concentrate will be supplemented from outside the Saindak Mine. The products and output of the Plant during the preliminary production stage are as follows:

Blister Copper:	15 500 t/year from Saindak Mine
in which	Gold 39 981 OZ
	Silver 35 622 OZ
Pyrite concentrate	79 688 t/year
Magnetite concentrate	62 333 t/year

Project Components

Open Pit

The open pit consists of the south ore body. The south ore body mainly occurs in tonalite/diorite porphyry and siltstone, belonging to a large sized low grade porphyry copper deposit. The ore is easy to be mined and amenable to beneficiation. Each block dimensions 25m x 25m x 12m and 0.25% copper is used as cut off grade in calculation. The

164

geological reserve of south ore body is 96.03 million tons; the copper grade is 0.413% and gold grade 0.441g/t.

The pre-stripping overburden quantity was 15.80 million tons (already removed) by MCC after removal of overburden level is at 938m, ASL. During the production period, the annual mining and stripping is up to 17.00 million tons in quantity, the ore is 4.25 million tons and the waste 12.75 million tons

There are three waste dumps which can contain 152 million tons of waste, in which includes ore for 35.34 million tons of low grade ore bearing copper from 0.25% to 0.15%, and 4.7 million tons of low grade ore in grade from 0.275% to 0.25% copper which is extracted as the waste from above 854m elevation in the early production period. These low-grade ores will be put into a separate dump during the production period, not mixed with the other waste, in order to utilize them later.

Tailing disposal and reclaimed water system:

The climate in the mine area is dry with little rainfall and significant evaporation. Therefore, the tailings are thickened for water reclamation before discharged at the density of 26.3%, and is directly fed to 27.4m high-efficiency thickener with overflow about 18 000 t/d; the underflow at a density of 45~50% is pumped to the West Valley Tailings Pond with a slurry pump. The transportation pipeline is 377mm in diameter and around 2800m in length.

The West Valley tailings pond is a comparatively ideal pond which is close to the concentrator and has a water catchment area of only 3.36km2; the process of upstream embankment is used in the design. The starter dam is 484m in length, 13m in height, with a crest elevation of 901m. The starter dam is a permeable stone-built dam. The final storage elevation of tailings is 955m ASL and the pond volume 68 000 000m³, so the tailings pond can store the tailings produced by the concentrator for over 19 years.

The reclaimed water system in the concentrator area consists of one pump station and one 500mm dia water pipeline from the pump station to the 5000m³ reservoir; the reclaimed water from the tailings pond is 5000 t/d based on the preliminary estimation, which will also be pumped to the 5000m3 reservoir via the pump station and 300mm pipeline, but in the first or second year, this portion of reclaimed water is not considered temporarily.

Smelting and Waste Heat Utilization

The smelter is arranged very close to the Southwest end of the concentrator; the copper concentrate is directly fed from the copper concentrate bins to the feed proportioning plant of the smelter.

The process of wet green concentrate smelting in a reverberatory furnace, converting in P-S converter and then blister copper ingot casting is adopted. This process is characterized by simple process, easy operation, high operation efficiency, and high copper recovery and flexible to materials. This smelting process adopted is suitable to the operation without Sulfuric acid-making from flue gas.

The smelter treats 90 000 t/a of copper concentrate and the concentrator of the Plant can supply 71 500 t/a (based on the average quantity of fun-of-mine ore from South Open-pit in 19 years); the shortage is supplemented from outside Saindak mine; the smelter requires 20 895 tons of quartz, 6 520 tons of limestone, 16 400 tons of heavy oil and 560 tons of refractory brick per year.

Two P-S 3.2 x 6.6m converters are available, one for operation, the other for standby and repair use. The matte treatment capacity is 100-115 tons per melt taking 12 hours as one converting cycle; the outputs of converter are blister copper, slag and flue gas. Around 32-35 tons of blister copper is produced per melt, containing 98.5% copper. The converter slag (88.5 tons per melt) returns to the reverberatory furnace for smelting.

Table 9.1: Payments to National Exchequer

Particulars	Rs. In Million (Estimated)
Royalty	251.591
Development Surcharge	62.898
Presumptive Tax	157.245
Total	471.734

Table 9.2: Financial Parameters of Saindak Metals

Total Sales Revenue (2004-8)	39253
Total GP	7283
Total CAPEX	14158 (236 Mn USD)(2004-2008)
Initial Capital Investment	13600(412 Mn USD)(1990-1996)
Total CAPEX	27758(648 Mn USD)
Royalty (% of Sales)	0.64%
Gp As % of Sales	18.55%

The outlet flue gas which is decreased from 750C to around 350C through cooler, enters into a 40 m^2 single chamber, four-field electrostatic precipitator, then the cleaned flue gas together with the cleaned reverberatory furnace gas is mixed with the environmental gas and sent to a 120m high chimney to atmosphere.

Table 9.3: Financial Highlights for Last Five Years

Year Ended 31st December	2004	2005	2006	2007	2008 (Estimated)
Sales Revenue	1,620.544	5,785.066	8,839.565	10,428.342	12,579.622
Profit Before Tax	133.810	297.218	1,918.559	2,432.999	2,500.000
Government Investment	1,925.814	3,904.334	3,143.833	2,987.405	(2,196.988)
GP as % Sales	19.87%	8.26%	5.134%	21.71%	23.33%

Note: Government has made capital investment of Rs. 14 Billion and all assets have been handed over to lease operator on annual rent of US $ 0.5 Million plus 50% share of surplus.

Financial Evaluation

SAINDAK METALS acquired a modicum of profitability, since 2006 only, generating a PBTAX stream of 1919, 2433, 2500 Million Rs. A total of 7283 Million Rs has been recorded as PBTAX. This is against a Capital investment of 13600 Million Rs made in the construction period (1990-1996), and a CAPEX of 14158 Million Rs during operations, to a total of 27758 Million Rs(648 Million USD).In recent years ,GOP seems to be reinvesting the profits, with practically no cash yield. One is not sure, in the absence of published accounts, whether the investment requirements would continue to be there, as an annual CAPEX affair. If that is the case, no cash profit would yield in future either. If that is not the case, with a projected annual stream of 2500 Million Rs. of PBTAX, a total of 32500 Billion Rs of PBTAX would be generated. Adding the accumulated profit till 2008, the total PBTAX projection comes out to be 39783 Million Rupees. Against a capital investment of 27758 Million Rs., the net PBTAX yield would be 12025 Million Rs over the entire life of the project.

A royalty payment of a total of Rs 252 Million has been made, which comes out to be a paltry 0.64% as opposed to the 2% royalty rate provided for in the National Mineral Policy. There is an alternative royalty rate of Rs 20.0 per ton of Copper ore. Based on this rate, an ore production of 12.6 Million Tons is indicated: an average of 2.52 Million tons per year. Based on a capacity of 12,500 tons per year of ore, annual production of 4.187 Million Ton of Copper Ore is indicated. At an average Copper grade of 0.4 %, a total of blister Copper production of 50,400 tons seem to have been produced over the period of 5 years(2004-8) , the period for which some financial data has been posted at MPNR website. Capacity level production of 14-15000 tons per year seems to have been achieved only in the year 20008. This gives a realised rate of 838,666 Rupees (USD 10,000) per of Blister Copper including the adjustments for Gold and silver. All this is of course, highly conjectural, due to non-release of published results with details on volumes and quantities.

Chapter Appendix

Copper is a mineral. As a mineral, natural copper (also called *native copper*) is relatively rare. Most copper in nature is found in minerals associated with sulfur, or in the oxidized products of these minerals. Copper also easily combines with a number of other elements and ions to form a wide variety of copper minerals and ores. Copper minerals occurring in deposits large enough to mine include azurite($Cu_3(CO_3)_2(OH)_2$), malachite ($Cu_2CO_3(OH)_2$), tennantite (($Cu,Fe)_{12}As_4S_{13}$), chalcopyrite ($CuFeS_2$), and bornite (Cu_5FeS_4).

Table 9.4: Copper Minerals

Mineral	Formula	Appearance	% copper in mineral
Cuprite	Cu_2O	Red earthy	88
Chalcocite	Cu_2S	Dark grey, metallic	78
Bornite	Cu_5FeS_4	Golden brown, metallic	63
Malachite	$CuCO_3Cu(OH)_4$	Bright green, earthy	58
Azurite	$2CuCO_3Cu(OH)_4$	Blue, glassy	55
Chalcopyrite	$CuFeS_2$	Golden yellow, metallic	35

10　The Balochistan Question?

Part I:　The exploitation issue;
#　　　　　myths and realities

Balochistan problem has been festering for more than three decades. However the bloodiness of violence from both sides has never been so gruesome. After the demise of Soviet Union, the warm water theories or threat had subsided to be recently substituted by international involvement from other sides. To top it all, a resolution has been moved in US Congress supporting an independent Balochistan, which the nationalist or liberationists in Balochistan have welcomed. Both sides would have to examine their premises and positions in order to be able to reach a middle ground and a peaceful and amicable settlement.

Our aim in this two part series is very limited. In the first part of today, we would examine the nature of the claims of the nationalists that their province and its resources have been exploited. We would also examine the extent and scope of realism in the claims and assessment that an independent Balochistan would be able to prosper due to its natural resources. In the subsequent second part, we would examine the scope and possibilities of awarding concessions to the nationalists especially a more equitable and acceptable approaches with respect to mineral resources and their incomes.

 After remaining on slow burner for quite a while, the issue acquired renewed momentum in the wake of the murder of Akbar Bugti and the concomitant misadventure, personal vendetta and manhandling of the Bugti and other hostile tribes. President Zardari apologized for the mistakes of his predecessors and launched an Aghaze-Huqooqe Balochistan package. From the perspective of the other side, there has not been much of a change, as the political governments both at the centre and as well as the province do not have either the powers or the

171

courage to take on the powers that be. Clearly they blame Pakistan army and the security agencies for what they call their bloodshed. On the other hand terrorist violence from the nationalist side continues unabated; be it blowing up pipelines or electric installations or murder of uninvolved civilians. Violence breeds violence, be it from any side; a people or the state. It is finally the politics and negotiation that delivers. Those who believe in violent or a military solution are denying the lessons of history. Sadly both the premises seem to be ill founded

Many well wisher Pakistanis are willing to accept whatever blames their Baloch nationalist brothers make in order to appease them and bring them on to a negotiation table. In the same vain, I would also be prepared to do so. However, it would not help the situation, if facts are not told. It would only further the misperception of our misguided youth in Balochistan. The claims of exploitation are highly exaggerated. We do not find any physical or palpable evidence to that claim .There is hardly any mineral project in Pakistan or in Balochistan worth its name. There is not a single mineral project of an international scale. All mining is at a small scale. Even Saindak Copper project is a small project .GOP has been losing money on it. The project was not financially viable and Chinese were reportedly begged to take it over to recover their project loan. Nevertheless the requisite royalty payments are being made to the provincial government.

For all his mistakes, General Musharraf corrected the iniquitous royalty and Sui gas price issue. Royalty used to be underestimated due to a gas pricing formula that may have been technically correct but was ill conceived. The situation has been corrected, even retrospectively. Arrears of Rs 110 Billion have been computed and there is an undertaking that all of it would be gradually paid off. But for the recent financial difficulties, payment schedule may have remained wanting.

There is no doubt among any responsible that it would be paid off rather sooner than later. Another popular misunderstanding is that Except for Quetta, natural gas has not been supplied elsewhere in Balochistan. The problem is technical rather than being in the realm of exploitation Balochistan is very sparsely populated. Nowhere in the world is pipelined gas supplied to such a low and geographically dispersed demand. Even with massive subsidies, it would not have been possible to meet the expectations of the nationalist circles. May be there are some limited number of places, where it may be somehow possible to take piped gas , which should have been done. But such opportunities would be highly limited, if at all. There could have been other solutions such as LPG etc wherein there are problems that are common to all of Pakistan.

Mineral resources have always been under provincial domain and after 18th amendment, provincial domain has been extended to all natural resources. This may take some time that the full fruits of 18th amendment would be available. As for the corporate tax and GST on Oil and Gas, GST is refunded in full (save collection charges) and corporate tax goes into the central kitty, whereby it is divided among the provinces on population basis. One may think, it is here that Balochistan may be suffering due to its lower population. However this is not the case. Balochistan is not the only province that produces Oil and Gas. Other provinces also contribute corporate income tax from their Oil and gas sector and Balochistan gets its share from that income as well. I have done some arithmetic which shows that income of Balochistan would have been the same if all its Resource income were deposited into provincial Balochistan account without going into a central pool. However, I would urge federal authorities to do some reform in this sector, so that this alibi for what ever its worth is also done away with.

And now the resourcefulness issue. At this moment, there is not much there on the surface. It will come when it will come. However, it should be understood that nations do not prosper and grow simply on the basis of natural resources. Most resourceful countries in the world are poor and underdeveloped. Let cash-full Middle Eastern oil countries not deceive any. They are cash flush, because oil is in such demand .And no Middle Eastern oil exporter is truly independent.

Poverty has not gone away from Iran, Iraq or Saudi Arabia, not to talk of the poor and "resourceful" countries of Africa like Niger, Congo, and Zaire etc. Resources or perception of these have invited coup, colonialism, war and strife. Oil rich Iraq and Nigeria are under threat of breakup. Nigeria was partitioned but got united again. Kuwait's oil invited Iraqi (Saddam's) invasion. Iran and Saudi Arabia have had to spend heavily on Military expenditure. Grass is always greener on the other side. Many people in Iran think whether they would have been better off without so much oil and gas.(Ask Pakistani elite what they would have done with oil , had they had it in that abundance). In fact Economist have coined a term called resource curse after studying the fate of some 30 mineral countries which are suffering and are extremely poor despite their heavy mineral export and exploitation. One may criticize the western countries (now China is a big importer of minerals from Africa) and their companies for the so-called exploitative policies. But it is Pakistan which may be able to negotiate and get a better deal for the resources of Balochistan than an independent tribal Balochistan, dependent and underdeveloped and so sparsely populated. Eventually, if all goes well, Balochistan may one day be like Queensland of Australia or Alberta or of Canada inside a prosperous Pakistan than an independent mineral dependent Mali, Chad, Zaire and others of the same lot. Baloch and Balochistan have a future within a united Pakistan and outside Pakistan; it is only a 'basti' of impoverished people.

The resource rich Europe, US, Canada and Australia have built their societies based on an integrated combination of technology and resources. They have not relied on exports of mineral resources. They have benefited from these internally. Resources need market and technology and human resources which will be provided by the brothers of Baloch in other provinces. Iran and Qatar are sitting on one of the largest resources of natural gas and are unable to sell their gas. There was no chance for gas at Sui to be developed even discovered.

Commodity based nationalism has interesting variations. In 1950 and 60s, Mujibur-Rehman made a big issue out of the Jute, the latter used to be called Golden Fiber. Jute was in demand and earned sizeable foreign exchange for the then United Pakistan. The notion was that jute would lead them into prosperity, which otherwise income would otherwise be shared. Nobody wants jute any more. Mujibur-Rehman was killed and Pakistan type political regime started prevailing there. There can be a similar fate for all those much wanted mineral resources. There is not going to be much demand for minerals in the days of recycling. GoP has tried for almost three decades to attract FDI in this sector. Nothing has happened and there is this talk of mythical exploitation. Mineral development has taken place more in developed regions and countries, where there is no dearth of such resources contrary to the naïve theories of the locals. Renewable energy and recycling is knocking at the door which may wipe out fossil fuels in the same way as plastic replaced the jute. In a decade or two, there would be much less talk of oil or gas .

Larger countries and markets possibly have more prospects for progress as the experience of China and now India and other BRICS countries shows. A united Pakistan may have delivered and could have been a part of BRICS today. Bangladesh was one thousand miles apart, but Balochistan is right under our belly, our garden and backyard. Baloch have more common with other parts than it was the case with

Bangladesh. It was easy wresting Bangladesh away from Pakistan in the wake of political unrest there, followed by external intervention. It would be too risky for the regional countries to repeat the same with a now nuclear Pakistan. The restraining factor would be the nuclear factor as opposed to the opening threat in West Pakistan then. All that can be achieved is to bleed Pakistan and make it weaker and throttle its growth and prosperity including that of our Baloch brothers and countrymen.

Additionally, all those living in Balochistan are not ethnic Baloch. There is a sizeable Pakhtoon population which certainly does not support independent Balochistan. This populous faction concentrated in northern Balochistan demands for separation from the province of Balochistan .And such demands may get stronger, if the present nationalist politics and violence continues. It would be futile and bloody and certainly not worth the cost to pursue a separation agenda, although one may condone it as a negotiating tactic to get a better deal.

However, it might be unfair to put all the blame on Bengalis earlier and now the Balochis. Politics and national interest have very wide and vague domain. National interest can always be conveniently and suitably defined to include or enhance the interest of the dominant elite. Both the centrists and separatist would be quite capable to appear to have pious intentions in the interest of their group or domain. Thus no proclamations are sacrosanct or worth the human blood and dignity. All political crimes and cruelties have been pursued under this cherished and publicized motto. Politics is too complicated to be assessed and dealt in black and white. It is all grey, relative and ephemeral. It is the art of the possible. Dialogue and negotiation as opposed to vengeance and vendetta is the key which many powerful groups do not recognize or appreciate and have a very small space in their style and agenda. If politics is allowed to run its course , and many of us on both the sides yearn it to be, without external threat and interference, even the mundane politicians of today, would be able to deliver a more united and coherent Pakistan than otherwise.

Tribal interests in Balochistan are too well entrenched in Balochistan. Pakistan's sate system is too fragile to take head on collision with these. Tribal influences would go down with economic development, education and employment opportunities. *Realpolitik* is required to deal with them. Once Pakistan's state system start delivering well, which unfortunately would be opposed tooth and nail, dependence on tribal affiliations may wither away. Those days may appear too far and so be it. Recourse and adherence to law finally wins moral battle in the minds of people. And that is the ultimate and final weapon against the forces of under development. Law enforcement agencies should have the perseverance and the discipline to remain within the ambit of law while tracing, tracking and controlling the culprits. Organized forces ought not to be guided or overwhelmed by vendetta and vengeance.

These argument have been made in the spirit of searching for truth and speak the truth and to counsel my Baloch nationalists to seek a peaceful solution of their complaints and grievances within a united Pakistan for their own good. The foregoing is not meant to justify any act of cruelty or injustice .All Pakistan, except for a small minority, are keen to listen to them and mix their voice and slogans with them. Media is free and is venting and supporting the genuine grievances. Even the small minority can be persuaded in favor of political negotiation than the language of bullets.

Part II
More resource distribution and economic development initiatives

Immediately political measures seem to be more important at this moment involving moratorium or termination of violence and hostilities and other confidence-building measures. In the last few days the PPP government has announced some additional economic measures as well. An all party conference APC has been proposed which may come through after initial political exchanges and reactions give way to more considered response from the stake-holders. One only hopes that a meaningful process and output results from this initiative.

While in the first part, we saw that the proverbial or mythical exploitation has not taken place. Except for Sui gas field, there is no mineral project and production at a world scale to warrant the allegation. We also saw that resource can be a curse as well, if one looks at the resourceful countries of Asia and Africa. Even the indication of resource is causing a curse like condition in Balochistan. It is unfortunate that Balochistan could not be kept happy and without sense of deprivation. Current economic problems have aggravated the situation. The arithmetic is alluringly simple. Despite problems, it should have been easier to help improve the lot of a 5% of the population. The reverse is true as well; no amount of exploitation of a 5% of population can make the remaining 95% prosperous. The rationale is abundantly clear; doing slightly more can cause immense change. It was different and difficult in the Bangladesh situation.

As they say, justice should not be done only, but it should be seen as well. Combined federal pooling and accounting has created doubts in the minds of smaller provinces. As a general rule and in the aftermath of the 18th amendment, straight transfer approaches may prove to be more credible than pooling and dividing. New approaches have to be looked into. It is in this perspective that the forthcoming proposals have been developed.

Beyond the Aghaze Huqooqe Balochistan Package

It has been quite some time now that the PPP Government announced the Balochistan package, in which significant steps have been initiated towards accepting provincial domain and ownership on natural resources such as oil, gas and minerals etc. Following are the most significant ones;

   a) Bringing a more equitable royalty system of uniform pricing.
   b) Retrospective correction of past mistakes and underpayment of royalties, by announcing to pay Rs 120 billion in terms of royalty receivables of the past..
   c) Dilution of federal ownership of the mineral projects such as Gold and Copper project of Rekodeq and Saindak.
   d) Bringing federal character in the boards of oil and gas companies by appointing representatives of Balochistan in the boards of the respective companies.

These reforms were overdue, and a lame start had been made by General Musharraf in 2002 by instituting a more favorable General Purchase Agreement (GPSA) of the Sui Gas, owned and managed by PPL, a GOP owned company to the extent of 78%. NFC award negotiations have resulted in a favorable determination for Balochistan with a consensus by all the provinces. For the first time other factor such as poverty and land size of the province have been factored in the NFC award. .While the oil production, despite reported potential, in Balochistan is practically none, Balochistan currently provides 25% of gas requirements of Pakistan. It used to be the sole source of gas from 1950s to 1970s when the gas was originally discovered at Sui, the home of Late Akbar Bugti.

Although the economic reforms are to be accompanied by proportional political reforms, the crux of the problem is economic. Without money and resources, no amount of political freedom and justice can bring improvements in the lives of the ordinary people in Balochistan. In that respect, announcement of Rs 120 billion in terms of the payment for gas royalty dues is a monumental step that has been welcome far and wide in the country.

Further improvements in Oil& Gas income sharing formula

Further improvements are possible. In the following, we would examine a few. There are five sources of income from mineral and oil / gas resources.
1. Royalties & Surcharges.
2. Corporate Tax.
3. GST.
4. Excise duty.
5. Profit / dividends.

Petroleum Policy 2012 has been finalized with the input of the provinces and the consultation in the CCI framework. It has not been a simple rubber stamping exercise but the provincial input caused some major changes in some significant aspects of the policy. The avenues for other income sharing have been increased. Totally autonomous provincial handling is rare and is not found even in strong federalist dispensations such as Canada and America and even in India. There is a question of capability as well. Can Balochistan provide and afford the kind of bureaucratic set up that is required for autonomous handling of issues and business. Even federal government finds itself lacking in terms of skills and human resources.

Royalties and gas development surcharges are already being paid to the provinces, although there have been some gas pricing problems of gas from Balochistan which have been partly resolved and partly needs to be still taken care of. Retrospective correction has been agreed to and a sum of Rs 120 billion has been agreed to be paid to Balochistan. Under new royalty regime, the province is expected to get royalty income of half a million US$ per day or 182 million US$ per annum, which prior to 2005 was only one-fifth as much. Under 1982 Gas Price Agreement (GPA) which had been replaced by a more realistic GPA in 2002, would be further improved. The 1982 GPSA provided for very low gas prices thus low royalties. Total income of Balochistan from the package would now be 26.73 billion Rs, while the current year's total budget of the Government of Balochistan (2008-9) was Rs 55 Billion o/w Rs 11.44 Billion came from gas royalties and taxes.

Balochistan is now getting Rs 32.71 per unit on account of gas revenues which includes a royalty of Rs 13.90, excise duty of Rs 5.09 and Gas Development Surcharge of Rs 13.72. Total gas receipts would amount to 25.53% of the total value of gas which has been priced at Rs 140 per unit. Interestingly, the foregoing can be verified from the latest annual report (2011) of PPL. In the adjoining we have compiled the results, both from PPL and OGDC annual reports of 2011.It would be readily noted from the table that Balochistan income from PPL has been reported to be Rs.26.8 billion despite the fall in output since 2008 when these estimates were prepared. The situation is far better than only a few years back when Balochistan gas was priced at about one-third of the present price. Petroleum Policy 2012 has proposed to enhance gas prices almost by 50%, which would further cause a concomitant increase in Balochistan's income as well.

Corporate tax is a legitimate Federal subject in almost all countries, although provinces are also authorized to levy some income tax as well in a number of countries e.g. USA. Some direct sharing formula instead of division through the current pooling and subsequent division practice might be more transparent and politically acceptable. Can Income tax on minerals be a provincial subject? Just as income tax on agriculture has been declared a provincial subject, can income tax on minerals be treated in the same way? Provincialisation of income tax on agriculture is perhaps a delaying technique to defer income tax collection on agriculture. However, agriculture being a provincial subject, the provincial domain in income taxation has been recognized in principle. Can the same principles be applied on minerals including oil and gas? In the US and Canada , provinces levy and collect state income taxes , but then state is not entitled to a share in federal revenue on the lines and proportions as it is practiced in Pakistan. If one wishes to offer palliatives to the nationalists, this could be a possible avenue to consider in place of the demands of sharing the resources on the basis of land size which is certainly self-centric and unreasonable.

 The problem is that mineral resources including oil and gas are the only significant resources; lacking industries and commerce and any significant agriculture due to lack of water .Perhaps reverse is the case with Punjab, having every other thing but energy resources. New Petroleum Policy 2012 declares intention to share all other incomes such as production bonuses and incentives to be shared with the provinces. Consideration could be given to share corporate income taxation on minerals under a direct formula rather than pooling and subsequent sharing on population basis. It may be noted that GoP earned corporate income tax of Rs.16.9 billion in 2011 from PPL. This belies the allegation that GOP earns more than GoB from the gas income of Balochistan. This might have been true earlier, but no more. GoB as it stands today earns 69 % more than GOP earns. However, a 20% sharing of corporate taxes may amount to additional revenue of Rs. 4.0 billion for GoB.

Excise duty is also being transferred in full to the producer provinces as per receipts. GST in general is a provincial subject and more so with respect to natural resources. Federal government collects it and transfers it to the provinces. We will focus on the issue of dividends / profit, which is normally, paid to the investor, in private sector, foreign companies and provincial or federal govt. whichever being the investor. While royalty is only 12% of the sales price, the total income from natural sources can add up to about 40-50% of sales value.

Transfer of PPL to GoB in lieu of Royalty arrears

Do we have the proverbial sacrificial lamb to break the ice? Yes, it is PPL, the company which was partly responsible and may have been in part the beneficiary of the underpayment; its net worth is almost the same as the royalty dues of Balochistan. GOP holds 78% shares in PPL, which can be transferred to Government of Balochistan in lieu of the overdue or arrears of royalty payments of Rs 110 billion. This solves many problems. The political issue of ownership of resources and the payment of royalty due at a rate that should be is affordable by the GOP. Alternatively, the proceeds from the proposed privatization of PPL could go straight to the coiffeurs of Balochistan government.

PPL's equity at book value is about Rs 94.4 billion and market value of Rs.202 and Rs 239 billion respectively on lower and higher market value. These are comparable figures with the royalty arrears of Rs 120 billion. If full ownership(78 %) is transferred ,GoB would be getting a dividend of Rs.9.0 billion in cash dividend and a retained income of   Rs billion. The royalty arrears would be paid in less than ten years. This would enhance the oil and gas income to Rs. 36 Billion as opposed to Rs 44 billion of total budget of GoB in 2008.PPL would remain a milking cow for GoB for quite a while as PPL is expanding outside Balochistan.

If transferring the ownership (78% of GOP Shares) of PPL to Govt. of Balochistan (GoB) appears to be difficult for political and strategic reasons, and due to the weakness of the provincial government, this could be done gradually by keeping the majority share of 51% and diverting the rest to GoB. However, a decision should be announced that all GOP profits from PPL hence forth would go to Balochistan. It should be understood that no new or additional monetary concession is being proposed. It is just a more dramatic and politically acceptable and understandable implementation of Balochistan package already announced by GOP. Baloch nationalists would realize that they are getting a fair deal and would calm down, allowing peaceful access to further oil and gas exploration activities, resulting in much needed energy for the country and income for the Balochi people.

It may also be considered that GOP reduces its share in both OGDC and PPL to the 50% of the current level initially, and transfer the 50% ownership to the provinces, according to some criteria, such as current and cumulate production of various provinces. It should also be studied as to what portion of equity has been financed from internal revenue generation, and how much of external equity had been injected by GOP. Revenue of 25 billion Rs would be generated for the producing provinces. Currently Sindh and Balochistan have major share in oil and gas production. Bulk of these proceeds would go to Sindh and Balochistan at the moment. Eventually NWFP would also benefit from it. Punjab does not seem to have much of an oil and gas potential, present or future. Agriculture and industry is Punjab's forte.

The longer term issues

The larger issue of sustainable and enduring provincial control on resources would remain to be deliberated and would include re-organization of Ministry of Petroleum and Natural resources, perhaps including the divestment of natural resources altogether from the parent ministry. The Directorate General of Oil and Gas may be converted into federal independent boards or authorities so that an economically fruitful and sustainable decentralization is brought about. Balochistan would however have capability issues, even if all role and power is entrusted. On this issue, Sindh has many reservations which are not vocalized now due to the same political party being at the center and the province. They would have been more vocal, had this not been the case. Control of Thar was wrested much before the 18th amendment. There are residual issues that ought to be examined to avoid problems and complications in future.

Other economic development opportunities

There are other economic development opportunities that ought to be explored. Although, 18th amendment puts a lot of responsibility on provincial government, it is obvious that without the external assistance, administrative as well as financial, not much can be achieved. Ironically, it is the smaller provinces which agitated for provincial autonomy and against the concurrent list. The caveat being there, the people on the street do not understand the constitutional complications. They want service delivery, employment opportunities and income.

There could have been four or five factors or axes of development in Balochistan ,which are;1) Industrial estate in Bela ;2)Quetta as supply point to Afghanistan;3)Gas producing regions such as Sui ;4) Gawadar-Turbat-Karchi axis;5)border trade with Balochistan;6)development of agriculture through water resource development, internal as well as external and 7)micro-enterprise development in fruit growing regions and mineral sector. Factors 1 and 2 have played their roles, although Quetta has benefit Pakhtoons more than the estranged Baloch. Around Sui gas based industries could have been developed. There is no evidence that efforts have been made in this respect .Although this not the time now to initiate this process in Sui for a variety of reasons, if and when gas is found in other locations in Balochistan, gas and mineral based industries SMEs should be promoted. There is quite an opportunity to establish development schemes and nuclei along Guawadr-Turbat-Karachi axis. Trade, fisheries, transport and possibly agriculture could be promoted. This axis is away from the troubled areas and there is quite some potential for growth of new settlements of the locals. Most investment has already been made on this axis, and very little money and resources should be required to get it going. Several water projects like Katchi canal and Turbat dam have been launched. .More effort could give good results. Water saving technologies such as drip irrigation has a lot of promise in Balochistan.

Table10.1: Financial Parameters of PPL and OGDC and Income sharing among Centre and Provinces 2010-2011

		PPL	OGDC	Total	
PLS parameters	**units**				
Gross Sales	Billion Rs	98.613	155.63	254.24	
Royalties& GDS	do	15.74	17.7	33.44	Province
Sales Tax/GST	do	11.17	13.2	24.37	Province
Net Revenue	do	71.703	124.73	196.433	
Production cost	do	21	35.1	56.1	Company
Profit Before Tax		48.365	90.98	139.34	
Corporate Tax		16.9	27.454	44.354	GoP
Profi After Tax		31.446	63.53	94.976	
Dividend		17	10.216	27.216	S.holder
EPS		26.31	14.77		
Balance Sheet Parameters					
Equity	Billion Rs	94.4	202	296.4	
Total Shares	Thousand	1194974	4000000		
Breakup Value per Share	Rs	79	50.5		
Market Value @low	Billion Rs	202	612	814	
Market Value @high	Billion Rs	238.8	720	958.8	
GoP share	%	70.66	75		
GoP vs Provincial Incomes					
Provincial Income		26.91	30.9	57.81	
GOP Corporate Tax		16.9	27.454	44.354	
GOP Dividend		12.0122	7.662	19.674	
GOP Tot. Income		28.9122	35.116	64.028	
Other Share Holders Dividend		4.9878	2.554	7.5418	

Sources: Compiled by the Author; data from PPL and OGDC Annual Reports

While infra-structure projects are capital intensive, micro and small loans could directly benefit the local populations. Non-tribal, private enterprise development can only come through such small credit schemes. As the target group is comparatively smaller, not a lot of money would be required; 5-10 Billion Rupees of such loans as opposed to gas royalty arrears of Rs 120 Billion is not much. However, peace would be required to launch such initiatives. Those who have personal agendas and want secession would not like any such initiative to be launched or succeed. They have managed to create scare and instability and the settlers and skilled persons from other provinces have mostly fled away. However, there would be sufficient number of people and political forces which may come forward and play their role and benefit from the economic opportunities so created.

Chapter Appendix

Center - Province relationship in Oil and Gas sector in federal countries

In this appendix, we provide an overview of the centre-province relationship in the oil and gas sector in several federal countries such as USA, Canada, Argentina, Brazil, Australia, India and Pakistan. Also useful data is provided in this respect in the form of tables and figures.

In the **United States** oil and gas and mineral resources belong to the owner of the land, even if he, she is a private individual. In the US, 30% of public land belongs to the federal government, hence 30% ownership. However, 90% of the rent, royalty and revenues go to the states. Federal government has more say in offshore production than on-shore one.

In the US, except for a 3 mile shore adjacent area, off shore land is in the ownership of federal government and as such all revenue/rents /royalty on offshore oil and gas is federal. Some 40%share of offshore oil/gas income goes to the states adjacent to the offshore area.

In the **Brazilian** constitution, oil reserves found off shore and on-shore belong to the Union (federal government). However oil income legislation has been made to grant 60% of royalties to producing states and municipalities. Currently debate is going on the division of income from off shore production, equally among all states / provinces, as oil belongs to all Brazilian people.

Argentina: Since the constitutional reforms of the 1994, oil, gas and other subsoil natural resources lie in the provincial domain; ownership, control and income. Provinces collect royalties on oil and gas and have the legal power to collect other taxes on economic activities and assets, like the gross sales tax, property tax, vehicles stamp duty on contract. Provinces also get a share in federal taxes or proceeds except on exports/imports. Federal government collects fuel taxes and shares the proceeds with provinces. Provincial government is empowered to grant oil/ gas/ mineral concessions, permits and licenses related with E&P.

India: Articles 294- 297 of the Indian Constitution provide that the ownership and natural resources located within the territory of a state rest with that state. However this ownership is not absolute and has been qualified by several parallel regulations. Management of the Oil and Gas sector is under control of the federal government. Royalties are decided by federal government and provinces cannot levy any tax on oil/ gas. Petroleum law "the petroleum and natural gas rules" has been federally promulgated, and has to be followed by the states / provinces. Although states may grant concessions and licenses and lease, these have to be cleared/ approved by respective federal ministry.

All offshore resources are owned by the Union (federal government). Except for royalty and a few traditional provincial taxes such as on property, vehicles etc all other taxes go to federal government/Union. There is no sharing of corporate income tax etc. Union's share in total oil/gas revenues has stood to be 84% and only 16% has gone to the states by the year 1996-2000. Thereafter the Union to states ratio of income became more balanced at the 67.33, two third (67%) going to federation and 33% to the province. The dominance role and clout of public sector oil companies have further diluted states authority and leverage.

Canada: For on-shore oil and gas, provincial ownership and domain exists. Offshore oil and gas falls under federal jurisdiction. Income is however remitted to adjacent province. Both federation and provinces levy income tax not on just oil and gas but in general. Thus in this way, provinces also share in the corporate tax.

Australia: In Australia, oil and gas production are not significant as compared to other sources, and not much attention has been paid on the subject. Under British Common Law oil/gas and minerals belonged to the owner of the land, be it private individual or province or federal government. Later government ownership was introduced. Provinces own and control on-shore oil and gas and receive royalty, lease/rentals etc, while in off-shore production, federation gets 4% royalty and states 8%.

185

Pakistan: Constitution of Pakistan (1973 and as updated 2010 through 18th amendment) puts oil and natural gas in federal legislative list Part 11. However, most revenues related to oil and gas including royalty, excise, gas development surcharge go straight to the provinces. Corporate Income Tax and GST however goes to the federal government. However there is no mention in the constitution regarding ownership of natural resources. Complete resource management cycle is managed by the federal ministry of fuel and natural resources and no provincial control or permission is involved.

Source: Pakistan's development challenges; federalism, governance and security (Akhtar Ali, 2009, Royal Book Co)

Table 10.2: Centre State revenue Share across exploration and production regimes.

Charges		Nominated	Pre NELP	NELP
Fees	Onshore	States	States	States
	Offshore	Centre	Centre	Centre
Dead rent	Onshore	States	States	States
	Offshore	Centre	Centre	Centre
Royalty	Onshore	States	States	States
	Offshore	Centre	Centre	Centre
Oil Industry Development Cess	Onshore	Centre	Centre	Centre
	Offshore	Centre	Centre(N OCs only)	-
Fines / Penalties	Onshore	-	States	States
	Offshore	-	Centre	Centre
Profit Petroleum	Onshore	-	Centre	Centre
	Offshore	-	Centre	Centre
Income Tax	Onshore	Centre	Centre	Centre After 7 yrs
	Offshore	Centre	Centre	Centre After 7 yrs
Minimum alternate tax	Onshore	Centre	Centre	Centre
	Offshore	Centre	Centre	Centre
Custom duty	Onshore	Centre	Centre	-
	Offshore	Centre	Centre	-

Source: Ligia Noronha and Nidhi Srivastava, Oil and Gas Management and Revenues in India, World Bank Conference, Oil and Gas in Federal Systems, Washington, D.C., 2010

Table 10.3: Oil & Gas Revenues (2009/2010) Billion Rupees

	Balochistan	NWFP	Punjab	Sindh	Pakistan
Royalty on crude oil	0	2469	1429	3915	7813
Royalty on natural gas	4443	2729	1214	18129	26515
GDS	5632	2159	1631	19915	29338
Excise duty on gas	1371	191	191	4545	6458
Total	**11446**	**7548**	**4465**	**46504**	**70124**
% of total revenues	17.0	6.6	1.0	14.2	3.0

Source: Gulfaraz Ahmedi, Management of Oil and Gas Revenues in Pakistan, World Bank Conference, Oil and Gas in Federal Systems, Washington, D.C., 2010

11 Energy Resource Development

Energy sector has a potential to drown Pakistan

Last oil price hike was among one of the major factors of devastating Pakistan's economy. What will another hike do is any body's guess? Great risk lies in there. Our dependence on oil is increasing despite such impending and known risk. Almost all power plants that have come on stream recently run on oil; more are to come. Domestic oil production is not increasing, despite some potential. Gas production is going down and in the process of being used up. New exploration and discoveries are hampered due to political and law and order problems in Balochistan and elsewhere. Despite Balochistan package and other palliatives and offers, political situation in Balochistan has only worsened. And do not think that only military can solve this problem. It can only make it worse.

There is no serious break through on Thar Coal despite great potential. It is difficult to imagine for outsiders like us as to what stalls progress on Thar coal. Probably Sindh has overplayed its card of provincial autonomy assuming exclusive control over an issue that has many interfaces. And now it is appearing to come close to a failure. Some new initiative is required to cause a breakthrough. Now floods would be a good excuse for every inefficient entity to hide under its cover. On the other hand federal bureaucracy, barring some settlement on "joint development", seems to be searching for options except Thar coal. Chinese have been prevailed to supply more nuclear reactors, which are three times more expensive in capital costs and associated with many other hurdles and political difficulties.

We must be clear in our minds that only Chinese can possibly develop Thar coal in the remote and scorching heat of Thar Desert. No other country or company can handle the risks involved in this size of the project. You can sign nth MOUs, nothing would happen. As a token World Bank has withdrawn support among criticism of financing dirty

189

coal. I hope we manage to put our act together before it is too late and financing coal is stopped altogether in the nearing prospects of solar power. The solution may lie in awarding a 5000 MW project to Chinese to include all the infrastructure development costs. Chinese may agree to it on suitable terms.

I heard nationalist leader spitting venom on hydel power and dams, despite being drowned in flood water. What more rationale and justification can be given of excess water to be stored in dams than these horrific floods in which 45 MAF (million acre feet) of water has over-flown in a few days as opposed to a normal flow of 100 MAF over the entire year? The combined storage of all the dams proposed to be built is smaller than this flow. It is hoped that barring these ignorant people in Sindh in general are not going to block dams any further. If they do they would be drowned again and again and resultantly the whole of Pakistan. Dams have long been used throughout to store water and prevent floods. Americans, Chinese, Brazilians, Indians and others have done it successfully. There is no colonialism about it. Let us hope that sense prevails ultimately.

And as for the pricing, GOP has been subsidizing electricity amounting to Rs 150 billion per year. It has not been able to pay it however, along with the non-payment of electricity bills by the provincial governments. This has given rise to circular debt of Rs 200 billion. It does not get paid off, as more amounts are added to it successively. And IMF is also asking to do away with these subsidies. If these subsidies are withdrawn, along with the uniform subsidized tariff, electricity rates in Sindh, KP and Balochistan would increase. In Punjab electricity rates are expected to go down? Why? Is it another so called" machination from Punjab" as many nationalists would be akin to term it? Not really the story is as follows. About 25 % of electricity is lost in T&D losses; a large part of it is theft. This T&D loss (theft mostly) is not uniform through out Pakistan. In Punjab, it is the lowest; around12% in northern and central Punjab and 15% in southern Punjab. Everywhere else, these losses are in the range of 35-45%.Currently these excessive losses are hidden and averaged out in uniform tariff. Without electricity subsidy borne out by the GOP, every province and user would pay for its losses. Thus Punjab having lesser losses would end up in lower tariff and the opposite will happen to the users elsewhere.

As it is electricity is expensive and kind of unaffordable for most of the people and even businesses, a Pandora box will open up. The issue may not end up in terms of the aforementioned cool and cold logic. The issue is far more complicated. KP will argue that you take away our (it is not theirs' solely) cheap hydro electricity at one Rupee a unit and sell it back to us at 6-7 Rupees. In Balochistan cost of gas fired electricity is Rupees 4 per unit and similarly Sindh produces a lot of gas for electricity production. What is the way out? Balochistan's consumption is quite low and could be jangled in a variety of ways. In Sindh, problems would be further compounded due to KESC vs rest of Sindh. More thinking is required on this.

However KP issue can be at least partly resolved by resolving the Hydel Profit/Royalty of Tarbela Dam produced electricity. No permanent solution has been implemented. Despite practical suggestions proposed by this scribe some 18 months back. My suggestion is simple. Give 12% of Tarbela generated electricity to KP free as royalty or alternatively pay 12% royalty at CPPA whole sale price. Both are more or less equivalent, transparent and simple to understand and not mired by the complicated calculations of AGN Kazi. It is being done in India, a country not disliked by Sarhadi Gandhi to say the least? Elsewhere the royalties are lesser. This maximum should be acceptable to the government of KP and even the other distracters. An early decision should be made in this respect in consultation with the stakeholders. These royalties should go towards adjustments of tariff increases. I would tend to support 12% free electricity which has a larger public appeal and would be politically attractive.

Finally energy conservation and efficiency issues should receive government support and attention. A unit saved is a unit produced and even worth more due to environmental reasons. In order to remain out of technical complexity, let me propose here to reduce the demand of air-conditioning to a more acceptable level. Two or even three piece suits have become unduly popular in Pakistan government and business circles, requiring chilling while the outside temperature may be 45°C or more. This is awfully expensive. Instead Bush shirts should be promoted, as one Japanese P.M. reportedly proposed for his country in the context of rising cost of energy. GOP has already taken steps towards reducing Ac loads. More should be done; How about reverting back to Kurta Shalwar.

In the medium term, several measures can be taken. Cheaper energy resources such as natural gas are running out and being increasingly replaced by expensive oil. More gas resources can be developed, existing and remaining ones put on fast track and abundant cheaper resources be put into the energy mix. CNG had been found to be a great way to at least partially insulate from high oil prices. Conventional wisdom popular among bureaucracy today is that CNG is to be discouraged, because we are running out of gas. I have a slightly different perspective. There is hardly any substitute to oil for the transport sector except CNG, while other sectors like industry and power can have alternative sources like coal, nuclear etc.

Oil and Gas Potential

Many reliable sources have indicated that there is much more gas potential, as much as six times greater, than has been discovered already. Exploration activities have been hampered by the poor law and order situation and lethargy and inefficiency of our companies like OGDC and PPL etc. Gas exploration and development is no secret or rocket science. If we put our house in order, activate and energize these companies and apportion some investment (almost the same as we would be spending on subsidies and higher oil prices).

One should not become complacent with the profitability of these companies, which is natural in high oil price environment. Their original mandate is Exploration and Development. Technology is changing. Those oil and gas resources that were marginal and were abandoned are suddenly becoming productive. In the US gas prices have plummeted recently due to the advent of new technology. The technology is available and can be further facilitated through the US AID programme.

There are many options even with the old technology. Thus with more gas and more CNG, the required insulation from higher oil prices for the transport sector is very much on the cards. More gas can also go into power sector. But there are other more appropriate options as we shall see in the following. Some crash action is required.

I am not the only maverick privy to all this information. In 2005, a presentation was given by the then chairman of the Planning Commission, to the then President and the Prime Minister in the presence of all the Who is who's of the scientific and petroleum bureaucracy. The presentation is available on internet. One of the major conclusions of the study/presentation was the Gas potential. It was projected then that there was enough Gas potential to generate 80,000 MW of electricity by 2030, as opposed to 5-6000 MW of gas based electricity generation today.

Even if the projection is dubbed as an over-shot, there is consensus that much more gas potential is there. Instead of developing local potential we are running after imported options, for which neither the government nor the people will have the resources to pay for. Be it LNG from Qatar or pipeline gas from Iran, the sellers are linking the gas price to 75-85 % of oil price and are in no mood to entertain floors and slabs, limiting the damaging peaks in prices. The imported gas will be more than twice as expensive as locally produced gas, and as much expensive as oil. Let us have a serious look at our domestic options.

Exploring non conventional gas (shale) resources

I would like to draw the attention of the readers and policy-makers on yet another vast potential, called Shale Gas. There are two types of Gas resources; conventional or core resources, the ones we are consuming now; b) non-conventional gas resources. The non-conventional resources have three further classifications ;a) Coal-based methane found in coal deposits ;b)Tight gas resources ,are the ones which have been abandoned earlier due to special problems and were not explored .On Tight gas resource GOP has issued a draft policy, which process is moving at a snail pace , and needs to be expedited. ; c) Shale Gas is a relatively new resource and technology that has not been discussed or evaluated much in Pakistan. My focus in this article is on Shale gas.

But before, I dilate on the Shale gas issue, I would like to say a few words about Coal-based Methane (CBM) gas resources potential and its exploration and exploitation in Thar Cola field. Currently Under ground Coal Gasification project is at an advanced stage of implementation. I would propose that the scope and domain of the project be extended to explore CBM gases as well. It is not a very difficult task, and drilling of only 100-200 meters is required as opposed to thousands of meters in case of conventional oil and gas. Foreign companies have earlier been awarded exploration licenses earlier, but were cancelled for unknown reasons. Sindh government would be doing a lot of good to the province, if it starts taking interest in this matter as well, by initiating policy processes and practical steps including the ones proposed earlier.

American Petroleum Institute (API) defines Shale gas as, "natural gas from shale formations. The shale acts as both the source and the reservoir for the natural gas. Older shale gas wells were vertical while more recent wells are primarily horizontal and need artificial stimulation, like hydraulic fracturing, to produce. Only shale formations with certain characteristics will produce gas. The most significant trend in US natural gas production is the rapid rise in production from shale formations. In large measure this is attributable to significant advances in the use of horizontal drilling and well stimulation technologies and refinement in the cost-effectiveness of these technologies. Hydraulic fracturing is the most significant of these.".... "Tight gas, coal-bed methane, and shale gas will make a major contribution to future North American gas production. Unconventional gas production is forecast to increase from 42 percent of total US gas production in 2007 to 64 percent in 2020. Despite the current economic conditions, the long-term need for US natural gas should be strong enough to support these anticipated future production levels".

Today, due to the emergence of these new resources, there is a glut of gas in the US. Instead of importing gas from Canada and LNG from the Middle East, there are talks of exporting gas. Gas prices in the US have plummeted to less than 4 USD per 1000 Cft. This is despite, rising oil prices. The US resources of gas are now forecast to extend beyond 100 years, at current rate of consumption and including these resources. We can have like of the same. We are also one of the significant gas producing countries of the world. Lethargy and despondency that seems to have taken over us must go.

Yet, there is another gas resource that has a significant potential. Stranded gas resource are those which could not be utilized for a variety of reasons; being of low heating value ,of not pipe line quality ; away from network; or not being in sufficient quantities. UCH gas resources were once considered stranded and were not utilized due to low heating value. It was used later by an IPP, which project is now being expanded after a very successful first installation. There are reportedly many stranded resources which could be put to use by creative policies. For example, rental or mobile power plants could be installed around such resources. GOP has reportedly announced its intentions to move in this direction.

Oil and gas sector in Pakistan is a victim of neglect for a long time now. There have been controversies in appointment of management and chief executive of such vital organizations like OGDC. Ministers have been changed, one after the other, and none of them had familiarity with the sector. Provincial autonomy issues have also caused uncertainty. Whatever is the political dispensation or the approach to slice the pie, the need for an organized core establishment in this sector cannot be over-emphasized. Issuing policies alone, although necessary, is not enough. Policies have to be implemented. Both Foreign Exploration Investment and as well as national one are required. As the former finance minister Shoukat Tarin, once said, we are following soft paths of launching energy import projects instead of developing our own.

The US government has expressed its willingness to share this technology with other nations and has taken certain practical steps in this direction. Global Shale Gas Initiative (GSGI) has been launched, and many nations including India and China have been taken as members of this initiative. Unfortunately, Pakistan despite being dubbed as most allied ally or lackey or care-taker of US interest is found nowhere in the list. Partly or mostly, the fault probably lies with us, of not showing interest and lobbying enough in this respect. Part of the problem lies in the under-development of our oil sector, and partly the law and order situation in our gas prone areas, which discourages involvement of external parties, agencies and companies.

We have to do something about these issues and work towards a political break-through and settlement with the disgruntled forces, and pave the way for initiating much needed efforts both to exploit conventional and new resources in the Oil and Gas sector. On diplomatic front, instead of almost a sole focus on acquiring arms from the US, or cash resources, technical and technological acquisitions such as in Shale gas development should be pursued.

I would also appeal to our US benefactors to be more willing and forthright in this respect, as we do not find much of the physical evidence of the promised US assistance and support to Pakistan in the Energy sector. Instead of forecasting or planning on how to deal with a potentially divided and anarchic Pakistan, (as one of my old friends Prof. Stephen Cohen of Brookings Institution and a well-known expert on Pakistan has recently written), it would be a good investment to take care of some of Pakistan's critical problems.

The Thar Coal

I will bring in the oft-repeated Thar coal issue, which is on the table for at least a decade. Almost all major experts and consultancies have prepared reports on it and have found it feasible. Thar coal is almost equal to the combined total of oil and gas resources of Iran and Saudi Arabia put together, in terms of its energy content. Worldwide coal base electricity is less than fifty percent cheaper. Imported energy will continue to be expensive than local resources, despite the role of all the rentiers classes. No serious move seems to be in the offing. If the ten point agenda deliberations only manage to find out a way for breakthrough on Thar, it would in itself be a major achievement.

The bureaucratic circles tend to show that there is progress on Thar coal. But the fact remains, that there is almost none. Allocation of blocks, MOUs and even feasibility studies do not mean much, as many such things have been done in the past. Under-ground coal gasification project has raised false hopes among the public. Without casting doubts on the scientific credentials of its eminent promoters and on the technological potential of the route adopted, the problem of scaling up would remain for which there is no capability in the country of a level that would be acceptable to the lending banks. While the existing gasification would yield useful data, we would be back to the square one, which is of requisite financing.

The bad news is that under criticism and pressure from international Green lobbies, World Bank has discontinued its technical assistance program on Thar coal, amidst news that government of Sindh has persuaded them to renew it. Even if they do renew, it sends us ample signals on difficulties that we are going to face towards financing Thar coal. With time, the opposition to coal would increase. Our problem is immediate and the renewables are still to be perfected and improved to be cost effective and competitive. In any case, renewables are projected to have a share of 20% even by the year 2050 .What are we to do in the meantime. The threat is that by the time we put our act together, although fossil based power age may not be over, the financing regime may become too difficult and hostile against coal.

The residual issue as it stands today is not the financing issue of the mining and power parts of the projects, however difficult it may itself be, it is the financing of infrastructure part which is proving to be a stumbling block. Various estimates put these requirements to between 1 to 2 billion US dollars. More money is required for infrastructure, than the first coal mine and power plant itself .Government of Sindh, obviously would not have such resources, nor would the federal government. And in these days of emphasis on provincial autonomy, where is the appetite for common projects. There are also issues as to the technical and management capability of the provincial bureaucracy, as the project continues to be run from the narrow confines of the Sindh secretariat. Apparently, there is no shaft of light at the end of this tunnel, although it is not the only one.

In all humbleness, this scribe makes the following proposals. There are two options. One is to tender for a large project of 5000 MW or so, which may be able to assume the infrastructural development costs. The cake becomes big enough to absorb all kinds of interests. This is not new. In India, these sizes of coal projects are being planned already. The feasibility of this proposal in Pakistan context can only be tested once it is actually tendered. The second option would be to float tenders for establishing a mining development company that undertakes to develop and finance the infrastructure and manages the Thar coal operations on behalf of Sindh government, within the framework of the relevant rules and regulations. The company recoups its investments by granting mining leases and charging a fee on coal production by individual companies. Obviously such a company would be a multinational which may have a joint venture with local private sector and government of Sindh's share in it. Such a company would offer many advantages. First of all to bring in finances, which appear to be well-nigh impossible for Sindh government to finance? Secondly, the operations would be more commercial like and would be on fast track. Ironically, I have made a case of yet another feasibility study? Not necessarily.

Wind Power

There is a 20,000 MW resource lying unutilized close to Karachi near Gharo. Wind Turbine prices are coming down for the last two years. There apparently is no move in this direction. If at all, it is quite likely that NEPRA would be approving projects at previously held high rates, as has been the case with a few other projects. India has been able to install 11000 MW of wind power capacity, at 50% cost of the international prices utilizing its low labor costs and other advantages. The same could have been done here, utilizing the underutilized capacities in the countries major projects like Heavy Mechanical Complex and Karachi Shipyard, and the private sector as well.

Inadequate Regulatory Structures and processes

Energy costs and prices cannot be reduced by mere pressurization of the political government or the regulatory agencies. However, they can be made more efficient and responsive. The whole Energy sector worth more than twenty billion USD in terms of output runs under a cost-plus system requiring efficient regulatory structures, mechanisms and processes. I t is a common knowledge that there is a considerable padding in capital costs of energy projects, especially electricity. It is not just the rental power alone. There is much more to that. NEPRA lacks the competence to deal with it, nor does it seem to be interested in going any deeper into this. It restricts itself to browbeat the proponents and perfunctory adjustments without recourse to independent advice and recourse to data sources. It is following an ill advised policy of making profit and investments in construction projects, instead of spending adequately on scrutinizing cases.

The situation is even worse in the Oil and Gas sector. Oil and Gas Regulatory Authority (OGRA) has not been given any powers by the relevant ministry and it acts hardly more than a bureaucratic calculator, without scrutinizing the underlying data. The reader can gauge the lack of regulatory process by the fact that it calculates/regulates the price of LDO only, which is not more than 1% or less than the total diesel consumption. The prices of the real Diesel (HSD) used by the public transport are surreptitiously posted on PSO web-site without any due process. To talk of the due process, OGRA does not go into the pretense of holding public consultation, except the two gas companies. In the US, which is an oil producer, oil prices are lower than the International prices by a good margin often of 10%.In Pakistan, although there is an explicit policy in this respect; OGRA has been kept at bay from scrutinizing payments to the companies. All oil transportation pipeline companies are beyond any worthwhile regulatory process, despite cost-plus payments. In a country which has consistently earned high ranking in the corruption indices of the Transparency International, one can only guess what may be happening. It certainly does not generate confidence.

Global Shale Gas Initiative: US Government

Overview

The Department of State (DOS) launched the Global Shale Gas Initiative (GSGI) in April 2010 in order to help countries seeking to utilize their unconventional natural gas resources to identify and develop them safely and economically. Shale gas is one of the most rapidly expanding trends in onshore U.S. oil and gas exploration and production. According to the U.S. Energy Information Administration (EIA), during the last decade, U.S. shale gas production has increased fourteen-fold; it now accounts *for 22% of U.S. gas production and 32% of total remaining recoverable gas resources in the United States. By 2030, EIA projects that shale gas will represent 14% of total global gas supplies, providing the reserve base necessary for expanded consumption in a business as usual scenario. Future climate policies could increase demand for shale gas since it is a lower-carbon "bridge fuel" to reduce CO_2emissions. Although the U.S. shale gas experience cannot be precisely duplicated, its application through GSGI can be instrumental in helping governments understand the complexities of shale gas development. Governments often have limited capability to assess their own country's shale resource potential or are unclear about how to develop shale gas in a safe and environmentally sustainable manner through establishing the right regulatory policy and fiscal structures. The ultimate goals of GSGI are to achieve greater energy security, meet environmental objectives and further U.S. economic and commercial interests.*

Country Participation

Countries have been selected to participate in GSGI based in part on the known presence of natural gas-bearing shale within their borders, market potential, business climates, geopolitical synergies, and host government interest. Within GSGI, priority countries have the greatest potential for benefiting from GSGI opportunities. Other, non-priority, GSGI participants include those countries that have expressed interest and meet GSGI criteria. To date, partnerships under GSGI have been announced with China, India, Jordan and Poland, with bilateral agreements possible with several other additional countries.

Government-to-Government

The GSGI uses government-to-government policy engagement to bring the U.S. federal and state governments' technical expertise, regulatory experience and diplomatic capabilities to help selected countries understand their shale gas potential. U.S. government agencies that partner with the Department of State under GSGI include: the U.S. Agency for International Development (USAID); the Department of Interior's U.S. Geological Survey (USGS); Department of Interior's Bureau of Ocean Energy Management, Regulation, and Enforcement (BOEMRE); the Department of Commerce's Commercial Law Development Program (CLDP); the Environmental Protection Agency (EPA), and the Department of Energy's Office of Fossil Energy (DOE/FE). A benefit of this government-to-government cooperation is the potential for establishing and strengthening long-term working relationships   at   the   technical   and   ministerial   levels.

Sample Activities

GSGI activities are tailored to each country's specific needs and availability of funding. Examples of GSGI activities in priority countries include: shale gas resource assessments; technical guidance to evaluate the production capability, economics and investment potential of shale gas resources; and workshops and seminars on technical, environmental, business and regulatory challenges related to shale gas development. Engagement with non-priority countries focuses on regulatory policies and fiscal structures challenges. At the request of these countries, DOS organizes conferences, meetings, training and public-private sector events in the United States. They are also invited to participate in select multilateral GSGI events.

Source: www.state.gov/gsgi

Energy Security Plan

Planning Commission of Pakistan prepared an Energy Security Plan (ESP) in 2005, and presented it with much fanfare to the then Prime Minister and the President. The Plan still remains operative in the books of the government departments, and is quoted and discussed annually in the Economic Survey. In practical terms, ESP was a non-starter. It was not implemented even by the previous government .By 2010, an additional 7880 MW of Electrical Power capacity was to be installed .Only a few hundred MW was installed and consequently we have a deficit of 4000 MW today. Why the "conscientious" Musharraf government was so derelict in meeting its responsibilities in this respect, is a serious question. Equally serious question is what the relevant bureaucracy was doing. Prime Minister Gilani fired the previous MD of Private Power and Infrastructure Board (PPIB) on this account, despite intense lobby in the favor of the latter's extension of the contract. More heads should have rolled and a serious review of official practices in power sector ordered.

What is known can be visualized by one single example. A veritable Chinese company spent two years in Thar Coal field, prepared a feasibility study, offered to make the investment and supply electricity at the rate of 5.5 cents per unit. The then military commander holding charge of WAPDA for the reasons best known to him opposed and rejected the offer. We are buying electricity today at twice the Chinese offer and Thar Coal remains unexploited. It so incensed the Chinese that despite many requests the Chinese do not return to Thar.

Returning to the Energy Security Plan (ESP), there is hardly any possibility that it would be implemented as per its projections and estimates. The Plan was so grandiose and unrealistic which could have only pleased a fascist agenda and ruling culture. One gets nervous on our Planning Commission's ability to become so frivolous in its planning practices. I will discuss the details a bit later in these passages, suffice it is to state here to support my contention that the ESP provided 4860 MW of generation capacity based on Natural Gas. Shortage of gas is in the country now for many years. It was known even in 2005, when the Plan was made. One may fail in long term projections, but what to term this kind of outright frivolity.

Long term projections can falter at the altar of reality especially in Pakistan's boom-bust type economy and polity, reversing it in seven years cycles. ESP projected requirements of 72,270 MW by 2020, by the way of installing an additional 50,000 MW in the period 2010-2020, and again half of it to come on Natural Gas. Realistically speaking, only half of that would materialize. We should be thankful and happy, if half of that is achieved. There is no way that the demand could reach a level of 72,270 MW by 2020 in a matter of ten years. ESP predicts an electrical demand of 162,590 MW by 2030, again half of which to come from natural gas: very grotesque and unrealistic projection. Where are they seeing the gas from? Even if both the projects of LNG and the Iran-Pakistan pipeline were implemented and more of the same are added, this kind of gas wouldn't be available.

Electricity demand in Pakistan has grown at a rate of 5% per year , and even at higher assumed rate of 7 % per annum ,the demand is to double every ten years , unless we become Chinese by some magic. By that robust formula, the demand would be 50,000 MW by 2020 , and 100,000 MW by 2030 , most of which should be planned to come from Thar Coal, Hydro ,renewables and nuclear and not from gas , as has been proposed in the ESP. There is, however, a potential of gas discoveries in Balochistan, if sufficient exploration effort and investment is directed. The prospects of such effort appear to be minimal in current political and law and order situation prevailing in that province. This may remain a much desired dream, and robust planning should not be based to depend so heavily on a break-through in that respect.

The problem with frivolous planning is that plans are not respected and a careless atmosphere ensues which results in shortfalls and other problems and inadequacies that we are facing today in energy sector. It is high time that ESP is buried with the kind of condemnation it deserves and a more realistic plan put into place and diligently implemented. Ironically, ESP was one of the rare indigenous planning efforts and failed miserably. Let us involve multi-lateral institutions in this as they do in all the other sectors to the chagrin of many nationalists and conspiracy theorists among us.

Table 11.1: Energy Security Plan (Planning Commission) – 2030: Electrical Power

	Nuclear	Hydel	Coal	Renewable	Oil	Gas	Total	Cumulative MW
Existing (2005)	400	6,460	160	180	6,400	5,940	19,540	
Addition								
2010	---	1.260	900	700	160	4,860	7,880	**27,420**
2015	900	7,570	3,000	800	300	7,550	20,120	**47,540**
2020	1,500	4,700	4,200	1,470	300	12,560	24,730	**72,270**
2025	2,000	5,600	5,400	2,700	300	22,490	38,490	**110,760**
2030	4,00	7,070	6,250	3,850	300	30,360	51,830	**162,590**
Total	**8,800**	**32,660**	**19,910**	**9,700**	**7,760**	**83,760**	**162,590**	

Source: Planning Commission of Pakistan / Economic survey of Pakistan 2008

12 Constitutional Issues in the Energy Sector

Some confusion persists as to the distribution of the roles of federation and provinces in the energy sector. Questions have been raised on the maintainability of NEPRA in its present form and the possible adjustments that may be required.

And there are other issues as well. It is highly desirable that constitutional issues and confusions, if any, be sorted out so that possible litigations of the future are avoided .Otherwise there is a danger that considerable time may be wasted in the legal adjudication process. Already cases are pending with the courts challenging the role of NEPRA in determining a uniform tariff in the country. There are demands for lower tariff s in the provinces (KP) which produce cheaper hydro electricity. In this space we will examine the contentious issues and look for possible adjustments and solutions in the pre-18th amendment energy regime that by and large persists even today.

Constitution of Pakistan divides subjects under Federal Legislative Lists part I and Part II. Subjects under Part I lie under exclusive federal domain which does not require any provincial role or consultation. Under 18th amendment, subjects under these lists have been changed along with the abolition of the much maligned Concurrent List. From the point of view of energy, only Nuclear energy falls under part I, and thus under exclusive federal domain. Subjects under Federal Legislative List part II are to be administered through Consultation s with the provinces under CCI (Council of Common Interest). Oil and Gas and Electricity fall under part II, requiring consultations with the province. Additionally regulatory bodies like NEPRA and OGRA also fall under FL part II. Furthermore, under 18th amendment, special provisions have been added which provide for much enhanced provincial role in Electricity. Provinces can now install generation and transmission facilities for provincial use. Provinces can now determine distribution tariff, which has hitherto remained a federal prerogative under NEPRA; easier legislated than actually done. Not much practical progress or implementation has been made with respect to the last item, even under much debated devolution scheme implemented in the wake of 18th amendment.

Electricity used to be in the concurrent list, the latter has been superseded by the 18th amendment. Although Electricity was in Concurrent list, there was hardly any provincial role in it. This could have been said for all items on the erstwhile concurrent list. This was perhaps the reason that the concurrent list has been eliminated altogether. Provinces in the earlier regime could have built power plants up to a capacity of 50 MW. The provision was minimally utilized by the provinces except for KP where significant activity took place in small hydro power under a provincial agency called SHYDO.

Table 12.1: Constitutional provisions in Energy sector

Eminent Federal domain (Federal Legislative List Part I)

1. Nuclear Energy and its complete fuel cycle
2. Taxes on minerals and oils (raw material inputs) for nuclear energy

Concurrent Federal domain (Federal Legislative List Part II to be administered by CCI)
1. Mineral oil and natural Gas
4. Hydro electricity and dams thereof
5. Thermal Electricity generation
6. Inter-provincial transmission network
7. All regulatory authorities established under Federal Law (NEPRA and OGRA).

Provincial domain under CCI and special provisions
8. Levy tax on consumption of electricity within the province.
9. Construct power houses and grid stations and lay transmission lines within and for use of the province.
10. Determine tariff for distribution of Electricity.
11. Coal (by omission; anything not mentioned in the federal list is automatically in provincial domain)
12. Renewable Energy (same as 11)

Source: Compiled by the author from the official text of the Constitution of Pakistan 2010 version.

As mentioned earlier, under the current (post 18th amendment) regime provinces can install any type or capacity of power plants out of their own resources and for use within the province. Also grid stations and transmission infrastructure could be handled or controlled by the provincial governments. However, it is seldom that a power plant of a reasonable capacity be restricted to local provincial use, except in Punjab where there is a large market. Investors and financers may like to have no restriction on this account. In most federal systems including India, Canada and the US, electricity is in provincial domain with independent provincial regulatory bodies.

However, there are regulatory bodies at federal levels like FERC in the US and CERC in India for dealing with inter-provincial and safety issues and performance standards. Borrowing from these countries, the role of NEPRA could be accordingly adjusted, meaning thereby that NEPRA's regulatory power is restricted to the federally financed projects and IPPs exceeding a certain size like 250 or 500 MW. Also the performance and safety issues may remain in exclusive NEPRA purview. The problem, however, is of capability and resources. Even at the federal level, performance of NEPRA has a lot to be desired not to talk of its future provincial offshoots. Then we have been talking of one window operation, which although could never be achieved, nevertheless remains a requirement for investor facilitation. The role of PPIB is another question in the new constitutional set-up. Then there are issues of sovereign guarantees as well which may cause complications and cross purpose processes. Although the sovereign guarantees are becoming outmoded, in some cases these may be essential. A clear organizational plan need s to be developed, whatever be the preferences and it has to be consistent with the constitutional provisions or constitution itself is amended or elaborated where it is found that there are inadequacies.

Even on Thar coal where there is a clear provincial domain and Thar Coal Board remained in provincial domain , reportedly there are issues and uncertainties that are vexing the potential investors .Who finances Thar coal infrastructure and accordingly what role is expected in lieu of the finances and possible guarantees provided by the federal government. Who approves Thar coal IPP's tariff, if it is for provincial purposes. On tariff of distribution companies, provincial exclusive domain has been provided by the constitution (18th amendment) and thus provincial regulator may be called for. It is another thing that some of the smaller provinces like KP and Balochistan may voluntarily transfer such a role to a federal body like NEPRA, for which there is a provision in the constitution. People in Sindh do not want to travel to Islamabad for approvals and may welcome the opportunity of installing its own provincial regulatory body.

On Oil and Gas, 18th amendment has not done much towards decentralization. There is eminent and exclusive federal domain on Oil and Gas which has been put under Part I of the fourth schedule. There are clear provisions of royalty and GST being transferred directly to the provinces. There is a case for looking into sharing corporate taxes with the producer provinces, especially Balochistan. At times corporate income tax may fetch much more money than the royalties, although this is truer in case of minerals where typical royalties are 1-3% as opposed to 12% of sales in case of Oil and Gas. Some nationalists or enthusiasts may argue for direct provincial collection of royalties which we would strongly oppose on grounds of transparency and institutional capacity issues. In most Africa, there is a lot of leakage in this respect in smaller African states. Federal collection and straight transfers would be in the interest of provinces especially smaller ones. Those who are aware of the problems and leakages in the provincial collections of vehicle tax especially in Sindh would agree with this proposal of continuing with the existing system.

There are much more complicated issues in the uniform prices of Electricity throughout Pakistan. Smaller provinces seem to be more vocal with respect to the proposition of doing away with uniform pricing. Uniform pricing is largely an off-shoot of the subsidy system. Its rationale may go away, if and when, the subsidies go away, which does not seem to be feasible in near term. One is not sure as to which province would be the net beneficiary or which one would be the net loser. There are counterbalancing factors. In Punjab, distribution losses are around 10-12%, as opposed to 30-45% elsewhere. But then Oil based expensive generation of electricity is more common in Punjab, while KP has cheap hydro power, and Sindh and Balochistan have relatively cheaper natural gas. New hydro power projects may not produce as cheap electricity as the existing ones due to much higher construction costs involved now. Hydro power from new projects may cost in excess of Rs 5.00 per unit as opposed to the current rate of Rs.1.50 per unit.

Royalties or net hydro profit issue has not been finally resolved. Constitution of Pakistan from the very beginning provide for the computation of the elusive term net hydel profit. WAPDA would like to pay, and as it is currently doing, on the basis of actual prices. KP, however, demands computation as per AGN Kazi formula and the tribunal's award, which calculates profit or benefit with respect to imputed prices and competing fuels. As per this formula, arrears of royalty/net hydro profit of Rs 110 billion have been computed. Present government in its initial euphoria committed to pay this amount and accepted the tribunals' award. It could not pay this liability, for obvious reasons. Only 10-15 billion rupees could have been paid yet. Either a more acceptable formula may have to be devised or Tarbela project may have to be partially given in the ownership of the KP government, which may be able to earn some profit as a substitute for interest on the arrears that is not being paid to KP. We have made a similar case for a partial transfer of ownership of PPL in lieu of the arrears of Royalty payment of Sui gas.

Concluding, there are host of issues on which policy decisions have to be made with provincial consultations and working rules developed in other cases. Also new organizational adjustments have to be made in the wake of and in consistence with the 18th amendment. There is a need of looking into the 18th amendment itself for some adjustments such as a possible sharing formula for corporate taxation from mineral s and oil and gas. Resolution of the issues and the required fine tuning would clear up the current confusion and future potential litigations marring the prospects of growth in the energy sector, which currently suffers from very dim prognoses.

SECTION-III

Science & Technology

13 State of Science in Pakistan

The merits and the role of Science and Technology in the development and self reliance of nations cannot be over-emphasized. Be it food or weapons, one requires the aid of science and Technology. However, there is a pyramid at the base of which is the primary education and at the top of which is Technology. The journey to Science starts from full access to a good schooling system and passes through stages of higher education. We cannot possibly ignore one for the other. Infact, if priorities are to be ordered, schooling is first both in chronology and as well as importance. However, development takes place simultaneously in all stages. One stage is not to be stalled or blocked for the other. A balance has to be maintained.

In this country, it has happened that while primary education suffered and languished due to shortage of funds, Higher education and Science got a lopsided emphasis, which resulted in the waste of precious resources. It is ironic the democratic movements and systems have universally emphasized schooling in preference to any thing else, while dictatorships have preferred early growth in S&T and higher education in furtherance of militarization and fascist agenda. It started with Hitler and probably ended with Musharraf regime. All democracies in the industrialized world spend enormously on school education which is usually free. In North Korea, Pakistan and some other countries this has been the reverse. My compatriots would mind bracketing Pakistan with North Korea. The reality is that there are many similarities between the two countries ;poverty , hunger, lagging development, nuclear weapons and missile technologies, persecution complex, exhibitionism and showy capitals, dictatorships, grave issues with neighbors, small elite and big armies . Only lately, we may be distinguished from them due to the nascent6 democracy.

State of Education

A DFID study done in 2009 has made startling and rather depressing revelations which should have a sobering influence among concerned Pakistanis. Some of the salient points are;

1) Half of Pakistani students cannot read a sentence.
2) 25 million children are out of school.
3) A third of Pakistanis have received less than two years of schooling.
4) 30,000 schools are housed in poorly maintained dangerous buildings.
5) 21000 schools have no buildings at all.
6) There are 26 countries poorer than Pakistan but manage to send a
   higher percentage of children to schools than Pakistan.

The situation should have gone worse due to the ongoing financial crisis and the recent floods, as public expenditure on education has gone down in recent years to around or just under 2% of GDP in 2010, from a level of 2.47-2.5 % in 2005. It used to be around 1.66-1.8 % in 1990s (subtract corruption and leakages, what little would have been lift). By contrast India spends 3.3 % on education and Thailand 5%. UNESCO recommendation is for a minimum of 4% of GDP which has been a long time demand of civil society and wish of many Pakistanis. In absolute terms, total government expenditure (federal, provincial and district) went up to 254 billion Rs 1n 2008-9 from Rs 132 Billion in 2003-4. However, almost all of the increase went to Higher Education (HEC), which got a phenomenal increase from Rs 21 billion to Rs.132 billion during the same period. In the 5-6 years period, 600 billion Rs should have been spent on HEC. There has been progress and output, but probably at a great loss to the primary school education. Also one has to ask the question, if the cost benefit ratio is positive or comparable. The expenditure level was definitely unreasonable and that is why all kind of wasteful and quixotic projects were conceived and launched. Present government has done well to restore the balance, although under severe financial constraints. This was certainly not sustainable.

Can you launch a meaningful Scientific program or campaign based on so poorly educated children as has been mentioned earlier, or higher education is meant only for the sons of the elite or the more fortunate ones who manage to send their off-springs to the private schools. A reasonable budgetary ratio should have been maintained between the budgets of primary, secondary and higher education. Otherwise not only poor science would result along with all kinds of social and political problems and deteriorating law and order problems.

While our scientific community recommends or demands more expenditure on S&T and R&D, amounting to 1%, 2% and even higher percentages of GDP to be allocated to their subjects, they should not lose sight of the basic and fundamental realities. They should not lobby or accept higher allocations at the cost of basic education. Unless total revenue as a % of GDP increases and different set of priorities are chosen, any meaningful increase in S&T allocation would be injurious to the very cause of science they are pleading; otherwise they would be considered a mere interest group .More output should come out from the existing allocations and we know that there is a lack of meaningful performance.

Also the elitist culture of proposing higher and higher benefits to the scientific and professor community must be shun in place of more reasonable levels. The draft S&T policy demands of higher and more lucrative SPS grades. Money is never enough. Those who run after money cannot apply their minds on science and students. In the center of technology the US, lawyers, artists and fiction writers make more money than the teachers. Most people in Pakistan live in financial distress and low living standards and university professors are better off than many. Those of science professors who want to make more should open their own businesses, as many of their counterparts do in the West quite frequently and successfully. One would like to support such facilitation programs such as incubators for this kind of expansion.

Scientific or Technological progress

Pakistan has made substantial Technological progress over the last 60 plus years or say since 1960s. Yes, it probably has. Technical change is not just high technology; it is the right and appropriate technology required at a particular stage of development. Even there, having made nuclear weapons, is an indicator of progress in high technology sector. However, in the terms of how economists measure technical change or progress, there has been a significant achievement as well, although more so in the economy and in industrial sector than in agriculture. Economists measure it through what they call Total Factor Productivity (TFP), although there is a group of respectable economists who criticize such measures as to its adequacy. Pakistan had a TFP growth rate of 1.66 % per year in the period 1964-2000.In some periods this rate was higher such as 3.39%p.a. in 1964-70 and 2.4 % in 1980s , shamefully under the dictatorships ; in other transitional and less stable periods technical change or progress has been rather slow. By comparison, India had a TFP growth rate of 2.08% p.a. in 1980-2000.OECD countries maintained an average of 2-2.29%p.a. in the war and post-war period of 1913-1980.Technical change slowed down in the 1970s, and was higher than average in other years, such as 3% for Japan in 1950s and later.

Table 13.1: Total Factor Productivity (TFP) growth rates (%p.a.) of selected countries

OECD (1913-1980)	Economy (2 – 2.29)	Agriculture	Industry
India (1980-2000)	2.08		
Japan	1.78		
Korea	1.82		
Malaysia	1.29		
Pakistan (1964-2000)	1.66 [3]	0.37 [2]	3.21 [1]

(1) In Ayub period, this was 4.00 and Zia period 5.38%. (2) Except for Ayub Khan's green revolution period, TFP growth has been negative % however; during 1990s it recovered to 1.52%. (3) In Ayub period TFP growth of overall economy was 3.39%, which came down in 1970s to 2.1% and jumped–up again 1980s to a healthy 2.45% and went down again in 1990s to 0.78%.

Sources: 1) TFP growth, Survey Report, APO, 2004. 2) A.R. Kamal, in Technology based Industrial Vision and Strategy for Pakistan's Socio Economic Development, by Dr Ataur-Rehman & AR Kamal etal, HEC, 2008.

State of Science and Scientific research in Pakistan is not very good, and not good at all. It improved significantly over the last decade, qualitatively and quantitatively. Its actual output, outreach and effectiveness may take time to be assessed and actually felt. However, if measured in terms of inputs, there has been an increase of several times over the last decade. All of it may not have been usefully employed and perhaps was slightly wasteful, as alleged by the detractors, but most of it should have enlarged the base and strengthened the roots.

Most of the improvement has been made in the higher education sector and the researches therein under local and foreign PhD programs. There are five types of R&D institutions and R&D activities; Military R&D, with military or civilian control; b)R&DIs under the control of the Ministry of Science and Technology(MOST);c) R&DIs under line ministries; d)R&DIs in educational institutions and universities; d)R&D activities in the Universities(HEIs) under M.Phil or PhD programs or independent research undertaken by the teachers, or in association with the former.

Table 13.2: Science and technology indicators in selected countries

Countries	Researchers R&D per million people	Technicians R&D per million people	S&T journal articles	R&D Expenditures % of GDP	Technology Products exports $ millions	Technology Products exports % of manu-factured exports	Patent applications Residents	Patent applications Non-residents
	2000-07	2000-07	2005	2000-07	2008	2008	2008	2008
Pakistan	152	64	492	0.67	275	2	91	1,647
Turkey	680	102	7,815	0.71	1,807	2	2,221	176
Malaysia	372	44	615	0.64	42,764	40	818	4,485
Indonesia	205	..	205	0.05	5,625	11	282	4,324
Iran	706	..	2,635	0.67	375	6	..	..
Egypt	617	378	1,658	0.23	85	1	516	1,589
India	137	86	14,608	0.8	6,497	6	5,314	23,626
Brazil	629		9,889	1.02	10,572	12	3,810	20,264
South Africa	382	130	2,392	0.96	2,011	5		5,781
China	1,071		41,596	1.49	381,345	29	194,579	95,259
South Korea	4,627	720	16,396	3.47	110,633	33	127,114	43,518
Japan	5,573	589	55,471	3.45	123,733	18	330,110	60,892
France	3,440	1,768	30,309	2.1	93,209	20	14,743	1,962
Germany	3,453	1200	44,145	2.55	162,421	14	49,240	13,177
Spain	2,784	1,029	18,336	1.28	9,916	5	3,632	252
Italy	1,499		24,645	1.14	29,814	7	9,255	870
UK	2,881	879	45,572	1.84	61,767	19	16,523	6,856
Russia	3,305	516	14,412	1.12	5,107	7	27,712	14,137
USA	4,663		205,320	2.67	231,126	27	231,588	224,733

Source: World Bank WDI-2010

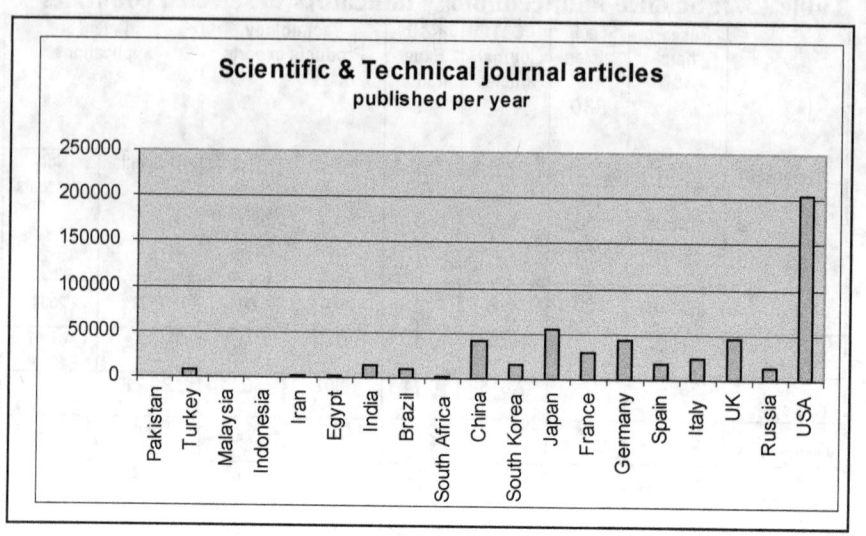

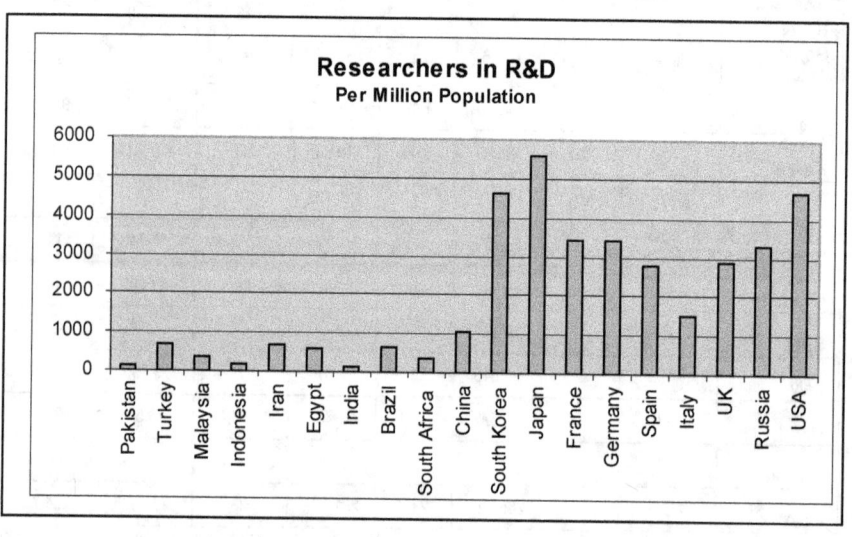

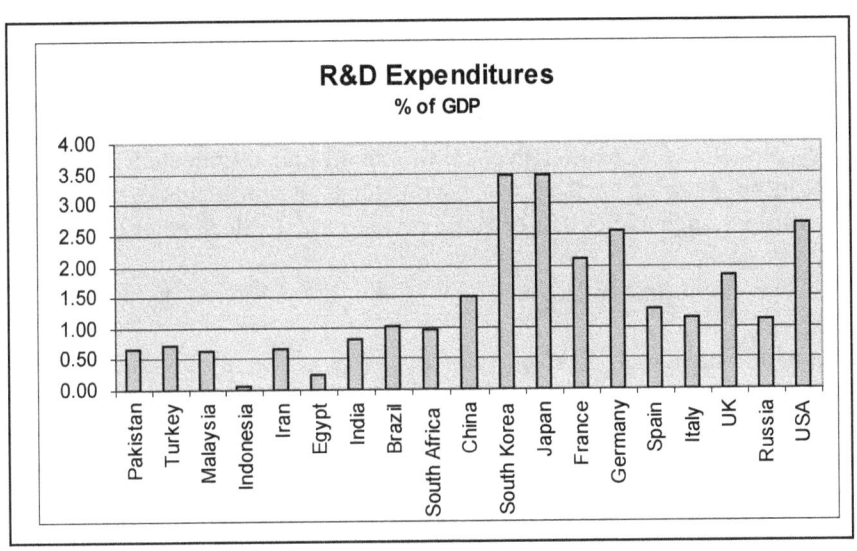

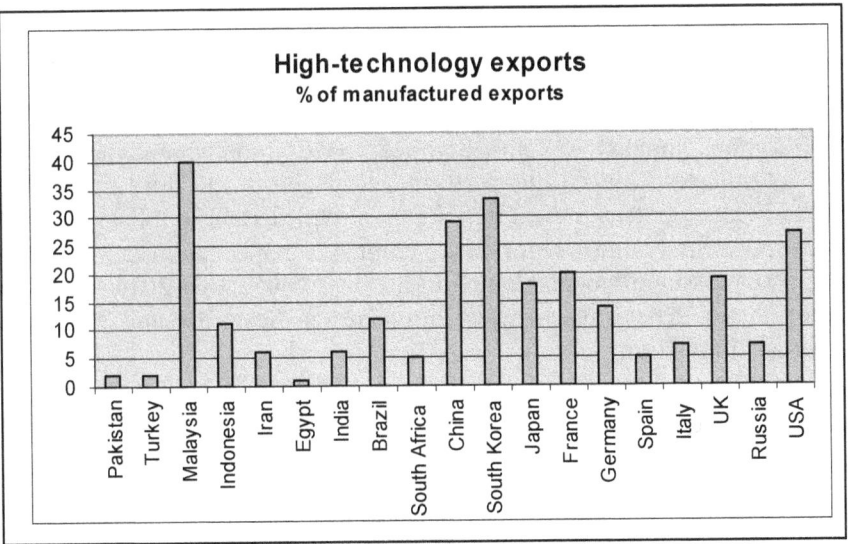

There are issues of relevance, duplication, output, effectiveness and efficiency, prioritization, spread etc. Some of the R&DIs are the relics of the past and have become ineffective and irrelevant or both and deserve either to be wound up or merged with allied institutions. While some duplication or lack of effectiveness may be tolerable, its extent is to be controlled by prioritization and resource constraints and supply.

217

Relevance may not always be immediately visible and can also be a transitional issue. A periodic strategic review taking may be required. Also, there is a need of a national research agenda. In some cases such as agriculture, it may be too obvious and determined by ongoing circumstances and issues. In other cases such as industry, it may not be very obvious. The market may be too small and fragmented. The issue would be taken up further, when we discuss the problems of individual institutions such as PCSIR, or National institute of Electronics (NIE) etc.

Measurement and Indicators

State of Science in Pakistan can be assessed by a few fundamental statistics. Following figures, mostly for the year 2006-07, in comparison with some selected developing countries may be noted;

1) Pakistan has 152 researchers per million of population, as opposed to 142 for India and 926 for China. Turkey has 680, Egypt 617 and Iran 706.

2) By the year 2001, research output in Pakistan was limited to 600 publications per year in international journals. Since then, however, research output has increased rather exponentially. The number of publications jumped to 2494 per year. Both funding and leadership seems to have achieved this performance which is still low, although. . World Development Indicators (WDI), a World Bank publication, has, however, grossly under-reported the number of papers published. May be there is an issue of nomenclature. In the year 2005, WDI-2010 reports, a total of 492 articles/papers were published in Scientific and Technical Journals in Pakistan.

3) A total of 23752 papers have been written since 1970s, bulk of which (83%) were in three disciplines; Biological Sciences (5136), Chemistry (9095) and Physics (4739). It is jokingly said about Chemistry papers that papers are the easiest to produce in this discipline. In agriculture, only 1814 papers, is really too little, keeping in view the number of researchers and magnitude of the problem that we have.

4) After considerable enhancement, R&D expenditure was 0.67 % of GDP in Pakistan. By comparison India spent 0.8 % and Brazil 1%. However, in this respect Pakistan compares well with Turkey, Iran and Malaysia.

5) Malaysia has 40 Billion USD of high technology exports, which was 40% of its total exports. By comparison Pakistan's corresponding exports were only worth 275 million USD, 2% of its total exports.

6) In terms of output performance of Pakistani Scientists and R&D institutions has been particularly disappointing. Patent applications filed are a good indicator, on which comparative data is available. In Pakistan, in the year 2008, only 91 patent applications were filed vis-à-vis 5314 in India and 3810 in Brazil. In Turkey 2221 applications were filed, in Malaysia 1267, and in Egypt 516.

Research and Development Institutions

There are 85 R&DIs (Research and Development Institutions) in Pakistan, which are exclusively focused on R&D. Research is also conducted in Higher Education Institutions(HEIs) and universities as well. Following are the major and eminent R&DIs, listed in random order;

1) HEJ Institute of Chemistry
2) Pakistan Council of Scientific and Industrial Research (PCSIR)
3) Pakistan Council of Research in Water Resources (PCRWR)
4) Pakistan Agricultural and Research Council (PARC)
5) National Institute of Biological and Genetic Engineering (NIBGE)
6) National Engineering and Scientific Commission (NESCOM)
7) National University of Science and Technology (NUST)
8) Sub and Upper Atmosphere Research Corporation (SUPARCO).
9) Center for Applied and Molecular Biology (CAMB).
10) National Institute of Oceanography (NIOC).

There are a total of 124 HEIs (Higher Education Institutes that include universities and degree awarding institutions); 68 in Public and 56 in Private sector. Bulk of the scientific manpower (researchers) are employed by HEIs .A total of 53621 Researchers are employed, out of which 44639(83%) are in HEIs and 8982(17%) in R&DIs. Out of this ,a total of 8982 researchers are employed in dedicated R&DIs, most of which are government controlled and funded.

Most Universities teachers have primary teaching assignments, and spend only part of their time in research activities. A more realistic and relevant number is of 17147 FTE (Full Time Equivalent) researchers. Thus HEIs have actually about twice the research manpower of R&DIs.

The real and realistic number of total researchers comes down to 26129.If one-third of these are productive enough, they should be able to produce about 7000 published or unpublished papers. Actual number of papers is less than one-tenth. However, to be fair, all useful research may not result into publishable papers, but nevertheless may be relevant, effective and useful. The reverse may also be true to some extent. Does this mean that most researchers are producing the output in right quantities and quality? This is an issue that we would revert elsewhere to.

There are a total of 5205 PhDs only in the country in total, half of those added in the last 7-10 years only. A total of 2033 PhD s are there in HEIs, and about 3000 in R&DIs. A total of 5164 students are pursuing PhD studies at various HEIs and even R&DIs as well.

A total of 43.039 Billion Rupees are spent on R&D conducted in Government S&T institutions, if PCST figures are correct. Another about 11 million Rs. is spent in HEIs on R&D activities. A total of 8.9 billion Rs (20% only) go to agriculture, where about 50% of the research manpower of government R&DIs is employed in some 44 organizations, which incidentally are also 50% of the total number. Without meaning to hurt or underrate the effort and value of others, in my view bulk of the actual and useful research is conducted at 2 or 3 premier institutions. In terms of per researcher cost, agricultural research is the cheapest. It is about Rs.1.5 Million per person as compared to the average of Rs 7.0 million per year per researcher. Funding for agricultural issues ought to be at least doubled, by doing away with some redundant research organizations, an issue we will take up elsewhere.

R&DIs generate only Rs.1.77 Billion, which is only 4% of their annual budget. It should be at least 10%, if not 20%, even keeping our circumstances in view. Partly government budgetary policies are responsible, whereby almost all budgetary appropriations to R&D are non-competitive and not contract based. Some percentage, say 5-6% of the budget should be in the form of contract research that promotes competition and wherein incentives are provided to the individual researchers and the associated workers.

Increasing the outreach of R&DIs

Under the nuclear weapons and missile programme, very significant scientific and engineering capabilities and institutions have been established. NESCOM is of particular mention here. They have been able to integrate basic science and engineering with processes and products, and have integrated and complete product development cycle. Not much detail is available, except some write-ups on Wiki that seems to have been released by official circles, and some revealed under personal publicity motivations. NESCOM is a civilian institution; however, it is shrouded in high security and secrecy. NESCOM's capabilities could be utilized to enrich local industries and other civilian institutions including the academia. Similarly other defence industries and institutions could benefit civilians. Secrecy and isolation is, however, styled in Pakistan on Communist lines ala-Soviet and North Korea. In open societies, despite adequate secrecy, defence development, if not research, is more open and integrated. Infact most of it is done in private sector. One could establish security procedures and clearance system that includes civilians as is a normal practice in the US. Such an integration of military R&D with civilians would have a multiplier effect and would not only strengthen and enrich Science and Technology but would also have positive effect on national economy.

Most agricultural research institutions have been doing pretty well. They know what is to be done, and what is expected of them. In short they have a research agenda. They have a supply source of trained manpower, which cannot possibly go anywhere but to these institutions. Their performance can, however, be improved by incentives and annual target setting. Agri-universities and R&DIs can also directly be involved in agri-extension system, which has been a weaker link hereto. It would enrich their own understanding of the problems of farmers and yield and productivity issues.

PCSIR has, however, faded into the background as it happens to quite a few pioneering institutions of its kind. New institutions emerge and the demands change over time. It survives more as a testing laboratory, which is no mean job. Its role as a reference and as well as customers lab can be very useful, if it acquires the necessary certifications, and continues with the process. Industrial research is a difficult field due to the variety and diversity of fields, unlike agriculture which does not face the same problem. There is a problem of scaling up. There is a missing linkage in engineering consulting organizations which could convert a process into the plant design. Large industries have the capital to acquire tried and tested and guaranteed technologies in a turn-key mode. However, there is a SME clientele, and a very large potential sector, that is in great need of PCSIR's support. SMEs lack capital to go and seek technology abroad. There are many local raw materials that could be put to use through collaboration with the industry, saving foreign exchange. However, they are reluctant to pay the nominal fee of the local R&DIs like PCSIR. PCSIR would be well advised to get some endowment to subsidize their fee under a contract research programme. It should also develop linkages with the local plant builders who are doing a successful business, but may be needing PCSIR's support.

The role and relevance of HEC under devolution

HEC is being devolved only, and some argue that it is being fragmented and practically disbanded. Perhaps initial government intentions were harsher or were misunderstood. Ministry of Finance has announced that it has released HEC funding for the Quarter, which was reportedly withheld earlier. Let us examine the controversy with some perspective, and try to look into the possibilities of a compromise or consensus approach. The arguments, as we shall see are divided along the classical fault lines of efficiency and continuity versus equity, autonomy and diversity.

Let us start in a lighter vane. I some times ask myself; are we an extremist nation? Rise of terrorism and fundamentalism tended to indicate it and extremist tendencies in our socio-political system? One government builds something; another demolishes it, instead of building upon it. Take the case of local governments, Awami Markaz, Housing projects, land reforms etc. All kind of clichés seem to be applicable to this syndrome; one step forward, two backwards, boom-bust cycles etc. Consistency is the virtue of an ass, as late Z.A.Bhutto used to often say defending his maverick economic policies.

Consistency is a virtue also. A less than optimum policy if applied consistently and constantly can yield far more beneficial set of policies suffering from inconstancies. Till yesterday, in the reign of Musharraf regime, HEC was a blue eyed institution. It was given so much funding, that it did not know what to do with it. HEC came out with all kind of impossible projects, inviting criticism for its wastefulness. Nevertheless Science and Higher education needed a jerky initiative to extract it from the prevalent dormancy. HEC did manage to do many useful things. Its single-most contribution seems to be the promotion and expansion of research programme and encouragement of private sector universities and educational institutions. There is concrete evidence for its achievements. There are 5164 PhD students and another 13592 M.Phil students pursuing their studies, as per data released by a Survey of Pakistan Council of Science and Technology (PCST). This is an unprecedented number. Prior to it, only 50 PhDs were produced in a year at the maximum. Initiation of local PhD programme will have a far reaching influence on the output and impact of R&D activities in Pakistan. HEC's other achievements are widely known. It did, however, become extravagant. Balance was later returned by the new government by making some needed budgetary cuts, making the needed hard choices, and shifted the emphasis on primary education.

There are following arguments against the so-called fragmentation of HEC. All University Vice-Chancellors have spoken in favor of maintaining HEC as a federal institution, and maintain status-quo. We must remember that despite 18th amendment, this is still one country. Even 18th amendment has kept all regulatory functions with the center. HEC has a vital regulatory function and does enjoy federal inclusion under the relevant clause. In all other federal countries, despite strong decentralization and devolution, Science and Technology and Higher Education are handled federally .Take the example of National Science Foundation of the USA, the citadel of federalism. Scale economies do not permit the division of HEC, as it is, even at federal level; it has been difficult to get sufficient number of qualified people to perform its function. Smaller provinces like KP and Balochistan would suffer most under the devolution or virtual disbanding of HEC. The two provinces do not have enough manpower resources to even run their schools.

In Pakistan state of Science and higher education and of education in general is already in appalling condition. It cannot afford to absorb the kind of jolts and discontinuities that are being tried on it. As reported in a recent report of UNESCO, available at its website, Pakistan's status in Science comes out to be very low. Its ranking in terms of number of publications comes at 20, the lowest among a set of developing countries of Asia, lower than tiny Morocco and Tunisia, and much lower than Iran, Turkey, and Malaysia. We are no more among the most developed even among our brother Muslim countries, like Iran, Turkey and Malaysia who today lead the Muslim countries in Science, Technology and economic growth. Having made a bomb (nuclear weapons) is not enough. It should not make us complacent. Even it would be a misnomer, if it is claimed that all of it was a totally indigenous effort. But it surely is an example and a lesson in constancy of policies. From Z.A. Bhutto to Ziaul-Haque and later , there was a one policy , that enabled Pakistan to achieve what it wanted to ,despite concerted opposition from powerful countries. Continuity and consistency has a lot of merit. One would require logic of huge proportion to break the continuity of HEC. We find that there is not much of an argument disbanding it, although devolution of sorts may have its own merit, as we shall see under the counter-argument later.

No doubt HEC is not an example of a marvelous institution. But it is a necessary institution and performs a useful function. HEC has to learn to be cost conscious, which it has under the new leadership which has shown great spine, courage and integrity. The incumbent, a distinguished academician comes from the ruling party itself and was its senator. It is not right to pursue vendetta against such a leadership and institution.

The counter argument for supporters of the devolution is that Education is a provincial subject under the constitution as revised under the 18th amendment that HEC is not just a regulatory institution, but also plays a major role in disbursement of funds to the Universities. It is the provinces which are to decide as to how much to spend on higher education and how much on primary education. If the argument that provincial politicians are inept, corrupt and inefficient is accepted, and thus would be mismanaging and damaging the cause of education, the whole idea of devolution of power is to be revisited. There is still popular support for the 18th amendment that has been passed unanimously by the constitution. The taste of pudding is in eating it. Let devolution be tried and implemented. It is too early for reversal and that piece by piece reversal and exceptions would be still more damaging. May be provinces, especially, the smaller provinces may want to pursue different resource allocation priorities matching their own assessments. Spending money is not a very difficult job. Some, particularly, Sindh may like to spend more than the population formula allows it otherwise.

On the other hand, the letter circulated by the architect of HEC, Dr Ataur-Rehman, does only repeat the arguments of provincial smallness, which may not have the capacity to perform the devolved functions. His argument would be valid in the case of KP and Balochistan only. Unfortunately the demand of provincial autonomy was louder and harsher in smaller provinces. Sindh might be able to benefit from the provincial autonomy. It is doubtful, however, that the smaller provinces would be able to effectively utilize the freedom and autonomy given under the 18th amendment .Lessons has to be learnt, but that would happen in due course. I would have expected more solid arguments in favor of maintaining the status quo and keeping the HEC intact.

Table 13.3: Distribution of Higher Education Institutions by sector and location

Region	Public	Universities / DAIs	Total
		Private	
AJK	1	2	3
Balochistan	6	1	7
Federal Capital	14	3	17
Northern Areas	1	-	1
NWFP	13	9	22
Punjab	20	16	36
Sindh	13	25	38
Total	68	56	124

Source: S&T Data Book 2009, PCST

Table 13.4: S&T Manpower (Head Count)

Description	Researchers	Technicians	Support Staff	Total
Higher Education Institutions	44639	4583	34989	84211
R&D Organizations	8982	8736	27894	45612
Total	53621	13319	62883	129823

Source: S&T Data Book 2009, PCST

Table 13.5: S&T Manpower by occupation - Full time equivalent (FTE)

	Researchers	Technicians	Occupation support staff	Total
Higher Education Institutions*	17147	2295	5101	24543
R&D Organizations	8982	8736	27894	45612
Total	26129	11031	32995	70155

Source: S&T Data Book 2009, PCST

Table 13.6: S&T Expenditure by type of organization (Million, Rs)

Field	S&T Organizations (Nos.)	Expenditure
Agricultural Sciences	50	8909.599
Arts / Design	4	429.246
Business / IT	23	4065.189
Engineering & Technology	32	10,815.954
Medical Sciences	13	23,126.271
Multi Discipline	60	59,123.476
S&T Services	11	3229.691
Total	193	109699.426

Source: S&T Data Book 2009, PCST

The stake-holders seem to be divided and have taken strong position. There is potential for academic unrest. PML (N) has taken an anti position on HEC devolution. The issue merits discussion among the stake-holders representing variety of positions and interests. A hasty and harsh decision would not be in national interest, would be polarizing and highly divisive. The truth, as they say, is always in-between. If a compromise is to be sought, between the two positions, it would be that HEC is allowed to remain with a regulatory and advisory mandate. GOP can assume its administrative budgetary responsibility, and it can receive international funding and grants to get its development projects go on. After all there are so many other institutions that the GOP keeps funding and maintaining. May be the next government has a different opinion and HEC reverts to its original mandate. Let us be flexible, reversals do occur in democracies. As we close this piece, the news is pouring in that a compromise formula is emerging.

Table 13.7: S&T Expenditure by type of University (Million, Rs)

Field	Higher Education Institutions (Nos.)	Expenditure
Agricultural Sciences	6	2826.144
Arts / Design	4	429.246
Business / IT	23	4065.189
Engineering & Technology	15	9656.235
Medical Sciences	8	22549.147
Multi Discipline	54	27134.377
Total	110	66660.338

Source: S&T Data Book 2009, PCST

Table 13.8: Research Expenditure by type of S&T/R&D Organization (Million, Rs)

Field	No of Organizations	Expenditure
Agriculture Sciences	44	6083.455
Engineering & Technology	17	1159.718
Medical Sciences	5	577.124
Multi Discipline	6	31989.099
S&T Services	11	3229.691
Total	**83**	**43039.088**

Source: S&T Data Book 2009, PCST

Science and Technology Policy

A draft S&T policy has been circulated among stake-holders to elicit feedback and input, which is to be commendable and appreciated. In this space we would examine the underlying issues and offer a few suggestions. There are a set of questions that need to be answered to be able to develop an effective S&T policy.

There are people who may put up a rather difficult set of questions, although I do not include myself among those. These are; "Our policy is to have no policy? Market and environment are too dynamic? We cross the bridge, when we reach it? We do not have fixed notions, we are open. We do as we learn and learn as we do? Policy is a paper shuffling exercise". The forgoing may, however, be too unique an attitude coming out of the conservative economists in the US, IFIs and elsewhere. They reject the role of policy and planning in development. The more serious questions, however, may be as follows?

What is an S&T Policy? Should we have S&T policy? What should be the role and purpose? What has been the role and output of earlier S&T Policies? What were the problems and what were the successes and achievements? What were the weaknesses and failures? What were the reasons of failures? What has changed in the meantime? Where is the gap, both in functional and operational terms?

Do we need technology and much lesser do we need Science? What ever technology is required is being bought and acquired and paid for? We need to grow fast, it is said, at the rate of 10% and more, may be based on low technology exports and merchandise? Let markets forces decide

227

what technology is required and let the market support it? If there is a demand, there is supply? It is a dynamic market. By the time any policy hits the ground, it may be outmoded?

What is the output of existing S&T institutions? Are they worth the cost and price? Should we write off some of these and build some new ones? Are we funding the dead wood? They are human beings, they can't be simply sent home? What to do for renewal? Is there too much fragmentation? May be undertake some merger?

Has market magic or its invisible hand worked in this area? What can be done to possibly guide the market? Does market fail also? Is making public sector institutions in R&D is a viable or the only solution? Is there a role for private sector? What can be done to energize and facilitate private sector? Should policy be broad and general or be specific and should specify targets? Should it be enforced or serve as a broad guideline only? What should be its time horizon? How often should it be reviewed?

There used to be a classical question; should we focus our R&D on Basic Sciences or in Applied Sciences and technologies? These questions have become more complex and tricky? Biology is a basic science but has so many direct applications? Physics is too intimately linked with electronics, materials and energy? And at a more mundane level, at PCSIR there used to be a debate, as to who should head PCSIR? A physicist or a chemist and a trade union type division developed. Perhaps Chemists won? I was too young at that time? Those were the old golden times, when in a naiveté, too much was being expected of scientists in a new and young country.

Pakistan spends 0.59 % of its GDP on Science and Technology. It is a sizeable amount. By comparison we spend only 0.8% of our GDP on health, and 2.5 % on education. In percentage terms, our R&D expenditure is the same as India, but in India there is a long list of achievements. Do we have the same? A lot of R&D funds, civil and military, are going to the military side and considerable scientific activity has been built around or inside the barbed wire. Can some linkage be developed and products, processes and know-how are passed on to the civilian economy. How to do that? Can we persuade the military –side to reorganize and restructure some of the facilities to achieve the afore-mentioned?

The draft Science and Technology that has been circulated for comments does not examine most of the afore-mentioned questions. The issue of output of the existing S&T and R&D institutions has not been given much of an attention and more institutes and organizations have been proposed. By spreading the resources on a wide agenda and opening one institution and the other, enough resources are not left to adequately fund the requirements of the existing institutions.

Duplication and Proliferation of Organizations

Furthermore there is a trend of establishing the so-called overhead organizations such as a National Technology Board has been formed with a mission to monitor the development of technologies in the world and select those for Pakistan_ a very broad agenda and duplication, indeed. It is not possible for a small organization to monitor technologies in all areas, sectors and discipline. It is the experts of these sectors and discipline who can do this and usually do this. The existing PCST could have done that job; if at all a separate unit or cell was required. In a circumstance, when GOP is facing grave problems of financial resources and liquidity, this kind of extravaganza is really unfortunate.

Similar trend must not be adopted in the implementation of the proposed activities in the S&T draft policy. A strong point of the draft is an enlistment of a "R&D agenda" in the form of proposed activities, which have been probably developed after taking input both from the demand and supply sector and institutions. Even if such a broad agenda may sound as a wish list, it serves a useful role in making the stake-holders aware of the needs and markets. However, the policy makers would do well to prioritize the activities into a Plan, with a schedule and estimate of resources and identifying the existing R&D/S&T institutions who could undertake those activities. Instead of proposing new organizations, the focus should be on the utilization of the capability and capacity of existing institutions .Even with the existing institutions, significant research funds would be required for the new projects.

Performance Review of R&D Institutions

A performance review of the institutions and their key individual and periodic and regular reports are an important element in keeping the system dynamic and productive. An external review, possibly done by foreign professors and researchers may be required; otherwise it becomes a back-scratching exercise, where performance is appraised in closed and cooperative mutually admired societies. Some institutions may have to be closed down or merged with appropriate institutions. There is a lot of moonlighting that goes on in the S&T institutions that must be controlled and curtailed and incentives and revenue sharing be announced for open and across-the-board consultancy assignments. There is a tendency to monopolize data and keep it secret from end-users and materially benefit from it, which not only is injurious to the industry and development but robs the institution of legitimate revenue and recognition. It has a corrupting influence on individuals and organizations.

In addition to the afore-mentioned, there is another class of elite scientists for whom writing research papers for international publishing is the only priority, and attending to the local needs and research agenda too mundane and ordinary. There is to be a balance in the two; both are necessary. The performance assessment systems should take into account this issue. The local PhD programme can play a very useful role in pursuing local research agenda. It should not be denigrated, because it may not be at the frontier of science, because local industry and end-user is also not at the frontiers. The phrase," contribution to knowledge" has to be adequately defined and interpreted to handle this aspect.

Concluding, reliance on cheap and raw exports and industries may be only an interim solution, the needs of a bulging population can be adequately met through the acquisition, development and application of Science and Technology that enhances the quality, scope and spread and quantity of output and services, while minimizing the use of resources and without or minimum impact on resource quality and sustainability. This has to come, sooner or later. Today gas is finished up; tomorrow water may not be enough. It is already not enough. One can build dams or line canals or adopt water efficient and conservation technologies minimizing water consumption in agriculture and so on. Science and Technology, appropriate and relevant, is indispensable. S&T policies can play a useful role in making this possible and speeding the process

Role of Engineering

There seems to be confusion about engineering; industry or engineering industry is being used interchangeably for industry. Engineering is a link between Science & Technology and the Industry which provides products and services. Engineering industry is a sector of industry which produces machinery, equipment, tools and devices. The discipline of engineering is used more in this sector, hence its name. However, this is

230

not only what engineering is. It is much more. It converts S&T into products and services. Loosely and for convenience, it can be taken as a part of technology. There are some overlaps as well. Developing a process may be a technology or could be called Chemical Engineering and hence the trade union dispute of the PEC with the recognition of the graduates of Chemical Technology as engineers.

Engineering has special needs and requirement for its development. Quite some S&T development could not be converted into the marketable products and processes because of the missing link, both of process and design engineering. Engineering has six main parts or phases; a) engineering education; b) design ;c) construction; d) manufacturing ;e) Operations and maintenance and f)engineering practice and profession ,often known as Consultancy .All are important, even the operations and maintenance.

There should be six sub-groups and a seventh integrator/coordination group that should put together the whole enterprise and handle the interfacial question. Six sub-groups and 6 technologies, makes it 36 cells. Would it be worth the time and effort is the last most important question that has to be answered first. MOST may not be that interested in such a detailed analysis, but Pakistan Engineering Council may do that?

Pakistan's engineering capacities and capabilities are quite limited both in terms of quantity and quality. And more so, these are concentrated in a few organizations; NESPAK, PTCL, NESCOM, ARL, HMC, KSEW etc. Even there most of the organizations do not undertake engineering design. Their activities are limited to do site studies, concept or preliminary studies, detailing of drawings and support activities. Most feasibility studies are done by foreigners. Many super-patriots may not like it and would start citing the making of nuclear weapons. Without going into much detail, and not meaning to belittle the great achievement, a lot of foreign input was involved in that as well. But, definitely, it was a masterpiece of local content and indigenous development. What ever little is done has been largely possible due to the afore-mentioned organization. There is a great need of building and improving design know-how. A working group should develop the priority and focal areas based on the market and development needs. Immediately, I see the following two activities that MOST might build upon and include in the recommendations in S&T policies.

1) Availability of Engineering Standards to engineers and their organizations may go a long way towards spreading and strengthening engineering design and operational know –how. Standards are in a way a culmination of technology and engineering and reflect consensus and can be used as a learning tool. I have seen outdated and copied Standards floating around in the organizations and monopolized by individuals. PEC?MOST can take a lead in acquiring bulk buying and distribution rights to selected and important Standards e.g. ISO,IEC,IEEE,ASME etc in a style that has been done by the HEC in promoting access to the Scientific papers of Journals.

Millions and perhaps billions may have been spent in doing studies on various subjects in various ministries, and government departments, autonomous bodies and public sector enterprises. Most of these reports are monopolized by the relevant and key personnel, quite a few of these ends up at homes in personal libraries. Immense know-how and details are normally available in these studies, normally multi-million dollar studies done by the foreign consultants and organization. National and provincial depositories may be built to safe-keep these reports and documents and access be provided to the engineering community, academia, practitioners and other eligible users. PEC may itself establish such a depository or assign National Library to build a section in its collection. An example of this could be found in the US in the form of NTIS (National Technical Information Service).Information on it is available on NTIS website.

Chapter Appendix

Strategic Thrust Areas & Activities in draft S&T Policy 2011

Metrology, Standards, Testing and Quality (MSTQ)

A52.   *Setting up NPSL as the National Metrology Organization as a separate entity, independent of PCSIR (subject to the enactment of a single cadre for employees of scientific organizations under MOST).*

A53.   *Strengthening PNAC in terms of manpower*

A54.   *Restructuring PSQCA and redefining its functions to remove Jurisdictional overlap with the functions of NPSL and PNAC through amendments in the PSQCA Act.*

A55.   *Increasing the number of mandatory standards manifold from its current figure of 85. These standards should also be enforced on imported goods to prevent the local market being flooded by sub-standard goods of foreign origin.*

A56.   *Harmonizing federal and provincial laws to ensure that the same standards are uniformly applicable throughout the country.*

A57.   *Involving the provincial setups in the enforcement of Pakistan Standards and strengthening them adequately for this purpose*

A58.   *Increasing the number of ISO 17025 certified laboratories in various sectors in the country to facilitate the availability of internationally acceptable certification to the exporters.*

Environment

A59.   *Development of cost effective sewage treatment plants*

A60.   *Development of Industry-specific biotechnological waste-water treatment processes.*

A61.   *Power generation through incineration of solid waste*

A62.   *Development of catalytic converters for retrofitting vehicles for minimizing the emission problems.*

A63.   *Assistance in meeting the objectives of Environment Policy – 2005, which inter alia, aim to:*
   i.   *Phase out sulfur from diesel and furnace oil.*
   ii.   *Establish cleaner production centers and promote cleaner production techniques and practices.*
   iii. *Provide alternate sources of energy, like piped natural gas, Liquefied Petroleum Gas (LPG), solar energy and micro-hydel power stations, to the local inhabitants to reduce the pressure on natural forest, and to substitute firewood in the upland ecosystems.*
   iv.   *Promote the use of Ozone friendly technologies; and phase out the use of ozone depleting substances in line with the provisions of the Montreal Protocol.*

v.   *Promote recycling of agricultural products associated with livestock production and use of livestock sector as an outlet for recycling of appropriate urban waste.*

vi. *Introduce adequate animal waste management system in peri-urban dairy colonies.*

Health and Pharmaceuticals

A64.   *Development of R&D capacity for producing active drug components and up gradation of drug quality testing laboratories.*

A65.   *Necessary steps for PCSIR-Peshawar to be WHO recognized Herbal Medicine Centre.*

A66.   *Establishment of new facilities for vaccines production*

Energy

A67.   *Harmonizing the efforts made in the energy sector by different Ministries, departments and research centers by creating an 'Energy Council' with heads of relevant organizations. The council will be entrusted to advice on priority areas for R&D and management of resources and to fill gaps.*

A68.   *Acquisition of technology for building nuclear power reactors through R&D as well as transfer of technology agreements*

A69.   *Constituting R&D task force for developing processes to convert Coal and Coal gas for environment-friendly energy productions and their conversion to economically useful products.*

A70.   *Development of pilot projects and their large-scale dissemination based on existing technologies such as solar water heaters, biogas plants, photovoltaic, etc..*

A71.   *Announcement of incentives (e.g. tax holiday) to the private sector for the manufacture of renewable energy products, components and systems, such as solar thermal power system components, wind energy technology components, biogas plants.*

A72. *Creation of an 'Renewable Energy Fund' for research into the development of new RE technologies such as hydrogen fuel cell, Fresnel mirrors and low-cost/high-efficiency photovoltaic panels.*

Biotechnology and Genetic Engineering

A73. *Revival of 'National Commission on Biotechnology' and charging it with the task of coordinating national-wide research programs in different areas where biotechnology can be applied.*

A74. *Reviewing the draft of 'National Biotechnology and Genetic Engineering Policy and Action Plan' and implementing it with the support of relevant organizations.*

A75. *Enacting biotechnology related legislations.*

A76. *Establishment of biotechnology incubation centers.*

Agriculture and Livestock

A77. *Development of genetic modification expertise for producing high yield/pest resistant crops*

A78. *Using new technologies such as remote sensing, laser land-leveling, bio-fertilizers and solar tube-wells for enhancement of efficiency in the sector of farm produce*

A79. *Producing, preserving and processing fruits and vegetables that satisfy food-chain requirements of international market.*

A80. *Establishing facilities for producing quality controlled Halal food for Muslim consumers in different parts of the world.*

A81. *Supporting schemes for modern techniques in poultry, live-stock and fish-farms*

Water

A82. *Providing help and support for the implementation of 'National Water Policy – 2009' and 'National Drinking Water Standards'.*

A83. *Completion of projects for establishing water treatment plants in all union councils.*

A84.   Implementation of water conservation technologies and assistance in the promulgation of water conservation Act

A85.   Development of inexpensive techniques for water desalination, purification for domestic use and treatment of waste water

Minerals

A86.   Provision of support for the implementation of National Minerals Policy 1995

A87.   Undertaking R&D work for utilizing the full potential of Thar coal.

A88.   Development of technologies for processing different indigenous ores to extract products of high commercial value

Ocean Resources

A89.   Mapping of oceanic resources in the maritime Exclusive Economic Zone as well as under seabed for assessing the potential of their utilization

A90.   Exploitation of tidal energy potential and sea-based minerals such as manganese nodules and gas hydrates.

A91.   Development of sea-based aquaculture and fishery industry

Electronics

A92.   Launching of specific programmes for the automation of local industry

A93.   Setting-up Electronic Facilitation Centers for providing advice, training and services to support production of electronics goods and electronics-based equipment.

Information and Communication Technologies (ICTs)

A94.   Support for the implementation of the IT Policy and Action Plan – 2000 (to be updated in 2011).

A95.   Establishment of a Public ICT R&D organization that will promote innovation and will provide a linkage between industry and research

A96.   Establishment of public ICT Industrial Parks

A97.   Enabling the ICT related industries to become internationally competitive

A98.   Deploying ICT across sectors, as a general purpose technology

A99.   Investment in ICT as an enabling and networking infrastructure

A100.   Introduction of an e-framework like Malaysia

A101.   Supporting e-commerce and e-governance applications

A102.   Encouraging entrepreneurial opportunities such as offshore call centers

A103.   Promoting open source software

A104.   Encouraging private-sector innovation in IT industry

A105.   Sharing of ICTs resources to meet large volume computing

A106.   Offering ICT-related financial incentives (tax holidays / introduction of special tax rates for software exporters)

A107.   Establishment of the citizen-centered e-state and development of the framework for customer-friendly business-to-consumer and business-to-business services

A108.   Making further improvements in;
    i.   liberalization of telecommunications market
    ii.   a well functioning regulatory environment
    iii. a high level of national education in ICTs

Space Technology

A109.   Launching of a coordinated effort by all relevant R&D and higher education institutions to develop indigenous satellites and expertise pertaining to space technology

A110.   Setting-up an institutional linkage between MOST with SUPARCO and IST.

Materials Science

A111.   Establishment of a National Material Science Research Institute

A112.   Revival of National Nano-technology Commission and establishment of National Nano-technology Centre

Engineering Sector

A113.   Help and support for the implementation of the proposals documented in the joint reports of HEC and PIDE, entitled 'Technology-based industrial Vision and Strategy for Pakistan's Socio-economic Development-2003'.

14 Education & Research

The antithesis

Universities have to teach, it is often argued, and the under-grad ones cannot possibly undertake research due to the teaching load. This may be only partly correct. Good teaching requires some participation in research and even if it is limited to observation and experimentation. Also as mentioned earlier, all research may not be on- frontiers and elegant high level. Collection of data, identifying wastages, studying quality issues, studying material substitution possibilities and a simple unashamed assistance in copying foreign imported products to our local industry and entrepreneurs is all worthy and valuable R&D. Japanese did it earlier followed by Korea and now Chinese are doing the same. Certainly graduate programs, especially, of PhD would be more helpful. To a varying degree most public sector universities have initiated Grad pro-grams already.

Unfortunately such research as has been described earlier has been derided by idle and talkative, chattering class teachers and professors. In some cases it has been opposed tooth and nail by university administrations. It is widely known that an otherwise reasonable and efficient Vice Chancellor of an engineering university almost auctioned a useful peace of power equipment donated to the university by some business party. Justification given was, it is an unnecessary diversion from "genuine" teaching. What was the actual reason or factors? But it is not too much out of the realms of possibilities. I would encourage the readers to post their feedback on it.

On the other hand among the engineering universities, NUST has probably the most active interest in applied and useful R&D. They are the most progressive and open, blessed by a stable leadership, institutional support and an optimal location. They have come closest to the scale economies and have ventured into technology incubators and consultancy. Pakistan's defence sector alone can be a good market and customer for their R&D. Bio-medical and communications requirements of the sector can provide enough of business, activity and funds. NUST is a part of Ministry of Science and Technology. Active consideration should be given to merge one or two R&D institutions controlled by the MOST on the lines and under the rationale that has been discussed elsewhere in this section.

Relevance, cost-effectiveness and not Elitism

Is University research relevant to our problems and socio-economic needs? Is research cost -effective and sustainable? Is research compatible with international agenda, and thus publishable in international journals, answer to our academic and research needs? Are our research institutes earning their bill on national exchequer? These are the questions and issues with which we would be dabbling with in this discussion.

As to the sustainability and cost-effectiveness, there is a news that due to budgetary constraints many PhD scholars enrolled abroad and in the midst of their studies may have to come back or may prefer to remain abroad and fend for themselves, if HEC is not able to continue to meet its financial obligations. They would be right as HEC would not be filling its legal and contractual obligations. Hopefully some solution would be found or USAID comes to our and their rescue.

What is patently clear is that the academic research and training program of our Higher Education is not sustainable. The heydays, and the misguided policies are not to return when higher education budget was increased to eight times its earlier levels, at the expense of primary education in a country which suffers from low literacy and one of the poorest levels of primary school enrollment. Wrong and elitist and shortsighted policies of a dictator surrounded by selfish and ambitious individuals could not have been sustained for long.

PhD training programs can only be feasible through locally relevant research programs. The developed countries are at a different level altogether. Their research agenda is different. It is universal and international and it is only they, who benefit from it directly and immediately, in the short and long run. We benefit only incidentally and at a cost of hefty payments. We cannot possibly contribute to international agenda by publishing internationally and sending PhD students at a massive scale abroad? Our research should be focused on local problems and issues, which certainly may not be as elegant as international issues? However local research has its own elegance.

Compiling a local research agenda is no mean achievement and on the top of it which earns some money and research funds from private and public sources. A PhD student is the most economic input to the research process, without him no academic research is possible and feasible. A foreign based PhD programme hence is neither affordable nor useful or relevant.

There are so many problems in industry, agriculture, water and energy sector, the whole issue of self-sufficiency and indigenization. Some of the problems and issues may not be amenable to research by our researchers and universities due to capacity and capability constraints. But some certainly would be and really are, many of which I can personally point out which can keep many a universities busy for years. A balance would, however, have to be maintained in academic standards of research and economic relevance and usefulness. You cannot possibly award a PhD on making a mundane silencer but an innovative design can infact consume many PhD dissertations.

In social sciences, both the quality and quantity of research, is awfully lacking, although, the funding requirements are too little as compared to natural and physical sciences. The whole society is a laboratory and the subject and the object of social science research. All one needs is the urge and sensitivity. Who would have more problems and unexplored and unknown issues than we have? We and our universities do not focus on them and the problems keep multiplying.

Financial difficulties of the Universities

Reportedly University Vice Chancellors have threatened to resign over their budgetary difficulties. HEC, under which universities operate, had its budgets phenomenally increased during Musharraf regime. In pursuit of elitist agenda, a crash program was launched to elevate the level of higher (university) education and Science & Technology. The assumption was that by throwing money at something, one improves its quality. All kinds of fancy programs were launched and money was wasted. Some of the programs like building new universities with foreign faculty simply could not take off at all, while other continued with varying levels of output, efficiency and achievements. It was widely accepted that a lot of money was wasted under egotistical and whimsical programs without stake-holders support and objective bases and criteria.

We do not want to go into the details .Suffice is to say that most of those programs are not sustainable and would have to be trimmed or curtailed altogether. Priority has to return to the primary and secondary education. Besides, in the aftermath of floods, a lot of humanitarian rehabilitation of flood victims has to be done. However, there would be practical issues in curtailing programs for which third party contracts have been entered into or the PhD students that have been sent abroad. Such cases would have to be sorted out on a case-to-case basis. Prime-minister has reportedly formed a committee to sort out the issue. HEC and its subsidiary institutions have to return to real life situation and condition away from the aberrations of the past. Vice Chancellors are mature and experienced people and should be amenable to reasonable adjustments. It is not easy and even not advisable to take sharp turns, while contractual obligations should be met.

The need of the hour is that apart from ending frivolous programs, universities should launch programs towards enhancing their incomes and budgetary self reliance. I would not recommend enhancing fees to unaffordable levels, but would make a case of increasing subsidiary earnings through contract research, endowment funds and fee and rentals. At least some (10-20%) of the budget should be earned through contract research. We have discussed this issue in detail elsewhere.

Ultimately Public Sector Universities would have to earn some money

Ultimately Universities will have to earn some money. There is an upper limit to what students can pay in terms of tuition fees. There is also a limit to budgetary sources. Primary schools have urgent needs as well to be taken care of. University research activities can provide the extra income. Not only this would improve university liquidity, it would enrich academic life. This is not a pipe dream or a mere utopia. It can be done. It is already being done in Malaysia and Turkey, as mentioned earlier: after all these are the Muslim developing countries who started their journey with the same socio-economic conditions. I only very sincerely expect that my readers do not still subscribe to the old and outdated perception that Pakistan is on the top among Muslim countries No more. Nuclear weapons, for all their benefit, have sent wrong kind of perceptions and signals to common man.

The Floods

Millions have suffered in the recent and continuing floods. Admittedly, such floods have never been experienced ever in the history of Pakistan, however, floods are a common cyclical occurrence with mighty Indus; lesser floods have always occurred. This is yet another area where adequate and ample research opportunities are available. Floods cannot be prevented but their frequency and intensity reduced through storage dam, which is a separate issue and has been dealt with elsewhere in these pages.

Floods impact can be handled and mitigated in a more organized and scientific manner much reducing the misery and sufferings of the affected populace, if Universities develop and maintain something that is called River Basin Models(RBM).Through such models one could predict the flow down the river and forecast, with the addition of GIS tools, the areas which would be inundated with a fair degree of accuracy and sufficient warning at-least for Punjab and Sindh where bulk of the losses have occurred. Universities of Peshawar, Jamshoro and Punjab are the directly relevant universities which could be involved with the work done by Pakistan Council of Water Research (PCWR).One wonders whether water research is conducted by our universities at all. Water is such a fertile and wide area of research that hundreds of PhDs can be absorbed in it.

Another related area where there would be no dearth of subjects and possibly even of funds is Environment which is no more a mere local issue and is integrated with the world environment. Research on the local environment, weather modeling, monitoring changes and trends are respectable issues of research, providing topics for research frontiers as is liked by the conventional wisdom on the campus in Pakistan.

Water & Environment

I have frequently mentioned about water and environment sector being capable of engaging the energies of our universities which are currently either idle or engage themselves on research subjects with no relevance or dividend for this poor nation. I further wrote that hundreds of PhD dissertations and research papers can be produce on locally relevant research. Fortunately I have come across a few passages in a landmark report of the World Bank on Pakistan's water problems. I would urge my readers to please go through the following rather carefully and see for themselves how we and our universities are wasting their efforts and resources in engaging in wasteful and irrelevant research. This is only water and environment. Similar opportunities can be identified in other sectors as well. Let me reproduce in the following, what the report says:

The Indus basin is a single, massive, highly complex interconnected ecosystem, upon which man has left a huge foot print. When a dam or a barrage is constructed, the water and sediment cycles are changed dramatically. In a system so massive and complex, the generation and smart use of knowledge are the keys to adaptive management. But there has been very little investment in Pakistan in building this knowledge base ....The country is literally flying blind into a very hazardous future.

The bottom line is that Pakistan needs to build a strong natural, engineering, and social scientific cadre capable of working with all users in defining the problem and developing solutions, monitoring, assessing and adjusting. This is a capacity which requires a wide range of disciplines_ those necessary for understanding climate ,river geomorphology .hydraulic structures ,surface water and ground water hydrology, limnology ,water chemistry ,sediment management, hydraulics, soil sciences, terrestrial and coastal ecosystems ,agronomy, plant physiology ,industrial organization ,conflict management, politics, economics and financing.

It will require an expansive and long term human resource strategy which will update the skills of a formidable capacity which exists in Pakistan , but will also strengthen the capacity of the universities and other scientific and training institutions to produce high quality applied research.

Let us try to build our research agenda in one of the sectors, keeping in view the thoughts as indicated in the above, which were conceived by a very eminent group of local and foreign scientists who have had the opportunity to have a closer look into our problems.

Clean drinking water and PCSIR products

Water gets contaminated in the flooded environment. And the victims are usually out of their homes without any pots and stoves and fuel to be able to boil their water. Disaster aid agencies and NGOs are often asking for donations of water cleaning kits that are imported usually and its supply uncertain. There are several solutions that may be implemented by the agencies:

Household bleach is one of the best disinfectant, approved by such donor agencies as DFID.A few drops per liter and 30 minutes waiting time does an excellent job. NGOs and volunteers should make these supplies available to the flood victims and do some demo and explaining. This practice can even be adopted as a routine as well

Another good disinfectant, quite effective and safe, was developed by our PCSIR. It was a pouch containing sand and silver halide. All one was require to do was to put such a pouch in ones water pot or filter, and drink safe water out of the tap. The product was developed probably in late 80's and was quite visible. Several of my friends and relatives did use it for quite some years when I was weaned on mineral water which I have stopped and have returned to the boiled water at my home. I wonder what happened to the PCSIR product. It is no more visible. It could have proved very handy for the flood victims. Why was it discontinued? May be it was due to lack of enough demand or having been proved undesirable for some scientific reason. Only PCSIR can tell? We would like to listen if they are listening to us.

Five Reverse Osmosis (RO) plants and three ultra-filtration plants designed and manufactured by EME Karachi garrison of Pakistan Army were dispatched today to various locations in Sindh. Ultra-filtration plants have a capacity of 25,000 liters a day and cost Rs.50,000/- per, while R. O. plants have capacity of 12000 liters a day and a price tag of Rs. 2.5 million. Naturally ROs are quite expensive as the water quality is almost mineral water irrespective of the input quality. We have earlier discussed the case of procuring such plants on rent or lease or outright purchase of even used plants. Some areas permanently require ROs or ultra-filtration plants where these can be dispatched to after the emergency. It is a good idea on the part of EME of Pak Army to have engaged in this kind of endeavor which would have multiple benefits.

Bio-sciences

Only if our science universities could engage in R&D in the bio-digestion process, and work in unison with the stake-holders and end-users, they would be doing a lot of good for every body. Let us go into a few small technical details. Bio-digestion processes are used in sewerage treatment, municipal solid waste treatment and a lot of food and Pharma industries. Most of the sewerage processing plants I have visited do not work or work very in efficiently. The problem is that various kinds of anti-bacterial matter is also generated in the process which slows down and degenerates the process. Often the material characteristic of the waste to be processed varies .Hence processes inputs and parameters cannot be standardized as is done in carefully controlled chemical industry. Active monitoring of bio-digestion process is required which manpower and know-how is often not available.

As a result we find that unprocessed waste water is utilized for plantation and nurseries. I normally spot DHA Karachi's trucks distributing untreated sewerage, although DHA has many sewerage treatment plants. DHA Golf Club is also supplied with this kind of untreated sewerage from a nearby sewerage treatment plant, creating mosquito problems for the Club, its members and personnel and in future would also affect nearby residents. This is the situation in a posh locality.

Similarly other organic solid wastes remain putrefying giving away often unbearable stinks and stench. Food and vegetable wastes abound and in food streets and markets. All such waste can be profitably processed. Universities R&D can play an important and useful role: solving the problem, earning money, enriching academic life materially and emotionally.

Not that our people, faculty and scientists are not capable.. Infact NIBGE has in the past made and even marketed some relevant bio-products out of these processes. We need a country wide systematic R&D system in our universities which is not parasitic. What is the use of R&D that is perpetually dependent on government, and comes up with show piece projects and output or generates some scientific papers which are published internationally add to the personal scores of a few elite scientists. We have belabored this point elsewhere and earlier.

Surely governments and not only federal government may have to provide some seed money or a portion of resources. But such public funding should be done on the basis of its applicability and usefulness of the country and not just to enable a few to earn academic laurels. Interaction and linking with the industry and end-users is a must for installing a useful and self-sustaining R&D process in our universities.

Agriculture

Agriculture is Pakistan's backbone feeding a large and ever increasing population. There is shortage of water and arable land. Agricultural productivity in Pakistan is very low, lower than India and much lower than Egypt, Turkey, Saudi Arabia and Mexico and many other comparable developing countries.

It has been reported that agricultural research and extension in Pakistan has stagnated for more than a decade now, which has resulted in low growth in output and productivity. It has also been estimated that expenditure on agricultural R&D in Pakistan as a percentage of Agri-GDP, is over 30% lower than in Bangladesh, India and Srilanka, and 40 % lower than the average for Asia-Pacific region. The same study has shown that Agricultural R&D spending went down by 40% between 1991 and 2003. It is no longer true, at least, for agricultural research to yield results in the long run. Applied R&D in Agriculture focuses on practical problems such as introduction of new seeds, farming methods, fertilizer recipes and other input packages and harvesting issues etc. Its rate of return is generally very high and time lag as short as 2-3 years. There are a number of agricultural research institutes and Universities with a pool of several thousand scientists and researchers. Due to low R&D funds, the research activities have suffered and so have the income and salaries of the research scientists.

Agricultural research has to be revitalized and strengthened, if high growth rates of 4-5% are to be realized in Agri-output. We have argued elsewhere that high growth in agricultural with a strong equity component is an answer to the endemic rural poverty and threatening food insecurity. Also the extension link has been always weak and rather bureaucratic. Some management innovations may have to be introduced to increase the output, outreach and efficiency of the extension system. Some element of privatization and incentives, performance payments etc., approaches could be tried and investigated.

Consultancy incubators could play quite some role, in off-loading the under-paid and under-utilized agri-scientists and marshaling towards offering extension services to the farmer. Such services can be subsidized by the federal provincial governments at least initially. But the scientists will get better paid work and agriculture will get technical input that would hopefully increase the agricultural productivity, even if the large farmer gets the benefit from such ventures.

What an engineering university should be doing at a minimum

Let me recount what an average engineering university could do to generate R&D work that can change the faces and environments at our campuses. This is from my own perspective. Others could add to the list.

1) Generate their own electricity and run a cogen plant/CHP to cater to the heating, cooling and hot water requirements. If it is a thermal power plant, it may come from a vendor, but it should be different to serve R&D needs, demonstration and experimentation facilities, simulators etc. It should not be a black box and a closed box. It should be open and sturdy and not too sophisticated. It should run on various fuels such as oil, gas, biomass, coal and solid waste. University should dispose its solid waste and of its close by neighbors. It may burn, recycle and produce biogas from organic waste.

2) University should have its own fresh water treatment facility including a reverse osmosis plant. It should treat its sewerage and effluent, produce useful products such as bio-gas and fertilizer and recycle water for plantation.

3) These days solar PV slabs could be made/assembled by the students and solar PV power systems installed.

4) There should be measurement labs to enable students to monitor operations and record data for later analysis and journal submission requirements. Graduate students could be involved in more creative, original and theoretical work, but still focused around the installed operational and monitoring and observational facilities.

5) In this manner universities can save a lot of money, provide a deeper insight into the subjects by direct observations and varying degrees of involvements with the installed systems.

6) Other nearby faculties of science in the area of bio-sciences for bacterial studies and input could be involved and engaged. Multi-disciplinary teams can be set-up

The afore-mentioned is but a small list with which a decent beginning can be made by virtually all engineering universities. Much more can be added in the area of electronics, electrical engineering and computer and instrumentation. Infact all these subjects could be built around these facilities and other similar facilities to be installed at the campus.

The incubators

An incubator as the name implies houses and keeps a new born in supportive and compatible environment, nurses it till the new born is able to survive on its own. Business incubators are well known and have had a mixed record of success. R&D often requires some business motivations. Either very large companies with deep pockets or government supported or owned institutions indulge in R&D based businesses. Research Professors and scientists are short of capital .Often capitalists and businesses are reluctant to enter into uncharted territories.

Incubators can prove handy in such situations. Physical facilities, furnished offices and even common facilities like labs or marketing departments, provision of working capital in the form of equity and arrangements of approved loaning schemes are the tools through which a business incubator operates. Sometimes it can be a smart way for privatizing a R&D institution. Governments can off-load the liabilities of salaries of highly paid unproductive scientists through converting a R&D institution into an incubator. It would be surprising that the private motive may energize a dormant Research enterprise. Universities can foster R&D through independent incubators on and off the campus.

The idea has remained on the table for many years now in Pakistan. Iran, Malaysia and Turkey have reportedly had some success with incubators. One could learn from their experience. Sustainability and output is to be assessed before jumping into it. The best guarantee for success would be an assured market. NUST is reportedly contemplating to launch an incubator project. NUST Consulting appears to be an enterprise with some of the features of an incubator. The solution is to be tailored to the conditions on ground. It may not be necessarily a great idea but not feasible. It can be small and mundane but feasible. The truth is always in between.

Market and marketing such projects and their outputs is the major issue. Normally Developing countries markets are at least initially too-small both of the input and the output. Bilateral or multilateral cooperation and networks can play a role. For example, a Pakistan, Saudi and Turkish network or JV can be formed. A larger network consisting of Indonesia, Malaysia, Egypt, Pakistan, Saudi Arabia and Turkey could be formed with one project each in the network countries. Islamic Development Bank could play a role in this. In the past, Dr. Anwar Naseem of Pakistan Science Society, a dear friend of mine has been working on these themes and got to have a lot of knowledge and insight in various Muslim countries. I indulged on this subject long time back, when Dr. I. H. Usmani assumed the charge of NEST (Network for Emerging Sciences and Technologies) with funding from Agha Hassan Abdi. A few concept studies were done. This kind of work requires money and peace, both of which are lacking these days in Pakistan. Saudis have both of it in abundance. They also need it. I would strongly encourage them to do so in collaboration with Pakistan.

15 Floods and Water Management

The Mighty Indus

Mighty Indus is being blamed for its ferocity; too big to be predicted or protected against? May be it is too convenient an excuse on the part of those who are blamed for inaction and mismanagement. And there are others who almost gave in to the mighty Indus and started worshiping it in the province of Sindh, celebrated a Devta Sindh day. Some participants offered milk and some kind of *Bhaint, it* was reported. Mighty Indus has responded with a lot of *bounty*. Indus river definitely important for us, as our *resourceful* country has only one river and the rainfall is too less on the average. Occasionally in monsoon period, excessive rains possibly in combination with excess melting of glaciers, we get floods as we are experiencing now. In future floods would increase in frequency due to environmental changes.

Let us see how big Indus is. Is it one of the largest rivers in the world, as super-patriots and conspiracy theorists would like to believe? Far from it, Indus is not big by global standards. It comes in a rank of 26th, take what ever criterion. Indus has a length of 3180 kms, drainage area of 0.96 square kms , and a mean discharge of 7160 cubic meters per second(250,000 cft per sec).

In the current floods, we have experienced 1 million cusecs (cubic feet per second).By comparison, river Amazon in Brazil, the greatest river on earth, has a drainage area of 6.915 square kilometers and a mean discharge rate of 219,000 cubic meters per second, almost thirty times as much water as Indus and 7.7 times the current flood discharge of Indus. Indian rivers of Gunga and Jumna are 2-3 time bigger in flow/discharge. River Congo in Africa is 41,500 cubic meters per second, more than five times that of Indus; similarly Yangtze of China with 31,900 cumecs. So let the size or might of Indus not scare people into submission and provide justification for inefficiency, if not insensitivity.

251

On the other hand death toll of floods, although lamentable, has not exceeded beyond 2500 or so. Perhaps disease may increase this number in future, God forbid. In previous floods death toll used be in the range of 30-40000.Certainly things have changed over the years due to technology, media, communication and development activities. New organizations have been formed, and there are national and international NGOs. World community and mutual inter-actions have expanded.

We are told that the low profile Federal Flood Commission deals with the flood issues. NDMA has not much to do with it accept for flood relief work. Did one notice the profile of FFC? It has been a total failure in so far as communication is concerned. They have put up a website which appears to be still in development phase. I could download their advisories with a lot of difficulty on my fast broadband internet connection, because instead of putting it in PDF, they scanned their letters and uploaded the same on their web-site, making the file heavy (several Mb).This explains more or less the outlook of the organization. This must change for the better.

There is nothing to download in the download section. The so called Flood Manual supposed to have been developed by this organization is not there, neither has it been made available elsewhere. Perhaps it is *confidential*! Flood maps, GIS, inundation forecasts and risks, perhaps are too much to be expected from an antiquated organization. A review of this organization into its functioning and output, organizational structure and outlook is highly recommended. The problem is that this time flood came after a gap of more than ten years. People forget floods and remember it when the next one wakes them. But these organizations are maintained throughout with ever increasing budgets and projects.

Provincial irrigation departments, although inept, corrupt and antiquated much more than the FFC, are receiving the public wrath rather exclusively. FFC must be included in this displeasure.

Flood dividends

In agrarian societies floods have always been considered and looked forward to. They brought much needed water and soil fertility and rejuvenated the land. Due to increasing population and human settlements and environmental degradation, misery, afflictions and losses have increased. In this blog, I have tried to examine if Floods have or would give some dividends as well and somehow balance the sheet. Some benefits will accrue to the economic and social life of the people, as we shall see in the following:

Firstly, it is being predicted that in Punjab, there would be more agricultural out put due to water and increased soil fertility. One is not so sure of Sindh, as devastation has been more intense and widespread. Will water recede soon in time and people rehabilitated in time to start their agricultural cycle, is an open question.

Secondly consensus on storage dams seems to be emerging in Sindh, as if we needed this much flood destruction to recognize the truth and the reality. No amount of obfuscation would convince people that there is no water to be stored, that people's lives and property could be saved by flood mitigation role of the storage dam and that human life is more important than the loss of land in delta .Already Bhasha dam is being built without opposition from circles in Sindh. Let us forget Kalabagh for the time being. There are psychological and political issues involved. It is difficult to accept too soon that one was wrong. Hopefully truth would have dawned on every body.

Thirdly provincial irrigation departments have been thoroughly exposed. It would be easier for the reigning government to introduce and implement reforms, quite a few of which have been sabotaged by these people. I have mentioned earlier and elsewhere of the telemetry system for water flow data that is in abeyance and many other reform measures in the pipeline. If government wants to break the water mafia this is the time.

Fourthly, people will come to realize that Environmental issues deserve attention. These are not mere fashion as has been generally perceived and that we are connected with the global environmental issues. Global warming may be hurting us more than others, as more floods and droughts are expected in the wake of the impending climate change. And the loss of biodiversity and the deforestation in the catchment areas contribute to flood peaks and gushes. Environment is a resource which feeds and protects us. May be more sensitivities may develop to pollution and environmental degradation.

Fifthly, there is to be more realism on international political issues and perceptions. Taliban announced that they would offer 20 million US dollars in flood relief, if the international aid is rejected by the

253

government. They might have looted and plundered to come with this kind of money. They in fact continued their atrocities even in the month of Ramadan. International technical logistic and financial aid came in. It is expected to go beyond one billion US dollars in humanitarian relief assistance alone. Other project aid and loan is also being discussed. Even IMF is loosening its conditionalities. We should be very thankless people if we do not appreciate all of this, and differentiate among friends and foes. I am sure this would also be a great source of public political education.

Floods and Dams: the right time for discourse and debate

While people in Sindh, particularly, would be affected by the floods, it would be the right time to talk about the dams. The role dams can play in averting the floods by storing excess water and that dams do not gulp the water away or consume it. Dams merely store excess water to be used when there is less water.

A very extensive study done by the UN has predicted that in the wake of climate change problem and the Green House Gases syndrome, there would be more frequent and intense floods to be followed by droughts. Our water storage capacity is already very low, and not able to meet the current demand of storage and consumption. What would happen, if we are not able to build sufficient storage dams in time? God has already helped us by giving us brains, knowledge and resources. We cannot expect God to help us out then somehow. The laws of nature fixed by him do not change; hence no room for delay, procrastination, destructive debate and inaction.

There are always side-effects of every remedy. There are no options other than dams. Fortunately Bhasha dam is not being opposed, at least for the time being, by the nationalist circles in Sindh. I keep my fingers crossed. Most of the arguments posed against Kalabagh dam, apply to Bhasha dam and others as well. Perhaps the opposition to dams by the nationalist is no more. And this should be a cause of some celebration. Still, while the floods devastate, the issue ought to be debated in electronic media to flush away the residual opposition.

There is some perennial problem and lack of communication and confidence between Sindh and Punjab, on classical lines of upper and

254

lower riparian. However the technology has come up to our rescue. Gone are the days when lower riparian user may be deceived or well informed of the water uses and withdrawals of the upper riparian. One can literally monitor the river and canal flows throughout the river basin on the internet. The technology is cheap and affordable it is not rocket science. Even off the shelf hardware and software is available to provide transparent data.

Admittedly some system is there. Apparently it is not sufficiently spread out to provide complete data. Any way the system can be and should be upgraded. The system can and should be even extended to the relevant rivers in India to resolve water disputes with India. So that another Kashmir like frenzy and division is not created among the two countries. Already there are enough problems. We need not add to the list of intractable problems.

There is 1993 water accord already. No accord is sacrosanct and can be dispensed with. However consensus is often difficult to come by on new accords and political agreements. There is a merit in sticking to the accord or suitably modify it with consensus. It is the PPP government which is in a better political position to deal and resolve the issue on a long term institutional basis, tying in all loose ends.

Pakistan is perennially short of water. Population pressure is going to make water shortage even more critical and unbearable. Water is too precious to be wasted and to be allowed to be wasted in floods and to the ocean. Thatta inundation by the sea water due to low water flows can be stopped by other means. Netherlands and others have developed technologies to retain sea water influx. It is said that half of Netherlands would have been under water had they not applied those technologies. Pushing water away by water is too antiquated and wasteful.

One last word of caution; Kalabagh dam is some how a contentious issue. Let us forget about the Kalabagh dam for the time being lest it generates destructive debate on other vital dam projects. Let the consensus sustain on dams like Bhasha. Others would ultimately come along.

Floods: water accord and discord in Pakistan

It is very interesting and yet depressing to note the diametrically opposite stands and positions of the antagonists from Sindh and Punjab. There is a wide difference of opinion as to the basic data such as river flow/discharge history. There is politics, skepticism and even mistrust. There is a chain of mistrust among the lower and upper riparian; Pakistan distrusts India as to the implementation of Indus Water Treaty and other possible foul plays: Sindh distrusts Punjab and Balochistan has grievances with Sindh. Ironically what one party is asking from the upper riparian is not ready to give the same to the lower riparian. Every now and then there is a water dispute, and vicious debate ensues. Small political parties make hey out of it, while large mainstream political parties get headache on how to resolve the issue without losing votes and support.

The differences are mind boggling. For one group there is no excess water. They say they require floods to irrigate their sailabi land and want to have adequate water flow into the sea to save Sindh delta and loss of coastal land. The other group says that 43 % of water is lost on the average, which could be saved in storage dam which would control and regulate floods and also provide for sea escapage. All I can see is misery in Sindh today due to the excess water and the consequent floods.

Water Accord of 1991 was a major positive development achieved in the short-lived reign of Nawaz Sharif government. The accord sets out most of the ground rules. A federal body IRSA (Indus River System Authority) with equal provincial representation has been formed to implement the accord and manage water distribution issue. One of the problems has been the absence of reliable real time availability of data on water flows and withdrawals. General Musharraf regime installed the most advanced telemetry system with a cost of Rs 360 million, with a sincere hope that the availability of reliable data would solve the problem. For one reason or the other, the system is not being used despite being operational. It would be eventually scrapped if not put to use. This is pathetically criminal attitude on the part of those who have a vested interest in continuing the water dispute. There are two parties to this state of affairs; one who fear to lose their stated antagonistic position if the reliable data is available; the other is corrupt officials and local politician's combo which would lose illegitimate income.

As a result there is total lack of transparency. IRSA does not even have a website. Primary data on water flows and withdrawal is simply absent. There is abundance of contentious articles carrying one sided stories and often inaccurate or convenient data. Some complain that WAPDA does not share with them complete data history on water flows. With to-days technology it is feasible to post on-line data in real time on the internet from all the points where sensors are installed. Today in Pakistan, there is a highly survivable and widely dispersed wireless mobile communication system, which is still working in all nooks and corners despite flood destructions.

Current PPP government is in an enviably convenient position to make a beginning in this respect. It is a main-stream political party having roots and representation in all the provinces and much credibility in Sindh. PPP has given to Pakistan the gift of 1973 constitution which every body except a few military generals of the past upholds and wants to abide by. The Eighteenth Amendment has been able to remove all the distortions that were introduced by the military dictators. In the wake of the martyrdom (shahadat) of Benazir Bhutto, *Pakistan Khappe* almost saved Pakistan from a potentially highly injurious civil war. PPP can deliver on this. Although, one is occupied with flood issue at this time, a beginning should be made towards the resolution of the water distribution problem. The framework is there in the form of Water Accord of 1991.Only the implementational issue s are there. Even flood problem and the dam issues are connected with the resolution of this. There are currently four major issues:

1) Implementation and operationalization of the telemetry system which also has a bearing on flood management capability.
2) Removing the lacunae in the Water Accord, such as a formula for distribution in drought and shortages and others.
3) Determination of water requirements for Sindh delta and creation of consensus on it.
4) Remove malfunctioning of IRSA and bring in an adequate conflict resolution frame-work.

Truth and impartiality appears to be the rarest commodity in Pakistan's highly politicized water issue. Only outsiders such as World Bank can prepare an acceptable regime. Foreign consultants are to be hired in which Pakistanis should not have a role and may possibly have a veto power of the provinces. Otherwise even foreign experts may also be rejected by the contestants. Outside help would be required even in implementing the system. Even a World Bank water auditor and arbitrator may be required for a period spanning a whole water cycle. World Bank has the money, technical capability, impartiality and the muscle. PPP would have to provide the leadership and handle the miscreants.

257

Review of FFC and Flood Management System

In Pakistan floods are no novelty. A total of 12 floods came between 1947 and 1995, giving an average intermission period of 4-5 years. This, however, is an average; it can come again in the next one or two years or in more than fiver years, but surely it will. It is important that we identify mistakes and shortcomings and take steps that these are not repeated again. Not only that, but potential future mistakes are avoided as well.

PMD reportedly did make a flood forecast early in June. But how credible these were? Apparently these were credible enough to lead into what one may be apt to call strategic pre-view. But does PMD system issues a formal probabilistic data, and the relevant agencies give credence to it and the formal follow up SOPs are tied to PMD, is not known. A clear indicator is that WAPDA did not start emptying its dams ahead of time, so as to make room for the coming flood water. Every body appears to have played safe to save his skin, and unsaved the system as a result. There are two remedies to it; formal system and protocols dealing with quantified uncertainty and operational coordination. Both have been lacking. Federal Flood Commission thinks that it is a scientific body only and has no extra powers of coordination, a claim that we would examine in the light of statutory and written role a bit later.

All of this indicates the need for a formal and independent third party review, to inter alia, include the following aspects;

1. Review of the PMD forecast system, as to how scientific and structured it is. How much of possible traditional safe playing is involved. Is there a formal stochastic procedure available to deal with the uncertainty e.g.99%, 95%, 90% or just 50-50 probabilities based predictions?

2. How good, inclusive and extensive is FFC (Federal Flood Commission) working. How simplistic or sophisticated is the so-called computer modeling; what are its variables; what is the scope of its output, quality, frequency and timeliness; does it limit itself to barrages only or goes down up to village levels; does it includes dykes and structures and their level and condition of repair; does it include topographical details at the required map scale to be able to generate forecasts for village inundations dynamically. Do they produce flood maps regularly and dynamically? Has adequately detailed flood zoning

been done and tied to flood scenarios? Most probably their system does static analysis and generates broad macro outputs of limited value in flood management, otherwise eleventh hour and totally improvised management by local administration would not have been there.

3. Where is the flood manual? It was not visible at all. Is it adequate? When was the last time it was updated? How frequently it was used? What were the problems using it?

4. NDMA/ PDMAs have apparently only a role in relief assistance and fire fighting, which it reportedly did with the assistance of Pakistan Army and Navy. NDMA was established in the wake of Earthquake of 1995? It has not been given much of a mandate and role in Flood Management. Every body including provincial governments believed that FFC is responsible for flood coordination and management, which FFC denies that it has such responsibility. FFC says it is only a scientific body. In that case it may be advisable that NDMA be given the responsibility of flood management and coordination, both in terms of planning and execution, while FFC continues to perform its purely technical functions it is capable of.

5. Consideration may be given to organize NDMA on the lines of FEMA (Federal Emergency Management Agency) of the USA. More centrist outlook may have to be adopted than the delay prone federalist structures in such emergency situations. There is certainly a major role of provincial and local governments in relief operations. However, the executive authority of emergency management may not be diluted by federal principles for the benefit of constituents themselves.

Floods; lack of a communication protocol

Federal Flood Commissioner claims that advance information was conveyed to government some times in June, more than a month before the advent of floods. The same info as not shared with public. It does not appear that even provincial governments were informed either. Had the issue been discussed widely even among government circles, the media would have picked it up. It is quite obvious that the flood info was kept as a closely guarded secret. There are three possible explanations; there is always a possibility, however small, that flood and weather forecast does not come out to be true; advance information may spread untimely panic among people; and that exact timing could not have been possibly predicted. Flood warning, as per routine, was issued 3-6 hours before. That is too short a warning for such a horrendous flood.

Even a guarded discussion in the media could have provided some time and guidance to the people to do some advance planning to save their lives and property. Floods are not like earth quakes. After all people know and have experienced floods in the past, especially those who live in riverine areas. Perhaps there is no Communication Policy in this regard. Such an issue should not be left on the whims and opinions of the reigning administrators. It should be a formal procedure based on research and evaluation. Communication is among many other issues that have been found wanting due to the lack of a formal Flood Management Policy substituting an obscure manual that is reportedly catching dust and no body seems to have access to it. We will discuss the Flood Policy issue in some detail later.

If nothing else cattle could have been saved. President Zardari has earlier spoken about fixing a micro-chip onto the cattle, in order to be able to locate them in emergency or in case of loss and theft. This could also facilitate cattle insurance scheme as a part of flood insurance or independent of it. Let us implement it sooner than later. NADRA's technology and infrastructure would prove handy in this respect.

Floods forecasts and Emergency preparedness

In "Dawn" daily of 23rd August, Chairman Flood Commission, was carried and I quote a part of it here: Pakistan Meteorological Department had issued an advisory as early as June 21 about the emerging flood situation and three separate meetings were held at the Armed Forces General Headquarter (GHQ), National Disaster Management Association (NDMA) and the Ministry of Water and Power between June 28 and July 28 had governments and relevant agencies into confidence about possible dangers and preparedness. The PMD had clearly forecast "very heavy rainfall" well in time. Following deductions are obvious from this statement:

Unless the language used by the Flood Commissioner was deliberately kept non-technical for the public, "very heavy rainfall" is too vague and "taking into confidence" too informal. There are two possibilities either the forecast was not taken seriously as it might have been taken as other forecasts such as of our intelligence agencies which routinely forecast trouble in order to save their skin. The other is and which appears to be the most probable is that Disaster Management protocols have yet not been formalized under which clear statements have to be issued in formal and technical language and made public and under which certain management measures on the part of various bodies become mandatory, so that the room for government discretion and vague procedures such as "taking into confidence" is not there.

Public came to know about the floods almost when these finally occurred. Had people been informed they could have taken some measures to protect their life and property. Administrative and social networks and NGOs could have had a premonition and they would have mobilized themselves and thus the loss to life and property could have been minimized and lesser human misery would have been endured. In other countries government and its departments would be sued by the public, corporations and insurance agencies.

Information Minister Mr. Qamaruzzaman Kaira had earlier in a press briefing had also announced that government would undertake a review of what happened and where the problems were. The focal agency in this respect is NDMA which should accept responsibility. It is the job of this agency to suggest and get lacunae removed and developed SOPs not only for its own internal working which it might already have done ,but for over all and administrative machinery .Even an act of Parliament may be required to bring such mandatory SOPs under the ambit of law, minimizing discretion and preventing inaction.

Flood Management & Map Phobia in Pakistan

In my blog,"Development Pakistan" I decried the absence of formal and even legal processes required in flood management. On technical side most elements and organizations are there and mostly reasonably equipped. There are weather monitoring stations, radars and real time river monitoring telemetry system. Pakistan Meteorological Department (PMD) and Federal Flood Commission (FFC) are old and established organizations, while NDMA is relatively young. Nor are floods new to Pakistan and neither are other disasters such as earth-quakes absent from our scene.

If one goes by the contents of a presentation arranged by UNDP for NDMA and made available on the internet, all kind of the required analysis of floods are done; from precipitation, river flow monitoring and forecast to flood zoning and mapping. But what happened on the ground, however, is quite different. People, communities and local governments were hardly in formed and were caught unaware. Flood Commissioner says we informed the governments, NDMA and GHQ.I have discussed earlier of the lack of clear and formal procedures in this respect earlier. Advance flood forecast alone in it is not sufficient enough. What one needs is a dynamic and timely data processing and information dissemination system. The situation on ground is that public was caught unaware on 3rd August when floods originated. Communities did not know till the eleventh hour whether they are required to move away from their settlements and to where. Once rainfall had occurred and no major one comes later, it is a fairly simple job to predict as to which areas and locations would go under water. Lower riparian populations could have been informed. Either there is vague and general info involving very large areas which no body believes or the local administrations finally decide on eleventh hour as to vacate or not, when it is too late and the consequent misery and catastrophe. As it is administrative structures are week and local governments dissolved.

First of all flood maps should be widely available based on the flood history, if not to individuals then to communities and local administrations. Flood forecast maps dynamically updated on a GIS internet based system ought to be available. Churning out maps in one month or more of time is of no use. Google Earth has also made life easier. If you make a commercial arrangement and fee payment with them, at least public dissemination aspect becomes very effective and economical.

There is however an out of sync map phobia in Pakistan at all levels from public to the defence and security agencies. Mapping and GIS has been actively discouraged and opposed. As a result Pakistan is very backward today in a number of fields due to lack of availability of the GIS infrastructure and tools. Volunteer groups disseminate some GIS data with a lot of fear of being harassed by the security agencies. It is almost illegal, although not quite. Copy right issues, permissions which are seldom granted are involved. It is some how in our psyche as well. Bangladesh frenzy was prematurely initiated when East Pakistan map was found in somebody's drawer. Similar was the Jinnah-poor episode. And lately Armed Forces Journal in America published an article doing a scenario analysis of the breakdown of state system in the Middle East and showed some maps. Ordinarily no body may have given attention to such an article as the like of which are published rather frequently and routinely in the U.S. But because maps were published, this caught our fancy and frenzy. Thousands of photocopies were made and circulated by concerned and well-meaning individuals.

Elsewhere maps are so common and freely distributed even detailed street maps are available on the internet. They all have security issues, internal and external. Cost of abuse and user benefits are to be compared. In today's satellite imaging regime what and where is the secret. Enemy knows every thing well; it is secret for the ordinary individual. In any case security zones, unless the whole country may be in some ones mind, could be removed from such data dissemination. Recently a Map of Emergency centers and camps was published in newspapers costing millions of rupees, which could have easily been done on Google Earth. It keeps media running and happy. So map phobia should go and an online real-time flood mapping system based on GIS be introduced.

Secondly, an issue of critical importance is the state of repair of the flood control infrastructure like *dykes* and *bunds* etc. In the USA Army Corps of Engineers are involved in building and even repairing major dykes and levees. Our irrigation department and officials are too corrupt, lazy and out of sync with time in terms of knowledge, technology and practices. Because public life and property is involved, independent monitoring arrangements of the stability and state of repair of dykes and levees should be established. Independent monitoring involving on-site examination may be farmed out to different civil engineering firms in the private sector. However a database of the *bunds* and *dykes* be maintained by FFC. The data base should contain all the technical data and civil inspection summaries on these facilities. A GIS of the data can be created on Google Earth and later on a dedicated network eventually. Actual major maintenance is entrusted to Pakistan Army or FWO.

Some kind of Flood Insurance scheme may also be introduced ,where in both private and public resources may go in, so that a long term saving and resource arrangement takes care of such emergencies at least partly and we are not totally dependent on emergency foreign aid and philanthropy for ever. A lot of commercial structures like grid stations, transmission towers and mobile communication assets have also suffered significant loss. Flood insurance would also force some standardization and regularity in the flood regime.

Floods control system and cost

People's misery in the floods has been also exacerbated due the failure and breaches in the protective *dykes and bunds*. These flood control infrastructure elements are in a poor state due to poor maintenance; corruption, over-staffing in provincial irrigation departments, under-budgeting and low *abiana* rates/ water tax. According to a World Bank study, in Pakistan *Abiana* rates are only 15 % of the requirements which do not cover even routine operating (O&M) expenses, not to talk of modernization and replacement etc. Where will the money come from? Land lords are not prepared to pay Income Tax, falsely arguing that Agriculture is already taxed heavily. We have seen how heavy is *Abiana*? And then one who earns the taxable income is to pay income tax. The untaxed and undisclosed incomes give rise to many social vices and exhibitionism also. So when you do not pay the tax and *abiana* as well, where will the money and resources come from? Today the houses and property of every body, rich and poor, have suffered. Misery is common, combined and pervasive.

Provincial irrigation departments have to be reorganized. These are corrupt, antiquated and over-staffed. It is widely alleged that they indulge in all kind of illegal practices in water distribution and are notorious in siphoning off the funds. For this purpose autonomous Provincial Irrigation Development Authorities (PIDAs) were made and a system of self management of *user-associations was built in.*

The whole irrigation network in all the provinces is in a state of decay which has exacerbated the flooding problem. Let me quote here from a recent World Bank Report: *Some recent events in the form of breaches in the first line of protective embankments in Sindh and the current condition of many distributaries, minors and water courses, and their related situation of Sukkur Barrage are clear evidence of accumulative neglect....The deteriorated structures such as gates and outlets...the delivery capacity of canals is 30% below design because of the cumulative effects of deferred maintenance and lack of rehabilitation.*

The major solution to control such extra ordinary floods is large storage dams, which would regulate water flow. It is only sincerely hoped that the opposition to storage dams in Sindh and NWFP would go away after these floods. However other steps should be taken in the meantime. The most important of which is a sustained and sustainable irrigation and flood management system. The total loss has yet to be estimated. It would exceed several billion dollars. Is it a good economics to suffer such losses and not invest much a less in loss prevention?

Most countries have large rivers. And all rivers tend to overflow. Nations have built protections against these overflows. Chinese used to experience such floods regularly in history, but no more.

Apart from standard irrigation practices and building storage dams in the north, other unconventional steps have to be taken. Government is already on building small dams where topology and geology permits. Consideration may be given to enlarge their volumes by broadening and deepening those as wells. Also water diversion channels around major population centers may be considered. I can readily cite two examples of such water channels; one in Austria and the other in Canada. In Austria on river *Danube,* a water channel has been made to divert flood water. *It is 21kms long and 70-210 meters wide. In western Canada* at Winnipeg, *Red River Floodway* has been built which is 47 kms long. A total of 2.75 billion cft of material had to be removed to provide for the flood storage and diversion. Also the silt load of the Indus should be reduced by controlling deforestation in the north.

Finally river-basin modeling and real-time river flow monitoring system building in details of dykes and *bunds* coupled with a rational and transparent decision-making system for emergency measures such as breaking *bunds* and dykes should be brought about. In the absence of a formal system the incentives for allegedly biased action are great and would be detrimental to harmony, peace and cohesion among the communities involved.

Finally all these measures require money and resources. International community can at best help in short term relief effort. Most of the rebuilding has to be financed by ourselves .If loans are taken, these have to be serviced. A consensus has to be built on the taxes and *abiana* issue. Every body pays according to his ability and usage of services.

Flood mitigation: Planning and community participation

Perhaps nothing can be done about the current flood victims, except the traditional relief activities that are being undertaken by the governments, civil society and the international bodies. Pakistan is a flood prone country. Next flood would not be far off. Average intermission period has been estimated as 4-5 years; actual may be less or more. We should learn the lessons, and take steps to reduce the misery and suffering that may follow in the next flood. Here are some suggestions;

1)Now that the water is still there and memories fresh, maximum flood water levels reached at all flood locations should be recorded ,not only in the books by relevant agencies but by the communities and the local administrations. Permanent Markings of water levels should be made on walls and structures and if such things are not available, permanent water mark pillars should be made.

2) Flood zoning should be done, keeping flood water depths in view. Simple building and land use codes should be installed, including prohibition on houses in certain areas where water depth has been excessively high. Raised houses, *kutcha or pucca*, one foot above the flood level should be encouraged and enforced. House clustering built on raised platforms should be promoted, around which there should be planting to prevent erosion. In riverine areas, where housing is permitted, brick housing may not be allowed; only temporary structures such as built of *Bamboo, Chatai and sarkanda* may be permitted. Even agricultural activities may have to be banned in especially precarious and vulnerable areas. Alternative land would have to be allotted to the often landless and poor people who engage in cultivation in these areas. We have dealt with the issues of Land and Housing reforms elsewhere. If for nothing else, then for good flood management purposes, some kind of Land Reforms resulting in land transfer to the rural poor and the landless has to be introduced.

3) All public buildings such as schools, hospitals, and administration houses may be built either on appropriately raised plat forms or entirely on first floor leaving ground floor un-built; only columns be there on the ground floor. Such shaded space can be used for many social and public purposes in the normal times.

4) A community center should be built in every village on an appropriately raised platform with an average size being 2-4 acres depending on the population and requirements. This need not be *pucca* construction. Sand and soil from the river and other excavations and some stones could be utilized for raising the plat form. Only perimeter may have to be reinforced and also protected through plantings. In ordinary times, this can be used as a community center and

during floods and other emergencies as a refuge center where humans and as well as cattle and other belongings could be accommodated. A store should also be made where valuables could be deposited under a locker kind system, where feasible.

5) All of this requires pre-planning and community involvement. Floods need not cause so much misery, losses and despair, if adequate planning is done and a structure for community involvement is ready for implementation. In our case, the whole community becomes a victim and gets paralyzed and converted into a begging and miserable case. Who would not like to contribute at least in terms of labor and other cooperation, who has suffered flood miseries? Community involvement and participation is a must; it means local administration, people's representatives as well as people. It appears that in all these days, relief agencies have been working mostly on their own, without an opportunity for people to participate and contribute, except some on-field improvisations that may have been there. I have noted a guideline document on preparing an emergency management plan on the web-site of NDMA. But I could not find any actual plan itself for different districts, except Jhelum. Even that plan would have been useless, as it involves a significant number of local government representatives, who are no more there. We have dealt with the unfortunate absence of Local Government system at this time of calamity elsewhere and made a case for the revival of previous LGs for a period of one year.

Flood victims: Emergency support vs sustainability

Charpai (wood and straw bed) has emerged as a very versatile and survivable asset of the flood victims. Many flood victims have used it as a boat and have improvised it to transport themselves through comparatively long distances. Charpai is a usual site around flood victims' temporary settlement. They use the Charpai in the day as a cover from the sun and at night sleep on those. It doesn't get dirty. Normally one doesn't require any extra bedding material. Charpai has survived. Victims could bring it with them and can take it back along with them when they return to their towns and villages. It is an ideal device for summers providing enough ventilation. And philanthropists may consider including Charpais and other sustainable items in their aid to the victims. Obviously Food, water and medicine is usually the priority.

Toilets and Hygiene is a very big issue in floods. People relieve themselves in water or nearby. Water gets contaminated and is rendered not drinkable. Thus drinking water is to be provided despite the ironical water abundance around. Bottled water is often provided due to its transportation and distribution ease. Low cost hygienic toilets can be provided relatively cheaply for communal common purposes. Women and girls suffer more than men and boys on the account of lack of toilets due to privacy reasons. Toilets should be of sustainable/survivable construction, so as to be incorporated in the ultimate dwellings of the victims. It is important that people do not relieve themselves at any convenient location, but should be required to do so at designated places where cover, water and shit-pot is provided. There are many creative solutions which we have discussed elsewhere. Used plastic containers of chemicals and batteries could be bought or acquired from SherShahs (flea markets). Otherwise a steel box of adequate size (15x24x12 inches) of riveted construction with handle and possibly legs can be procured in abundance from local market. Again this is survivable and can be incorporated in later day toilets in the dwellings ultimately.

Containerized Reverse Osmosis plants could be handy and effective and could be installed where electricity is available. One plant per tehsil may be sufficient and could meet cooking and drinking needs. When emergency is over, these can go back to the donor agency for use elsewhere or redeployed in far -off deserving areas where it may be required on a routine basis. Such plants can be even rented or acquired on lease. And a good supply may always be available in traditional global markets.

Pots and pans for kitchen and water storage are also highly survivable and a good gift for the flood victims which they could incorporate in their homes when they return. Most of them may not recover whatever little they had in their houses when they return to salvage their household items. TV channels are reporting that if food somehow becomes available, they are short of pots and pans, which may also result in food wastage.

Floods and the Local Governments

Local governments are no more, when we need those most. People and flood victims have complained of inadequate and inefficient relief activities. Government circles respond that they are doing whatever they can. Actually government is severely handicapped due to non-existence of local governments which were dissolved some six months back. Obviously no body knew then, that there would be floods, and we would need the local governments badly. In any case keeping local governments in long abeyance is not a good policy. After a successful grounding in period of local government's traditional provincial government's linkages and organization is no more. Although there is LG civil bureaucracy and administration in place, the representative efficacy and efficiency is not to be found.

The argument that the LG bureaucracy is there to look after the state of affairs is not a fair and right argument. If we accept this argument, it can go very far and would be obviously inconvenient to its proponents. One could then argue that there is no need of civilian democratic government because the army and civil bureaucracy can and is doing what is required. Mobilization of people and keeping in contact and in touch is usually done much better by peoples representatives and hence the rationale of local governments. This is no time and place to repeat the debate in favor of local government. It is obvious and that is why we have adopted it along with most countries in the world. Unfortunately in Pakistan, provinces and political parties have not found peace with local governments. There is a deep seated suspicion and sense of rivalry even antagonism. Military dictators have used local bodies for their false legitimization by bringing in local bodies as a substitute for civilian rule and as a parallel focus of power.

No doubt there is a loss in direct exercise of power. It is still their but routed through local representatives. To enjoy and have peace with indirect power requires some practice in democratic traditions which have not been allowed to take route due to successive military interventions and long absence of civilian and democratic rule. It is wondered why PPP government should have problem with local government. It is adequately represented usually in rural Sindh. In Punjab and NWFP it shares local power with other major contestants. In Punjab there is currently a personal style of administration prevailing and hence procrastination to return to local governments. PPP does not seem to have this kind of problem in particular in Sindh.

What to do now. There are floods and the aftermath. Local governments have been dissolved on the completion of their terms. There was an intermission and procrastination due to certain changes that the new PPP government and also others wanted to bring in. Consensus among partners does not seem to have emerged. It may be difficult and inopportune to organize and contest elections when whole cities have come under water and are totally submerged. It is time to be creative and think of the out-of-box solutions. Think about reviving previously elected local governments for the next one year. The legal modalities could be worked out at-least in Sindh. After all it is a provincial subject. Others may follow or be persuaded simultaneously.

Pakistan Meteorological Department - a Ministry of Defence entity?

It may surprise many, but it is true that Pakistan Meteorological Department (PMD) is part of the Ministry of Defence(MoD). What direct relevance is there of weather with matters of war and peace should be known to those who put that department where it is now. Perhaps nowhere in the World is this department associated with the military or Defence except for antiquated regimes like North Korea and Myanmar. In 19th century days of Clausewitz, weather data may have had strategic value requiring security and secrecy. Today in the age of satellites and international weather modeling, there is hardly any notion of sensitivity about this data.

But why should one bother about where a department is located hierarchically, so long such an association does not cause any problem in its functioning, output and liaison with the users. There is an implication and a serious one. Due to being a MoD installation, there has always been an aura of secrecy about it. PMD has been found wanting in disseminating the data with the required facility and readiness. There is always some hesitation and number of questions asked and forms to be filled to get simple meteorological data which everywhere is available abundantly on the net without charge. Now bureaucracy has discovered another convenient device of hiding behind user charges and has started charging discouragingly high commercial charges for the data. It may be awkward to call the data to be sensitive and easy to deny and discourage access through demanding payments. And then making payments is not easy. You have to get an account number from the department, go to the State Bank of Pakistan, make the payment, repeat the process if there is some discrepancy and the cycle goes on.

Similarly Federal Bureau of Statistics (FBS) does with its data. They hardly earn any money and contribute towards financial sustainability, but manage to discourage data use and development. And in case of

PMD, save the so called," sensitive' data. The consequence is that many scientific, economic and environmental applications that could have been developed and published could not be done, a number of which I can readily cite. Most EIA applications involving air pollution such as of power plants cannot be done because of the data restrictions. Expensive software like AERMOD has been made free by other countries, but for the ready availability of data. Flood modeling and water inundation cannot be made online because of restrictions on GIS.A lot of economic analysis is not undertaken on various regions of the country because population census data is not made available in the required format or even made available online. A lot of flood information and analysis and forecast of flood flows could have been made available to the public in the form of flood maps, but for such restrictions especially on GIS.

In the case of PMD and its role in flood forecasting and organizational interfacing with the user departments, the jury is still to be out. The net result has been a lack of coordination among the relevant organizations. Did PMD's special status as a MoD entity prevent or discourage readily interacting directly with other departments or it had to go via? These questions would be and should be reviewed at the earliest opportunity. In any case PMDs association with the MoD and its secretive behavior is an anachronism which must change. It should be reorganized along open lines and appended to Ministry of Science and Technology or MINFAL. PMD itself should not have too much of a say in it, as they may not be objective about it due to the real estate advantages that come with MoD affiliation.

And lastly appending civilian institution to defence sector has many disadvantages, the most important being the budgetary issues. Defence expenditure unnecessarily becomes high and bulky reflecting poorly in political terms inviting undeserved criticism and hostility. Genuine requirements of Defence sector are too many and do not justify further agglomeration.

The need and rationale for a Water Policy

One may decry the need of a policy and argue that there is already a defacto policy and dispersed over many documents and rules. And the sophists may argue that *our policy is not to have a policy. We want to be free of constraints and be dynamic.* Although policies often are vague and broadly drafted affirmation of principles and targets and often remain unimplemented, yet in some areas policy affirmations and determinations are vitally required, especially where many agencies and sectors may be involved. We have seen how power policy has attracted IPP investment and Export policies have promoted and expanded exports. Policy makes decision making easy on the part of the bureaucracy and saves time and effort of the stake-holders in sorting out issues.

We do not have a water policy, although we do have elements and components of water policy; an elaborate drinking water policy has been prepared; there is WAPDA's water vision 2025,which also goes by Planning Commissions water vision, which is essentially a WAPDA's strategic plan outlining its investment programme and strategy over the period. These are parts of a potential water policy but not a policy in itself. A policy is a holistic document, enunciating principles, objectives, goals and targets, resolves and intermediates cross sectoral issues, lays out priorities and may even provide guidance to working rules.

It would be relevant here to point out that some of our flood management problems are due to the non-availability of a policy document; the issue of coordination between PMD,FFC and WAPDA on operation of the dams; the fixing of priorities, storage vs hazard and human life. An archaic Flood Manual could not possibly resolve the question in time. Thus there is a need of an integrated policy drawing upon existing framework, improving upon it and gather support around it. Water is an important issue, especially when it is getting scarce requiring prioritization and choices to be made. There are many issues which remain to be straightened such as royalties and user charges, water allocation among various user sector, investment schemes, strategies and targets, around which much needed action is to take place. Although, one may like to add a caveat here that in the presence of water sector reports of the lending agencies such as ADB and World Bank, what is the need of a policy? Policy without the backing of money has no teeth. They have the money and teeth as well. This was a mere caveat. A nation of 160-180 million people needs much more.

Our neighboring country India introduced a Water Policy as early as in 1987 and revised and updated it in 2002.Our Ministry of Water and Power should make an immediate beginning in this respect. The honorable minister will get a feather in his cap, as well as the government. After all it is a highly competitive political and democratic environment wherein achievements are to be made and demonstrated as well. The immediate contribution of a political government is enunciation of policy. Implementation keeps following. Even after 62 years of our national existence, there are still new horizons and virgin territories.

Pakistan Drinking Water Policy

Ministry of Environment has prepared a draft policy for drinking water, which is in the process of government approval. Work on this policy was earlier initiated by the ministry of health almost a decade ago under some UN initiative. Nothing of substance perhaps is initiated in our beloved country unless the impulse comes from the UN system. Finally the policy process was taken over by the Ministry of Environment. It is a good omen and an elaborate policy.

The draft policy announces certain policy principles the most important of which is that access to safe drinking water has been recognized as a basic human right, the existing inequities working against the poor are to be removed and that the drinking water allocation gets precedence over all other uses. The policy also lays out time bound targets related to water access, water treatment etc. It is an elaborate draft, painstakingly prepared, most probably with the assistance of foreign consultants, as is indicated by its relative sophistication, its emphasis on gender and financial sustainability.

The draft, however, contradicts itself when it deals with financial sustainability and user charges. It should be patently clear that the poor cannot pay. One third of Pakistan is abjectly poor and does not get the required daily nutrition. Most water policies and the associated literature, I have come across, argue in favor of recouping of O&M costs and not the full cost recovery. If drinking water is a basic human right, water is to be subsidized either through external or cross subsidies, for the poor. There is a strong case for differentiated water rates as is currently being done for other services such as electricity. I wonder if the policy makers would make the requisite adjustments in this respect. Similarly, one would suspect the role of private sector and private-public partnership, however elegant and fashionable these terms may appear to be. Private sector requires more than adequate return, while in water sector, ROA/ROE are relatively unknown terms. One could however see the role of public-ally subsidized cooperative schemes.

However, drinking water policy coming from the ministry of environment, which is a kind of staff ministry having advisory functions and no implementation resources, may remain a stumbling block. I wonder if the Ministry of Water would have been more appropriate agency for drinking water policy which could have issued it as a part of the broader Water Policy. Perhaps drinking water standards and testing routines, water and waste water plants standards could be more appropriate for the environment ministry.

If the policy is not to have the fate of just a *good document*, it has to have ownership of the line ministry concerned which in this case is Ministry of Water and Power. I am not sure whether the delay in announcing the policy might be due to these issues that I am raising here.

Our Water woes

A World Bank report on "Pakistan's water economy" makes the following statements:

Pakistan is one of the most arid (water less) countries of the world with an average rain fall of 290 mm a year. It is one of most water-stressed country as well and it is expected that the situation would worsen with the passage of time, when by the year 2035, per capita water availability would come down to a low level of 100 CM per capita per year. There is no additional water to be injected into the system. There is no feasible intervention, which would enable Pakistan to mobilize appreciably more water than it now uses.

Pakistan's water situation is highly risky; in being based just on one river Indus i.e. no scope of error, as there is no compensating source or river. Large scale degradation of water resources base has occurred due to salinity and pollution. Ground water has been over exploited over many years and its quality is deteriorating. Flooding and drainage problem are going to get worse, especially in the lower Indus basin. Climate change (CO_2 effect) is going to exacerbate the problem due to excessive expected flooding and successive decrease in river flows. There is an inadequate knowledge base of the eco-system underlying the Indus river basin, and the knowledge base has deteriorated over the years. The country is literally flying blind into a hazardous (and unknown) future. Much of the water infrastructure is in a state of poor repair. The quality of project implementation is low and the system is financially unsustainable.

Pakistan has to invest and invest soon in costly and contentious large dams. Most arid countries have large storage. The US and Australia have 5000 CM per capita of storage and China 2200 CM, while Pakistan has only 150 Cubic Meters. The dams of Colorado Rivers in the USA can hold 900 days of river run-off; while in South Africa storage of 500 days is provided for its Orange River. In India the corresponding figure is of 120-220 days, while in Pakistan it is only 30days.

The two main storage dams of Mangla and Tarbela are already silted significantly .Water productivity (use-efficiency) is low due to one of the lowest crop yields in the world and other reasons. Within Pakistan, there is a large variation among efficient and inefficient farmers and among head-enders and tail-enders. Tail-enders (lands which are situated at the far end of the canals and water courses and their distributaries) crop yields are 40% less than those of the head-enders, speaking volumes about the inadequacy of the irrigation system.

Table 15.1: Comparative water and economic productivity of wheat and rice crops

	Wheat	**Rice**	**Ratio Wheat: Rice**
Crop water productivity	1.48 kg/M^3	0.23 kg / M^3	6.43
Economic water productivity	17 yen / M^3	3.7 yen / M^3	4.59

Source: Pakistan Economic Survey

Pakistan's farmers consume 60% more than Indian farmers and 100% more than Californian farmers with respect to wheat production. However there is hope, ironically, because we are so low in crop-yield and water productivity, there is a large potential to be exploited of doubling and tripling the output with the same amount of land. And more, if more land is brought into the system of which there is greater scope, if not much in the case of water. Increase in crop-yield is going to have doubly important impact. Firstly solving the food shortage problem and secondly improving the welfare of the poor and subsistence farmers, with direct impact on reducing poverty among a large section of our population. It would have many other salutary side effects; increased supplies to agro-processing industry resulting in-higher value added and savings of foreign exchange. Water rights should be tradable, through an efficient water market, where water efficiency is rewarded and the proposed water rights for the landless and share-croppers bringing additional income.

Ironically Egypt has the lowest water availability in the sample of 794m3 per capita, but consumes highest in terms 17000 m3 per ha. Canada, Malaysia and Australia are super water rich being in excess of 20,000 m3 per capita. China, Indonesia, Canada and have comparable water resources in the range of 2700-2800 Km3.Low population of Malaysia and Australia contribute to their highest per capita water availability. Pakistan lies among the lowest per capita water countries along with India, Germany and Iran. In absolute terms, Egypt and Afghanistan have the lowest of water resources of 58-65 Km3, while Turkey, Pakistan and France have comparable water resources of around 200-229 Km3. Most frequent (medium) size of water resource in the sample is around 400-500 cubic meters per capita. Bangladesh, China, Indonesia, Canada and USA, all have 2200-12000 cubic meter plus per capita water resource, but have different predicaments due to different populations.

High per capita withdrawal of 1250-1682 m3 of Canada, USA and Australia can be explained by high wages and industrial output. In those three countries, raw material processing industries consuming water are preponderant as opposed to Europe. Pakistan's withdrawal of 1187 m3, falling in the same high consuming category is somehow not explainable, except perhaps in terms of its low water use efficiency level. However Afghanistan, Egypt, Iran, also have comparable per capita withdrawals. In these countries per capita water withdrawal is twice that of China, India, Indonesia, France, Germany and Turkey.

High precipitation (1600 m+) and watershed areas in China, India, Canada, and USA are responsible for high ground water resources of 400-1300 Km3 range. Malaysia, Thailand, Iran and Pakistan have comparable ground water sources of 40-50 km3, among one of the lowest. Pakistan has one of the lowest precipitations in the world, 218mm, as opposed to 2168mm of India and 2366 mm of Malaysia, 1400 of Japan and 1201 mm of USA. No wonder Pakistan is classified among arid/semi arid countries, despite claims of our patriots classifying Pakistan among resourceful countries. What is their criterion or source of confidence? It is mind boggling. The net message is that Pakistan should improve its water productivity and efficiency, which is lower than comparable countries and thus offers a lot of scope for increasing agricultural output and food availability for the ever increasing population and for decreasing malnourishment.

Conclusions and recommendations

1. More water storages should be built, may be postponing Kalabagh dam for the time being and initiating other possible projects like Bhasha and Bunji dams as is being already done.

2. Speedy implementation of the projects, as more than two decades has been lost in Kalabagh controversy.

3. Improve the irrigation system and the physical infrastructure, solving tail-enders problem.

4. Improve agricultural R&D and extension services, introducing technology packages more frequently than has been the case.

5. Introduction of water efficient on -farm irrigation technologies such as sprinklers and drip irrigation;

6. Reduction of water losses and lining of canals and their distributaries;

7. Improving water rights system making it more fair and transparent, reducing corruption and influence-peddling; Award at least some water rights to the share-cropper and the landless tenants, in addition to the land owners. Currently water rights are for the land owner only. Consequently all increases in water supply go to the benefit of the "haves" only and have-nots remain without right or an asset.

SECTION-IV

Post Script

16 Terrorism; towards an intellectual deal

Will terrorism, extremism and violence go away if and when Americans leave Afghanistan? Is there some innate conflict in Pakistan and contemporary Muslim societies that push them to a trigger ready violence? What are the causes and origins? What are the dimensions of this conflict and who are the parties to the conflict? What is the nature of this smoldering conflict and irrespective of history of 9/11, Iraq and Afghanistan, is there any scope of dialogue, compromise and reconciliation? It would be too foolhardy to venture a solution or formula at overall Muslim nations' level .However, in a limited way, in a Pakistan context, one may like to explore the issue and posit some possible solutions or the tracks thereof.

It is not difficult to discern that in Pakistan and elsewhere, there are two conflicts that seem to have merged and have fed on each other. Extreme poverty and disparities should have naturally unleashed an unending conflict that may not be too visible. There is a vast body of people who are disgruntled and alienated and are despondent. Despite their profession of patriotism, they are not part of the system and have no sympathy with it. They would not cry, if the whole thing winds up. Many wonder that colonial powers were better rulers. Deteriorating economic and social conditions have perhaps exacerbated these feelings. The other conflict that is visible vividly is among modernism and the religion, and among the so called liberals and the fundamentalists. Apparently the two forces or phenomena have combined and are presenting themselves as a unified syndrome. Poverty and extremism are natural allies and likewise liberalism and affluence are bedfellows.

The conflict can perhaps be ameliorated or resolved by progress in two domains. Firstly, reducing and eliminating the grinding poverty and improving the general social conditions. Secondly, a compromise, intellectual, political and administrative, among the liberal and fundamentalist or say Islamic values and their followers needs to be worked out. In this space, we explore the prospects of a compromise on such a social order.

There is an influential strain of thought in Islamic thoughts and a belief, having a foundation in basic teachings of Islam that condones even incites violence for opposing and mitigating vice, Nahaq and Batil and opposing oppression. While vice may be clear, Nahaq and Batil and even oppression can be relative and even vague and subject to a very broad interpretation. There is a diversity of views on it, and therefore there would be groups that would be akin to adopt a violent path. Ikhwanul-Muslimoon chose it in early 1950s and has gradually come to adopt more peaceful and democratic struggle and processes as is seen in current Egyptian politics. Their counterparts in Pakistan started with affirmation to democratic process but have gradually moved to either tacit support to violence and terrorism or an outright and shameful display of terroristic muscle. The social and political conditions in Pakistan and elsewhere in Muslim societies may remain as these are for some time which will give continued justification of violence which may have many forms including terrorism.

Sometime back, a conference of Pakistani Deobandi scholars and Ulemas had been called by the government circles to garner support (and a declaratory supporting statement) against terrorism and suicide attacks. The organizers could not succeed in getting any fatwa or statement against terrorism unleashed by the Taliban, led by TTP and other factions. Indeed as reported by the daily Dawn newspaper and by its editor, everybody else was criticized and condemned for their failures; drone attacks, the US action in Afghanistan and Iraq, and the non-Islamic character of government in Pakistan. The conference reveals confusion in the minds of Deobandi scholars, if not outright support for terrorism. Earlier there was the Lal Masjid episode, in which demand for Islamist system was pushed by the extremists who occupied a children's library and created a severe law and order situation. Unfortunately excessive force was used which resulted in many deaths and disappearances of the female students of the religious seminary. It is often said that this show of force by the rulers at the time resulted in further alienation of the extremists from the existing system and the Pakistan Army and impelled them towards a deadly terror campaign that materialized soon after the Lal Masjid episode. Subsequently the Swat peace deal did not succeed and was followed by operation Raahe Nijaat, in which the whole city had to be evacuated and the infiltrators and terrorists had to be wiped out after a deadly military campaign.

Some winds of change have also started blowing in Pakistan with the popular opinion being explicitly against terrorism, replacing a confused and muddled attitude earlier, in the wake of excessively barbarian terrorism unleashed by TTP.. Most fundamentalist scholars of Deoband School seem to have ended their quiet confusion and have condemned terrorism and suicide attacks. Ironically they put the blame on US, India and Israel in a classical allegiance to conspiracy theories. In their Juma prayers sermons they condemn both the government and the unknown perpetrators alike. The fundamentalist mind is still confused though.

Keeping in view the deteriorating situation and even expanding and intensifying terror campaign by the militants, the choices before liberal forces are not too many. They may risk a future war of attrition at best and a take-over at worst. Pakistan's states' security cannot be left to the whims of a handful of liberals who may idealize western cultures and values, but are totally out of tune with the minds and attitudes of a largely uneducated populace living in harsh and difficult conditions. Poverty and extremism are usually best friends.

Attempts to force the change in seminaries curriculum and the associated pedagogy would not succeed. However, enmasse induction in these seminaries could be completed away by offering alternative education facilities to the children of the poor. Financial and modernization assistance such as libraries, computers and internet, provision of teachers of modern sciences such as economics, philosophy and natural sciences could in the medium to long run may dilute extremism and help produce more balanced and seminary graduates and scholars.

There may be a scope for compromise among well meaning liberals who wish to bring about an egalitarian system replacing the existing unjust and feudalistic order under the garb of democracy, and the Islamists, if not the die-hard terrorists. The common cause among the two, otherwise diverse groups could be a "just socio-economic order'. Liberals may have to forego or postpone their emphasis on Western values of wining and dining, flaunting and exhibitionism, vulgar and obscene media etc.
Elimination of hunger, poverty an injustice can be the compromising agenda, if the two sides are faithful to their ideals. The recent revival of the judiciary should not be confused with the social justice. The former is legislative and even elitist while the latter is real, enduring and all pervasive. Liberals could never have the wherewithal to change the system while the Islamists have a wider base and can mobilize support, mass appeal and street power. Islamists need respectability and

acceptability in the corridors of power, national and internal, and a marketable outlook. Jamaat e Islami originally, perhaps, offered a potential vehicle, but has now chosen an extremist path. Many in this country dread a collapse of the system and sudden surrender at the hands of extremists in the form of a hurriedly organized compromise. The alternative prognosis of a pervading war of attrition with extremists led by TTP is not a good prospect either which may leave us divided and under developed, with our neighboring India looking forward to reap the benefits. An intellectually negotiated consensus should reside as an option of the State of Pakistan.

The Islamists may have to forego or postpone their emphasis on initiating Islamic interpretation and implementation with "cutting hands", caning the defaulters, mishandling women and restricting their participation in economic life. Ziaul Haque's Islamic rule came with trying to impose "hand chopping" punishments without arranging and providing for the poor and hungry (the latter) as enshrined by Islam. Talibans in Afghanistan did violence to women coming out of their homes and interfered with relics of other religions. Pakistani Taliban flogged a girl and routinely destroyed girls' schools. On the other hand, liberals insist on flaunting sexuality and nudity, even display of sexual acts on television and media, and all that goes with it. Both the diverse penchants can be delayed or if not totally, foresworn permanently, till happy and workable solutions are found.

If we look for the common thread in the demands and the conduct of the extremists, and the participants of the Deobandi scholars' conference, we can conclude the following:

1. Resentment against immorality spread through the media and films, CDs etc with the assistance or benign neglect of the government(s) of Pakistan.
2. Establishment of some obvious manifestations of Islamic system especially a fast-track legal system based on Qazi Adalat and Shariat.
3. If they have their way, they would also demand several anti-woman initiatives, stress on beard and salaat etc.

On the first two, even liberals may like to support the extremists. Many of us would not like to show us on TV, what is being shown e.g. vulgarity and raw sexuality. All kinds of near x-rated films and songs encouraging flesh trade are not the grievances of the extremists but also have a common cause of conflict with an average law abiding and progressive Pakistani.

That the existing legal system of Pakistan is highly inefficient, corrupt and time- consuming and absolutely inadequate for the needs of an average Pakistanis well known and almost undisputed. Without sacrificing the fundamentals of the existing legal doctrine and regime, it may be possible to induct a fast track effective system which is available in the form of a Qazi system on which there are procedures and consensus. Small cause courts, felonies and personal laws like marriage, divorce, inheritance etc., could be entrusted to Qazi courts, wherein both lawyer and police are avoided and side tracked. Most people cannot afford lawyers and police and want to have immediate recourse to an institution which is readily accessible, without intermediary and un-necessary costs and whose quick adjudication can be achieved. Qazi / Shariat adalat system could be introduced first in NWFP, in the districts where there is excessive demand for the new system. Localized referendum can be organized to ascertain the will of the people. In Punjab and Sindh also initially some rural areas could be given to the Qazi system.

Concluding, some way has to be found out of the social and political polarization that has threatened our national fabric and very existence. It would not go away with the withdrawal of U.S. troops from Afghanistan. It is an intellectual and social challenge. There has to be a way out, or we would be consumed by the controversy and the conflict. Will the grand compromise evolve gradually before it is too late?

17 The Enduring Budget Realities

Budget has been announced rather triumphantly by the PPP government in the backdrop of alleged attempts to roll back democracy and the government much earlier. In other environments, governments tend to call it off and be relieved of the job in search of new coalitions and adjustments to face new realities and architect new courses and strategies. Apart from low growth scenario, the budget is a familiar story of deficits; more expenditure and less income and more imports than exports resulting in the need for internal and external borrowing in the backdrop of accumulated debt which has reportedly doubled over the last 4-5 years. Many a practical economists argue that deficits are all right so long as the economy is growing fast enough. And it has not been doing so, despite the high growth rates in the economies of the region. However, the finance minister wants to hide behind the recession in world economies.

Pakistan, its economy and the budget are suffering from a number of issues that have not been tackled over the years and the cumulative burden of it is now showing up and threatening the very fabric of this country. The issues are well known and I would focus on the following in this space; Energy, Military expenditure, income tax on agricultural landlords and waste and inefficiencies in government.

Energy is both a budgetary issue and as well as economic growth issue. GOP has been subsidizing energy sector annually by injecting Rs 200-300 billion, and still the economy suffers from shortages and people protest in disgust and pain. Energy shortages have been causing a growth loss of 2% in the economy. It appears that if only this problem had been resolved, many other problems would have been prevented and the economy would have been growing at a minimum required rate of 6% or so. Easier said than done; the PM one day announces that in the next three months there would be no energy problem or shortages and in the next one challenges all and sundry to come up with a solution to energy problem. To compound structural issues, Oil prices have been misbehaving and reached a level of 136 USD per barrel to be followed by a very recent drop to 103 USD , still higher than a usual of 60-80 USD of Musharraf years. Oil prices hurt the economy in many ways, especially because Pakistan has become very dependent on it. All economies are dependent on oil and energy but either they produce energy or consume less of it. Most countries consume oil only for transport needs as there is no other alternative to Internal Combustion engines used in the automotives of today. It is a gift of Musharraf regime which installed or put into pipeline many oil based power plants neglecting investments in gas discoveries and putting Thar coal on a back burner. Unfortunately, he and his coterie did not know, as is usual when going is good, that he was digging a grave for Pakistan's economy. Thus high oil prices, dependence of power sector on oil and low capacity of people to pay for real energy costs resulting in theft and low energy tariff result in unpaid subsidies and circular debt; a vicious cycle that has to be broken somewhere. This can be done if a government is spared of challenges in other sectors extracting and diverting the resources from powerful sectors. A besieged government cannot do that. And all other governments which don't manage to extricate themselves from blackmailing will continue to suffer and will end up as failures in the dustbin of history.

The present government had its share in adding to the crisis. It has failed to act swiftly and decisively towards the development of indigenous energy resources like Thar and local gas. It has instead tried to take soft and urgent courses. It indulged in much defamed Rental Power only to know later that the crisis was not of capacity but was of energy resource. Rental Power, through inferior efficiency would have only worsened the crisis and would have contributed to the circular debt Thank God, it could not be implemented in full as originally planned. And they have been wasting time and energies in pursuing LNG projects that the economy could hardly support. Already, government has defaulted on IPPs and has been threatened of international litigation. This would not send a good message to international investors who alone are capable of financing the capital intensive energy projects. On the other hand, energy bureaucracy has been left alone to decide on its own without central policy coordination. Bureaucrats are enhancing and showing their personal efficiencies at the expense of the total sector's performance. This is like somebody polishing the furniture of a ship that is sinking. Excessive tariffs (Wind Power) are being awarded to powerful groups which would only exacerbate the financial crisis of government. People think that wind is free, while they would be forced to pay through their nose a price that is twice more than elsewhere in the region and the world.

Three steps could reduce budgetary deficits, theoretically speaking; reducing military expenditure, taxing agricultural incomes and reducing waste, inefficiency and profligacy in government. It is the last one which government could have done with relatively lesser threat although it may annoy bureaucracies, political and influential leaders and many other beneficiaries of such waste. Finally it robs the ruler of the only pleasure it enjoys; pomp and pleasure bought through spending free money. I t is the easiest and also the most difficult job requiring discipline, expertise and self-sacrifice. Waste reduction requires a lot of technical expertise as well in addition to the political will..It is not reduced by showy acts of riding on bicycle to ones office or to relinquish a newly constructed office building.

Military expenditure has remained a permanent burden and drain on national economy and resources.
The FY Budget 2012-13 has allocated formally a sum of Rs 545.3 Billon towards Military Expenditure (MILEX). Reportedly; it is a 10% increase over the last year without the asking of the defence sector. A good 42.1% (Rs.229.5 Billion) go towards payroll and employment related expenses, another 26.23 %(Rs 143.5 Billion) go towards operating expenses and Rs.120.5 Billion (22%) go towards physical asset, some kind of PSDP for the defence sector. It used to be a one line budget in early days. Happily, slightly more is known now about it. There are other declared and non-declared expenditures which have been excluded from the formally declared allocation. A sum of Rs 98.2 Billion for military pension comes out of civilian budget due to an innovation in understatement techniques. Several organizations of military nature are either budgeted from civilian sector or are simply not declared. It all adds up to an estimated figure in the range of 800-1000 Billion Rupees. This should be compared with a total outlay on PSDP of a mere Rs. 360 billion and net revenue receipts of Rs1774 billion.

To an extent, it is necessary and unavoidable and even desirable. But a significant part of it is undesirable and uncalled for. It is widely believed that there is lack of transparency of many kinds in it. Whatever be the exact figures, it is obvious that MILEX is a very large amount for a country which cannot manage to send half of its children to school, has more than one-third of its population living under poverty line and where fuel cannot be bought to run its power plants resulting in 10-12 hours of electricity blackout. On the other hand it is argued by military circles that MILEX has come down, if measured with respect to the percentage of GDP or the total budget. It is high time that transparency is brought about in this respect. That should be the first step in bringing reforms in this sector so that useful and objective discussion takes place on the subject devoid of self-perpetrating logic or emotionalism.

It is often considered unpatriotic or even immature liberalism to talk of reducing MILEX. There are political parties in the countries often encouraged if not propped by the establishment, who make a strong case for a national security state, high foreign policy agenda, wresting Kashmir from the clutches of India and the like along with a welfare state and subsidized energy and food prices. To top it all, these forces and the establishment have apparently turned against the Samraj which used to be milked to finance high military spending and import of weapons. History has shown that a security state crumbles under its own burden and challenges and agendas. Soviet Union is a recent example and starving North Korea another. The similarities between North Korea and Pakistan are getting more and more vivid and clear, as India leapfrogs its economy and technology on the development trajectory of South Korea. It may not become or equate with South Korea any time soon but may be able to reach a level of prosperity, cohesion and national power that may eventually make the dream of Pakistan look a bad dream. When this happens, collapse is automatic and imminent as happened in Soviet Union when no amount of nuclear weapons is able to save the system and its dispensation. Many argue that Soviet Union crumbled but Russia lives on. Others argue that it is the march of history; people and their valleys and streams always sustain. I would not further elaborate on this fateful and dangerous logic any further.

It is ironic that even Military dictators start talking and thinking about reducing military expenditure when they consolidate on power and develop an understanding of the national problems. Ayub Khan spoke on strain on people in this respect and active discussion towards reducing MILEX started taking place in the hey days of ZiaulHaq when the powerful general and minister Abdul Qadir of NLC fame argued that there was a fat of 25% in MILEX that could be reduced and removed. This has been the classical position of many a knowledgeable retired military experts who argue that reductions are possible without affecting military preparedness and compromising on genuine national needs. However, defining genuine national needs can be quite contentious where after Kashmir, Afghanistan and its predicament and the strategic depth have occupied quite a place in the security vocabulary, while visiting Afghan leaders argue that Pakistani leaders, civil and military, should stop treating Afghanistan as their province.

It is argued that a large and strong (and I would argue that strong is not necessarily large and profligate) military organization and establishment is essential for a Pakistan that is suffering from many divisive challenges. On the other hand, the recent Supreme Court campaign on missing persons in Balochistan has revealed that military power (or its off-shoots FC etc) is the part of the problem and not of the solution. Many vested interests are created from the cess-pool of violence, whether it is emanating from the state or from a people and their disgruntled groups. It would be only pertinent if I quote here from the book of Percival Spears who wrote in his insightful book (Oxford History of Modern India, OUP, ND, 1965) thus;

an undisciplined state possessing disciplined troops may have far more anarchic possibilities than one resting solely upon a complex system of personal loyalties, as the fate of Sikh Kingdom showed. A group of chiefs broke up within ten years a powerful kingdom through lack of inner cohesion and the existence of a fine military machine only make the collapse more violent and complete. I first quoted this in one of my books written in 1987 when the relevance may have appeared to be futuristic and remote to many. Ironically, in the mean time the scenario that appears to have evolved does not make it that remote and futuristic.

A lot has been written on income tax on agriculture. I do not have to belabor this point. Suffice to mention that this should not be confused with taxing agriculture .This source should be able to generate a well deserved government income of Rs 200 Billion. There has been a lot of beating about the bush by successive governments such as throwing the ball in the court of provincial governments. Income tax is a federal subject. If income tax on agriculture is a provincial matter, the tomorrow Balochistan would ask the same treatment on corporate income taxes on minerals. Combined ,reduction in Military Expenditure and waste and profligacy in government and a sincere attempt at levying and collecting income tax on agricultural incomes is estimated to yield Rs. 500 Billion which may go a long way towards not only meeting the budgetary targets but expand spending on much needed social sector. Energy initiatives towards development of indigenous resources would result in lower cost of generating electricity and reduction in subsidies without unduly enhancing electricity tariff. This would help both budgetary and as well as current account deficits. Without a serious attempt at introducing and implementing these reforms, it is almost impossible that the deteriorating budgetary imbalances may be repaired.

Lack of adequate land reforms, immunity from agricultural income tax and high military spending has given rise to two very powerful groups in this country; one of agricultural Land lords and the other of Military establishment, later having a euphemism of establishment. Excessive financial muscle has created a very large military organization which competes and is often superior than the civilian sector. Military establishment can offer sound advice in many sectors which is often converted into often interference. This has created a great imbalance in the national power structure which is responsible for many a current mix of problems and issues. No initiative or reform can be launched without the concurrence of the two groups. Often most reforms or political stances would be somehow affecting the interests of these two groups. Similarly large land holdings and surplus enjoyed by the landlords enable them to enjoy an undue influence on the politics of this country. Instead of utilizing their surplus and scale economies in expanding agriculture, enhance productivity and technology, they have chosen to get hold of power and extract income and advantage through unfair means. Siphoning some of their income to taxation to be followed by meaningful land reforms has to be an important part of the reform agenda.

It would be naïve on the part of the political parties and the politicians to hope for improvement in the lives and living conditions of the people, by continuing their beating round the bush approaches. Free and fair discussion and debate has to precede any reform effort. If they are scared of even talking about the real issues, they would reach nowhere and would demean themselves before the masses. Musa is born in the house of Pharoah. We have to hope that eventually sense would prevail and realities would be recognized. And we pray that some individuals out of these two dominant groups would show leadership and pave the way for much needed reforms. It is not necessary that a military coup (of which we had had more than our due share) is required to effect such reformation. Turkish Army realized lately that they had to let it go, and that real and true democracy (without their shadows) should be allowed to function and flourish. We have seen how Turkey came out of its problems and has converted itself to a vibrant, harmonious and prosperous society and economy. Let us, for a change, act to be genuine.

18 Improving Governance; a Proposal for Political Parties' Manifestoes

Pakistan has been beset by governance failure from its very beginning period. While most comparable countries of Asia which have prospered started from a comparable low initial levels of socio economic conditions, but have over the period of several decades, created much more sound and stable society conditions. Even India has managed to come out of the classic image of low performance and governance ills, while Pakistan deteriorates on a continuing basis, despite   claims of successes (military) regimes of good performance and success little do such regimes understand that their very existence and recurrence is a governance failure. The starkest reminder is the eruption of terrorism menace and the apparent inability of the government and the military to deal with it.

A good governance system is expected to be effective and efficient in overseeing, guiding and regulating economic activity and social development, with democracy, consensus, participation of the people, in a transparent manner, keeping people informed of its decision, under a set of rules and laws to be adjudicated by an independent judiciary, and having a role for media, NGOs, civil society etc. Good government has to be protective and mindful of the religious and ethnic minorities. It should not rule by brute majority and force. It should be sensitive to the historical and heritage issues of its people. It should also be able to conduct itself with its neighboring countries and participate constructively in the international system, meet its obligations under conventions, treaties and UN resolutions.

Progress, development, improvement in socio-economic conditions, internal and external peace etc are outputs of good governance system and not the good governance itself. As has been proved by international experience, those countries and societies which are high in economic and competitiveness ranking and are socially more developed and are advanced than those which rank low in governance scales. Because governance is an input to the socio-economic development process and activities and not the output, and pertains to many aspects, most often qualitative in nature, it is difficult to measure it, as one is used to measure and define GDP, literacy, growth rates etc. However, in order to be able to judge performance of governments and their governance, there has to be some measure, coefficient rating etc.

On most of such issues , opinion surveys of the stake holders, business executives, social and political actors, media, civil society, NGOs etc. have become very popular and found a broad acceptance at various national and international levels. UN system has also started taking interest in these issues, as it has discovered that its success in fostering and promoting economic development and implementing its various programs and projects. Most of these assessments have commonalities as well as differences. They mostly draw upon similar if not same, data sources. However, their concepts of governance can be either minimalist (World Bank Governance Indicators), limited to government issues such as regulatory quality, effectiveness, etc. in addition to the rule of law. Others such as FnWG adopt a more inclusive, expansive and maximalist approach to include questions of human rights, civil liberties, environment sustainability, human resource development etc.

Large countries carry much grave consequences of their failure on the populace, region and on the world. Pakistan, Iran and Iraq are such countries. Pakistan with nuclear weapons and large army poses highest threat perceptions to the world community, the same two factors may however, prove to be its source of survival and bargaining weapons, as Madelaine Albright (former US secretary of state) conveyed the feelings that Pakistan was an "International Migraine'. What to do with a country which is smart enough to make nuclear weapons and yet weak and incapable of managing itself on a satisfactory level as demonstrated by all listings. No wonder Pakistan has been successively classified at best among "worst governance performers" and at worst among Failed States, and at the bottom side of such lists. The evidence is so massive that it would be preposterous to hide behind conspiracy theories and patriotic appeals. Yet, such discussions need not create despondency and pessimism, but should incite debate, discussion, introspection and result in consensus approaches towards improvement.

Governance can deteriorate security divisions into a military organization that is cruel, insensitive, oppressive, and predatory, while reverse is also possible by boosting social and economic multiplier through a civil-military partnership through indigenization, creation and promotion of social sector in far off areas.

Fortunately democracy has returned and dictatorial rule is gone, hopefully forever, but a continuous threat for its return persists. Military in this country goes away when it is unbearable, lets democratic rule return while waiting in ambush to come back once again, on one pretext or the other. And even in this interlude, presses its agenda and priorities. Tall claims of salvaging the country are made, but in essence more problems are created. It is ironic that growth rates in the economy have been consistently higher during military rule, than during civilian rule, partly legitimizing the former, in the eyes of many, if not all. Why does this happen? This must be investigated and answered.

Social and economic problems are the main problems and remain as such, irrespective of military or civilian governments. Dictators manage to bring short term improvement through sheer coercive power, often putting to use, unutilized production capacity. Military rule is often endowed with stability and peace of mind that is often denied to civilian rule. It was hoped that this time, we would give some peace of mind to the new civilian government of PPP. This has not happened. However, PML-N has acted wisely, because their suffering at the hands of military dictator in the immediate past.

Despite democracy, we are not amongst one of the 89 countries which have been declared Free by Freedom House, the latter measures and evaluate the state of freedom in various countries and issues an annual Freedom Index and classification. Those who think that conditions in Pakistan and India are the same in this respect, may be hurt by knowing that India has always been grouped under "Free" countries with high ratings on political rights and civil liberties. Fortunately, after the elections in 2008, removal of Musharraf and assumption of office by a democratically elected government, Pakistan has been classified as a "partly free county", by Freedom House. For half of the life of the country, we have been under military rule, and in those periods earned the stigma and disgrace of living in a "not-free" class of country, although we struggled for our independence and believed that we got it in 1947. We neither were (are) free nor independent. But partly we are, and should pray that we continue to enjoy this without break or discontinuity in the coming days.

Political parties are an important link between people and the system, and an essential player in democracy. Without strong political parties, there is no strong democracy .Our political parties are weak in many ways, and that is the reason that every now and then, an ambitious and selfish and egotist general manages to call off the democratic system and locks the prime-minister up in a jail, or even hangs them or exiles them.

Policy prescriptions are abundantly available. Some may require change of emphasis, such as the previous government's profligacy on higher education etc. There are few options, but hard choices. Solutions can be found only in national consensus including the military. It is unfortunate but they are to be on board if a major policy break-through is to be made; be it vis-à-vis India or reducing military expenditure. The two major parties have to play a role in building the consensus that is so vitally needed but also because of the fact that the next government would also be facing the same issue.

However, State structure is   intact in Pakistan, although beset by problems; strong military, adequate bureaucratic structure if not performance, a rejuvenated judiciary and healthy trends of cooperation among mainstream political parties are the positive elements, on which hope can be placed, to initiate the reform process. Elections are close by. Political parties should involve themselves in intensive discussions on identifying problems and developing priorities and solutions. Manifestos are generally not taken very seriously in Pakistan, both by the public and as well as the parties. Some writer types are assigned the task of "writing" the manifesto" instead of involving various sectoral experts. I am proposing the following as my humble suggestions to political parties to consider incorporating the following in their manifestoes. In the coming days, we will select some of the more important issues and elaborate upon those.

● **Elimination of Corruption**

1) Elimination of corruption to be the first and foremost objectives; all ills emanate from this mother of ills.
2) Reinstitute **justification of assets** clause in the NAB Act.

3) Whistle blowers serve a very useful purpose against malpractices and corruption. Protect *whistle blowers* in government services under an act of Parliament.

● **Politics, Freedom & Democracy**

4) Introduce and affirm a Bill of Rights for the citizens.
5) Broaden and strengthen freedom and liberty consistent with morality, decency and religious or ethnic sensitivities; discourage monopoly and tyranny even of the majority
6) Diversify political participation by promoting and legislating the representation of class interests of workers, tillers, crafts and trade, teachers and professions, both in political parties and as well as representative institutions like local bodies and assemblies.
7) Strengthen political parties and the political processes leading towards their institutionalization. Assist them financially by awarding estates, commercial plots for building income bearing projects including their offices and meeting halls. Possibly, make a Foundation and name it democracy foundation (Bunyad-e-Jamhooriat); launch Training programmes for political workers and office bearers, leaders and representative.
8) Broaden political participation by Including school teachers and professors of the public sector in the political process by permitting them.

● **War & peace**

9) International relations should be conducted on the basis of national interest, mutual respect and reciprocity, non-interference, pursuit of peace and fostering of economic and cultural relations especially with neighbors.
10) While support for the oppressed is obligatory on Muslims as per injunction of the Holy Quran, the issue can be postponed for better times on Sulah Hadibia model .The conditions are comparable today.
11) There is however a great threat for Pakistan to go down piecemeal (ala Soviet Union and other similar states) under social, political and economic complications and undiluted security agenda. We should introduce a state structure and positioning that builds an economic (social welfare state) based on Islamic principles of social justice in place of a Security State System that thrives on conflict and war; rather Focus Jihad against poverty and illiteracy and corruption.

12) Nuclear deterrence to be an active part of the defence policy and not just a background in which conventional forces operate. It is with the active and credible threat of use of nuclear weapons that the adversary can be dissuaded from adventure or planning for it. There should be no shame in the implied barbarism. In fact it is the only positive fallout of the undeserved image that we have. Adoption of such a posture should enable us to save significantly from the conventional expenditure. Adding for both (nuclear and conventional) simultaneously, as the case currently is, would cripple our economy and our society.

13) There is no winnable war and victory esp in a nuclear age which has dawned in South Asia. Disguise pursuits must be abandoned with reciprocity. 12) Pursue Kashmir issue on the model and pace ala Hongkong.

14) Abstain from expensive and naïve military pursuits of Siachen and Kargil.

15) Reduce Military expenditure by 25% in the first go and ultimately to 50% of the current level; right size the forces and introduce cost consciousness in forces; bring in public oversight and transparency; do away with hidden and indirect military expenditure and declare the true figures.

• Economy

16) Build a self reliant economy utilizing local resources and inputs and focused on poverty Alleviation

17) Balance the budget through collection of due taxes(including agricultural incomes) and reducing military expenditure and eliminating waste in governmental processes.

18) Collect due taxes without excessive taxation; all new capital and industries have been built under a permissive tax regime; but thus far and no more.

19) Reorganize and rejuvenate Planning Commission, modernizing and updating its project approval and monitoring processes, possibly expanding its presence at the district level

20) Cut energy imports by developing local resources such as Thar, Shale gas etc.

21) Reduce interest rates through banking reforms reducing the banks' intermediation charges (difference between avg lending rate and the deposit rates).

22) Construction sector has great potential to create demand and generate employment; small infrastructure schemes (through self help and without contractors and intermediaries) at Tehsil level and urban low cost

housing are to be promoted. Provide public land for housing schemes at attractive projects to construction cooperatives and projects.

23) Economy is always stimulated by consumer demand (in a populous country) more than it can be done through public sector expenditure and investment.

24) Build economic and trade linkages with India irrespective of political problems.

● **Industry & Business**

25) Introduce Board of Supervisors for oversight of large corporations in private and public sector

26) Promote cooperatives as a form of business organization to promote public and larger participation in economic activities by the consumers, workers etc. Selectively convert public sector into cooperatives; e.g. health delivery, R&D institutions etc

27) Promote SMEs by launching high-rise (3-D) industrial estates.

28) Don't take the documentation issue too far so as not too cripple the small businesses.

29) Textile sector deserves support and attention due to its backward and forward linkages, resource base, sector's size and share in employment and export.

30) Engineering sector is a mother industry that produces machines which in turn produce machines and so on. There is a large export potential. It can help promote self reliance and self sufficiency in other sectors. Power producing equipment esp Wind Turbines and Oil Drilling rigs should get immediate priority for local production.

● **Poverty Alleviation**

31) Introduce Land Reforms through following actions; a) Upper limit on land holding b) taxation differential on large holdings; c) public purchase of land at reasonable and affordable prices or compelling (legislating) the large land owners to sell excess land to the market in small plots of 2-5 acres; d)Encourage land donation(ala Qarz utaro mulk sanwaro!!!) , where in women donated their jewelry) to public land provision initiatives. e) Allot cultivable waste land among the land less in small plots of 1 acre, ala India House and Garden Scheme; e) encourage and enforce permanent and inalienable settlement of the tillers on the land they till, in large land holdings exceeding 100 acres. Tillers entitlement to be one acre each family.

32) Introduce differential agricultural tax on incomes, discouraging large land holdings above 100 acres.

33) Promote work-at-home especially for women office workers, IT etc

34) Register workers in the informal sector and bring them into the ambit of insurance such as **EOBI.** Construction workers and house-hold workers are to be given priority. Impose **Construction workers cess** on Cement production to collect imputed EOBI contribution of the employers in the cement downstream industry. We have provided some calculations in this respect elsewhere.

35) Launch urban housing schemes for the poor and the industrial workers on public or subsidized land. Promote house building cooperatives for the poor and the lower middle classes involving loan and saving schemes and credit unions.

36) Expand workers training and institute literacy programmes at Tehsil and district levels.

37) Expand nurses and health workers training programme, protect them from sexual harassment and exploitation widely prevalent in the health system.

38) Revive the old time Ration Shop system (computerized) to funnel food subsidies to the very poor; install these in poor areas.

• Government & Civil Service

39) Introduce public service (bureaucracy) reforms; enforce information act; b) mandatory reporting on websites of material and significant activities ;c) preparation of annual reports and work plans

40) Introduce specialized rather than general bureaucracy; promote lateral entrants by introducing **Senior Executive Service (ala-USA),** inducting talent at grade 20 and above, involving a shorter service span of 10-15 years.

41) Seek extra-ordinary powers from the Supreme Court for handling major issues such as corruption, as had been bestowed upon General Musharraf.

42) Revive and strengthen local bodies accommodating the positions of the provincial stakeholders; expand its local courts and dispute resolution functions.

43) Introduce oversight committees for all public institutions, esp at the village or local council levels, schools, police station, land records offices. Classes and Professions be represented in such committees and not just powerful political interests.

44) Bring transparency in the Establishment division's operations by building a Board of senior executives, serving and retired, both from private and public sector.

45) Computerize land records and eliminate patwaris role and machinations.

46) Popularize and institute modern working tools such as e-govt and videoconferencing, the latter having great potential in saving time and money.

47) Remove the gaps and make adjustments that have become necessary after the incorporation of the 18th amendment.

● **Energy, Water and Food Security**

48) Food, Energy and Water self-sufficiency is to be the cornerstone of development policy and a principal criterion in resource allocation.

49) Bring competition and transparency in the energy sector; b)fast track Thar coal; c)build an international energy hub at Gawadar, to fuse Iranian and Arab interests and facilities and access to South Asian countries; d)Reform tariff system , doing away with excessive pricing e.g., as in Wind Power.(details in my books)

50) Promote conservation and efficiency in water usage; introduce and popularize drip irrigation. It is a misnomer that all water saving technologies is expensive.

51) Present electricity Crisis is a cash crisis (circular debt) than of generating capacity .The crisis can go away by substantially reducing the circular debt by some form of cash injection. However new debt stock would be created due to the Tariff not fully recouping the production cost. Tariff cannot be raised so much as to wipe out the gap completely. The problem is to be solved gradually (in midterm) by reducing the T7D losses and bringing in cheaper and local energy sources.

52) Gas crisis is however of capacity and resource which can only be solved through developing local and cheaper resources both of gas and coal. All imported energy is very expensive which price cannot be paid by low income consumer. There is enough gas and Coal (Thar). Gas requires impetus on E&P and Thar coal requires fast track approaches. Also hydro resources like Bhasha and others would be comparatively much cheaper.

● **Education & Research**

53) Expand Education and Promote Quality, Equality and Uniformity devoid of class structure and preferences.

54) Double the spending on education and health; focus on primary education rather than Higher education which has already received much preference in recent years. Resources are few; priorities have to be laid out.

55) Close down dead-wood R&D institutions, and curb the tendency of establishing paper-shuffling institutions as the case has been over the last decade.

56) Rejuvenate and Reorganize the ones that remain after the clean-up.

Focus esp on agricultural research.

57) Build linkages between Education and R&D institutions.

58) Close down all suspected and questionable research that may be violating international conventions such as Biological or chemical weapons.

Natural Resources and Provincial Rights and issues

59) Revisit 18th amendment from the perspective of centre-provincial coordination (concurrent list) on major subjects possibly with provincial domain in implementation. No purported revolution has occurred in the aftermath of 18th amendment and none is in pipeline in near future. Two of the provinces are too underdeveloped to utilize absolute autonomy in a meaningful manner.(look at the HEC and Drugs control issues; more may be coming; we have gone from one extreme to the other; for details pls see my book ; Pakistan's development challenges; federalism, governance and security). However autonomy and ownership of natural resources may not be compromised during the revision and reformulation. Constructive and non-exploitative engagement is required in these sectors as well. Only Punjab can develop autonomously, but it does not have natural mineral and energy resources.

60)12% free electricity to hydro electricity producer country or equivalent as royalty ; 25% share on payment at normal price; producing regions(districts) to be paid a share of such income;100 free units for 10 years (out of the 12% free electricity) to displaced or disturbed households consequent to the development

61) Adequate (internationally competitive) royalty rates on mineral extraction and a share in corporate tax; 50% share in other incomes under production sharing arrangements.

62) Adequate priority rights (say 20-25% of the production) in resource usage of the producing province.

Internal Politics and Issues

63) Eradicate terrorism (regional and religious) through persuasion, dialogue and legal and police action replacing military action. Hunger and deprivation are the biggest alienators. No military campaigns against a whole population; it has never solved any problem. It has always failed and added to estrangement and alienation.
64) Evolve a cultural profile based on consensus bringing together religious and liberal forces.
65) Religious minorities' rights to be respected based on good international practices and within the confines of Islamic injunctions bringing them in national mainstream.

Bibliography

Akhtar A. Badshah, Our Urban Future, Zed Books Ltd – London, 1996

Akhtar Ali, Nuclear Stalemate or Conflagration, REAP – Karachi, 1987

Akhtar Ali, The Political Economy of Pakistan, Royal Book Company – Karachi, 1996

Akhtar Hossain, etal, In Quest of Development: The Political Economy of South Asia, University Press Limited – Dhaka, 1996

Anthony H. Birch, The British System of Government, George Allen & Unwin Ltd – London, 1967

Arun Ghosh, etal, Indian Industrialization: Structure and Policy Issues, Oxford University Press - New Delhi, 1992

Ayesha Siddiqa, Military INC: Inside Pakistan's Military Economy, Oxford University Press – Karachi, 2007

Benazir Bhutto, Issues in Pakistan, Jang Publisher, Lahore, 1993

Bhabani Sen Gupta, Regional Cooperation and Development in South Asia, South Asian Publishers - New Delhi, 1992

Dilara Choudhury, Constitutional Development in Bangladesh: Stresses and Strains, Oxford University Press – Karachi, 1994

Dr Akmal Hussain, Poverty Alleviation in Pakistan, Vanguard Books Pvt Ltd – Lahore, 1994

Dr. A.S.Nasir, Planning, Strategy and Strategic Measures for Development, Royal Book Company – Karachi, 1999

Durga Das Basu, Introduction to the Constitution of India, Prentice Hall of India - New Delhi, 1987

Feroz Ahmed, Ethnicity and Politics in Pakistan, Oxford University Press – Karachi, 1998

Ghulam Kibria, Technology Acquisition in Pakistan: Story of a failed privileged class and a successful working class, City Press – Karachi, 1998

Goh Tianwah, Doing Business in Malaysia, Rana Books – Singapore, 1986

Ijaz Nabi, The Quality of Life in Pakistan, Vanguard Books Pvt Ltd – Lahore, 1986

Ishrat Husain, Pakistan The Economy of an Elitist State, Oxford University Press – Karachi, 1999

Ismail Serageldin, etal, Overcoming Global Hunger, World Bank - Washington, D.C., 1994

J. Denis Derbyshire, etal, World Political Systems, W&R Chambers Ltd - New York, 1991

Jan Van der Linden, etal, Karachi Migrants, Housing and Housing Policy, Vanguard Books Pvt Ltd – Lahore, 1991

John Blunden, Mineral Resources and their Management, Longman Group Limited - New York, 1985

John G. Stoessinger, Why Nations go to War, Random House, 1971

John Groom, Mineral Resources a Blessing or a Cause, 8th ICARD Conference, Skelleftea, 2009

John Middleton, Adrian Ziderman, Arvil Van Adams, Skills for Productivity: Vocational Education and Training in Developing Countries, Oxford University Press - New York, 1993

John P.Lewis, India's Political Economy, Oxford University Press-New Delhi, 1995

John Pierre, Debating Governance, Oxford University Press - New York, 2000

John Retallick, etal, Transforming Schools in Pakistan, Oxford University Press – Karachi, 2005

Justice (R) Muhammad Ilyas, Up-dating the constitution of Pakistan, Vanguard Books Pvt Ltd – Lahore, 1998

K.K.Taimni, Asia's Rural Cooperatives, Oxford University Press - New Delhi, 1994

Kamal Siddiqui, Local Government in South Asia : A comparative study, University Press Limited – Dhaka, 1992

Kamal Siddiqui, Local Government in Bangladesh, University Press Limited – Dhaka, 2005

Keith M. Lewin, etal, Education all the Children, Oxford University Press - New York, 1993

Khalid Baig, First Things First, Open mind press – California, 2004

Kumazawa Makoto, Portraits of the Japanese workplace, Westview Press-USA, 1996

Louis D Hayes, The Crisis of Education in Pakistan, Vanguard Books Pvt Ltd – Lahore, 1987

Lt. Gen. Gul Hassan Khan, Memoirs, Oxford University Press – Karachi, 1993

M. Khalid Masud, etal, Islamic Legal Interpretation, Oxford University Press – Karachi, 1996

Mahbub-ul-Haq, Reflections on Human Development, Oxford University Press - New York, 1995

Mahbubur Rahman Morshed, Bureaucratic Response on Administrative Decentralization, University Press Limited – Dhaka, 1997

Mahmood Hasan Khan, Underdevelopment and Agrarian structure in Pakistan, Vanguard Books Pvt Ltd – Lahore, 1981

Marlaine E. Lockheed, etal, Improving Primary Education in Developing Countries, Oxford University Press – USA, 1991

Mian Muhammad Jamil, Local Governments in LDCs: and some related issues, Ferozsons (Pvt) Ltd., Lahore, 1996

Michael R. Dove, etal, Sociology of Natural Resources, Vanguard Books Pvt Ltd – Lahore, 1992

MINFAL, Agricultural Statistics of Pakistan 2001-2002 & others years, GOP Islamabad, 2003

Muhammad Azam Chaudhary, Justice in Practice, Oxford University Press – Karachi, 1999

Muhammad Waseem, The 1993 Elections in Pakistan, Vanguard Books Pvt Ltd – Lahore, 1994

Mushahid Hussain, Pakistan: Problems of Governance, Vanguard Books Pvt Ltd – Lahore, 1993

Mushtaqur Rahman, Land and Life in Sindh, Pakistan, Ferozsons (Pvt) Ltd., Karachi, 1993

Mustafa Chowdhury, Pakistan Its Politics and Bureaucracy, R.K.Paul – India, 1998

Narmeen Sheikh, Slums, Security and Shelter in Pakistan, Vanguard Books Pvt Ltd – Lahore, 1998

National Commission on Terrorist, The 9/11 Commission Report, W.W. Norton - New York, 2002

Oliver E. Williamson, The Mechanisms of Governance, Oxford University Press - New York, 1996

Paul Caro, Water, McGraw-Hill, Inc - New York, 1993

Paul R. Dufour, etal, Science and Technology in Japan, Stockton Press - New York, 1984

Pervez Hoodbhoy, Islam and Science, Zed Books Ltd – London, 1991

Peter Hennessy, etal, Ruling Performance, Basil Blackwell - New York, 1987

Peter James, The Future of Coal, The Macmillan Press Ltd, London, 1984

Ponna Wignaraja, etal, Participatory Development, Oxford University Press – Karachi, 1991

Raul A. Deju, Extraction of Minerals and Energy: Today's Dilemmas, Ann arbor science – USA, 1974

Rehman Sobhan, Governance and Development, University Press Limited – Dhaka, 1998

Roy W. Bahl, Johannes F. Linn, Urban Public Finance in Developing Countries, Oxford University Press - New York, 1992

S.Akbar Zaidi, Regional Imbalances & The National Question in Pakistan, Vanguard Books Pvt Ltd – Lahore, 1992

S.K.Das, Civil Service Reform & Structural Adjustment, Oxford University Press - New Delhi, 1998

S.M.Naseem, Dilemmas of Destiny, Vanguard Books Pvt Ltd – Lahore, 1998

Shahida Wizarat, The Rise and Fall of Industrial Productivity in Pakistan, Oxford University Press – Karachi, 2002

Shahrukh Rafi Khan, Basic Education in Rural Pakistan, Oxford University Press – Karachi, 2005

Shahrukh Rafi Khan, Fifty Years of Pakistan's Economy, Oxford University Press – Karachi, 1999

Shahrukh Rafi Khan, etal, Initiating Devolution, Oxford University Press – Karachi, 2007

Stephen P. Cohen, The Pakistan Army: 1998 Edition, Oxford University Press – Karachi, 1994

Steven Vago, Social Change, Simon & Schuster Company, New Jersey, 1996

Sugata Bose, etal, Modern South Asia, Sang-e-Meel Publication – Lahore, 1998

Syed Nawab Haider, etal, Land Reforms in Pakistan, Pakistan Institute of Development Economic-Islamabad, 1987

T.N. Seshan, etal, The Degeneration of India, VIKING – India, 1995

Tanveer Azhar, The Quest for Power: Pakistan's Policy options for the Nineties, Ferozsons (Pvt) Ltd., Lahore, 1991

Tariq Husain, etal, Farming Systems of Pakistan, Vanguard Books Pvt Ltd – Lahore, 1992

Tariq J. Banuri, Shahrukh Rafi Khan & Moazam Mahmmod, Just Development: Beyond Adjustment with a Human Face, Oxford University Press – Karachi, 1997

Tariq Rahman, Language and Politics in Pakistan, Oxford University Press – Karachi, 1996

Tasneem Ahmed Siddiqui, Towards Good Governance, Oxford University Press – Karachi, 2001

US Congress, Nuclear Proliferation Factbook, US Congress, 1977

World Bank, Water Resources Management, World Bank - Washington, D.C., 1993

Zafar Azeem, Competing Choices, Aries Publishing House – Karachi, 2007